UNIONS IN A GLOBALIZED ENVIRONMENT

UNIONS IN A GLOBALIZED ENVIRONMENT

Changing Borders, Organizational Boundaries, and Social Roles

Bruce Nissen

Editor

M.E. Sharpe

Armonk, New York
London, England

Library of Congress Cataloging-in-Publication Data

Unions in a globalized environment : changing borders, organizational boundaries, and
social roles / edited by Bruce Nissen.
    p. cm.
Includes bibliographical references and index.
ISBN 0-7656-0869-3 (alk. paper)—ISBN 0-7656-0870-7 (pbk. : alk. paper)
    1. Labor unions. 2. Foreign trade and employment. 3. Globalization—Economic
aspects. I. Nissen, Bruce, 1948–

HD6483.U66 2002
331.88′091—dc21   200149525

Printed in the United States of America

MV (c) 10   9   8   7   6   5   4   3   2   1
MV (p) 10   9   8   7   6   5   4   3   2   1

CONTENTS

LIST OF TABLES AND FIGURES

Tables

Figures

UNIONS IN A GLOBALIZED ENVIRONMENT

1

THE LABOR MOVEMENT IN A NEW GLOBALIZED ENVIRONMENT

AN INTRODUCTION

BRUCE NISSEN

In the late 1980s and the early 1990s the U.S. labor movement received little scholarly attention. Much of what was written about organized labor treated it as a relic of the past—perhaps an impetus for innovation and positive change in the period between 1935 and 1975 but no longer an important force to be reckoned with. Influential industrial relations scholarship, such as Kochan, Katz, and McKersie's (1986) *The Transformation of American Industrial Relations*, depicted the labor movement as unsuited to the modern environment: a dying and reactive force stuck in outmoded adversarial attitudes and relations.

As mainstream industrial relations scholarship drifted ever further from unions in the direction of human resource management, academics with a stronger attachment to the labor movement found their concerns and research increasingly marginalized (Goddard and Delaney 2000). But a 1995 changeover in leadership of the AFL–CIO opened the possibility that the fortunes of both the labor movement and labor-oriented scholarship could improve in the future. New AFL–CIO leadership inspired hope and increased interest from progressive academics. A number of recently published books analyze the state of the labor movement and/or provide prescriptions for its future course (Fraser and Freeman, eds. 1997; Mantsios, ed. 1998; Mort, ed. 1998; Aronowitz

3

1998; Tillman and Cummings, eds. 1999; Nissen, ed. 1999; Meiksins-Wood et al., eds. 1999).

Most analyses of organized labor's prospects note that it faces a very different environment than the one it confronted in the immediate post–World War II decades. Some of the many environmental changes are not central to the analyses of the essays in this book, but one is central to them all: the "globalization" of the U.S. economy. In many obvious ways, the growth of transnational business investments and trade has served to undermine traditional segments of the U.S. labor movement. Corporate investment abroad and growing import penetration of markets have been major stimulants to "corporate flight" and "deindustrialization." Plants close in the United States and either reopen in foreign countries or abandon the market entirely to foreign producers (Bluestone, Harrison, and Baker 1981; Bluestone and Harrison 1982; Rothstein 1986; Browne and Sims 1993; Craypo and Nissen, eds. 1993). Major U.S. unions like the United Steelworkers and the United Auto Workers lost hundreds of thousands of members in the 1980s for these reasons.

The *threat* of relocation was often as potent a weapon against organized labor as was the real thing (Bronfenbrenner 1997). Concessionary contracts were forced onto unions by triumphant companies, well aware that they were in a position of power vis-à-vis their unions in the 1980s and 1990s.

The massive growth of transnational trade and investment has been accompanied by a worldwide political trend often referred to as the "neoliberal agenda." According to neoliberalism, markets unhindered by political interference best solve problems and promote the welfare of the population. Free trade pacts, reductions in government social expenditures and programs, deregulation of industries, denationalization of nationalized industries, lowering of tariffs and import barriers, and the like are all examples of this general political trend, which has swept most of the world.

None of these trends has been favorable for the U.S. labor movement in the near term. By any measure of power and influence, organized labor in this country has been losing ground (Goldfield 1987; Moody 1988; Robinson 1988; Moberg 1989; Nissen, ed. 1990; Freeman 1992; Craver 1995). By the mid-1990s, union density (percentage of the workforce that is unionized) was less than half of what it had been in the early to mid-1950s. Politically, the labor movement was unable to keep the U.S. Congress from turning Republican in the 1994 election and was finding that the Democratic Party was more and more a business party that could not be relied upon in crucial issues such as trade policy.

Domestic changes causing divisions within the U.S. working class also negatively impacted the labor movement. Examples include increasing suburbanization, which dispersed previously cohesive working-class communities; a "white male" backlash against affirmative action and other programs perceived to be unduly benefiting minorities; the "culture wars" over issues such as abortion and gun ownership; the rise of religious fundamentalism and right-wing religious movements such as the Christian Coalition; technological and sectoral changes in the U.S. economy that decreased the importance of traditionally unionized industries; and the like.

But unions in the United States have begun to respond to the unfavorable environment by experimenting with new ideas and directions. The change has been slow and halting in many respects, but there has been a clear change, the most visible element of which was the changeover in leadership of the AFL–CIO in 1995. A "New Voice" team led by John Sweeney, previously president of the Service Employees International Union, has made organizing the unorganized its number one priority.

Other initiatives aim to develop a more independent and powerful political presence and to give workers a voice in the community and at the work site. Politically, the AFL–CIO began to abandon its traditional role of endorsing and giving money to Democratic candidates, no matter how conservative or pro-business they may be. The federation is trying to become a more *independent* political force requiring much greater accountability from politicians, who are expected to adhere to a "working families" agenda. While the rhetoric on this score often exceeds the practice, the trend is nonetheless evident. Organized labor is also putting much more of its effort into face-to-face, one-on-one outreach to members and their families *on the issues*, with less reliance on simple mailings and exhortations to vote for a particular candidate or party (Rosenthal 1998; Garin and Molyneux 1998; Eimer and Zullo 2000; Bruno 2000).

In the community, the "new" AFL–CIO has worked to revitalize its central labor councils throughout the country. The "Union Cities" initiative attempts to make these local central bodies more effective in organizing, mobilizing, local political action, and voicing community concerns (Kriesky, ed. 1998; Ness 1998; McLewin 1999). A combination of cajoling from the national federation, financial incentives to central bodies undertaking innovations, and conferences and gatherings to spread "best practice" information appears to have had some effect by the year 2000 (McLewin 2001). In 1999 the national AFL–CIO convention endorsed a "New Alliance" resolution that foresees a major restructuring of AFL–CIO state federations and local bodies. The goals are to increase affiliation of union locals to these bodies and to combine a number of smaller labor councils into larger and better staffed "area councils" presumably better able to accomplish the traditional goals of state and local bodies.

Greater voice for workers at the work site is to be achieved in a number of ways. Through new mechanisms such as the Center for Workplace Participation and the Working for America Institute, the AFL–CIO is trying to influence workforce development policies and create union–employer partnerships that achieve more union influence over the running of enterprises and the training afforded to union workers. The effort to create partnerships with employers is by far the most controversial aspect of the AFL–CIO's new program among left-wing union militants and allied academics. It is also the most welcomed aspect among many liberal and mildly social democratic unionists and academics (Lazes and Savage 1997; Parker and Slaughter 1997).

Overall, most reaction by labor-sympathetic observers and academics to the new leadership of organized labor's peak organization has been positive. Nevertheless, tangible progress in achieving more power and greater numbers was not readily apparent by the year 2000. American unions face the twenty-first century in a precarious position. Their capacity to institute needed programs and initiatives is in doubt, and it is not even readily apparent what exactly is needed to make unions once again central to the lives of working people in the United States.

The essays in this book do not attempt to answer all questions about what is needed or the likelihood of accomplishing needed change. Rather, they confine themselves to questions primarily raised by the challenges arising from globalization. Three categories capture most of the issues discussed: (1) "crossing borders"; (2) "opening organizational boundaries"; and (3) "transforming internal goals and operations." The three sections of this book are divided into these three categories.

Crossing Borders

First, how well are unions "crossing borders"? Are they developing ties with workers and unions in other countries and making common cause?

Is cross-border solidarity actually developing? Is it aiding in efforts to organize the unorganized? Is it building power for unions on both sides of national borders? Given the globalization of capital, the globalization of labor would seem to be a natural response. Yet despite the logical nature of such a move, U.S. organized labor is having more than a little difficulty achieving its own "globalization."

Some of the reasons for this are historical. They include the legacy of the Cold War, when the communism–anticommunism divide colored every international activity of unions, leading many labor movements on each side of the divide to support repressive governments aligned with "their side." Also, the personal histories of many top union leaders in the 1950s–1980s were closely tied to the same historic divide. Red-baiting or (much more rarely) the defense of the right of "reds" to participate in union affairs frequently became a crucial issue determining the individual fate and leadership longevity of a union leader. In addition, U.S. union successes in the 1950s–1970s without international solidarity bolstered the inclination to ignore this particular source of strength. Finally, the apparent payoffs to U.S. workers from the growing U.S. economic empire in the 1950s–1970s and a dominant "business union" practice during those same decades solidified an outlook far removed from or based on international or class solidarity (Nissen 1999).

Other reasons for the difficulty in achieving cross-border alliances have to do with current international realities and the internal state of U.S. unions. Labor movements in other countries take on a bewildering array of types and roles. Many are in varying degrees of dependency on their government, calling into question their independent role in defending worker rights. Others are split into mutually antagonistic blocs, making relationships of solidarity with each bloc difficult. And the atrophied state of many U.S. unions makes solidarity with other unions in this country difficult to achieve, much less to find common cause with those in other countries.

The first three chapters in this book deal with current attempts to overcome the U.S. labor movement's absence of strong ties of solidarity with unions and workers in other countries. In the opening chapter Steve Babson provides a detailed look at a specific industry and growing attempts to make common cause across national boundaries. The auto industry in the United States and in Mexico is almost a textbook case on the need to develop common strategies and forms of solidarity between labor unions on both sides of a national border. Following a review of the North American auto industry and its unions, Babson assesses the critical opportunities for, and obstacles to, cross-border solidarity. His deeply knowledgeable review of the various types of transnational solidarity is quite thorough, including union local-to-local meetings, worker-to-worker meetings, "solidarity funds," health and safety training, crisis support in times of struggle, North American Free Trade Agreement (NAFTA) labor side accord filings, union councils at a particular employer, and broader strategic alliances. Babson's prognosis for auto cross-border solidarity is both sober and encouraging: much is possible but nothing is automatic, and much must be done to change old cultures and ways of doing things for such ventures to succeed.

In the next chapter Henry Frundt compares and contrasts the different types of cross-border organizing that have been recently attempted between U.S. unions and those attempting to organize maquila plants in Mexico, Central America, and the Caribbean. Frundt examines four models: international campaigns based on consumer pressure; clandestine targeting based on local organization building; federation organizing committed to bilateral organizing; and coalition organizing, which includes organizations well beyond the traditional union movement. His conclusions are tempered by a knowledgeable assessment of the strengths and weaknesses of all four models. But they do provide relatively clear guidelines as to which forms of organizing are most likely to lead to sustained local union organizations. Those analyzing or attempting cross-border work would do well to utilize Frundt's analysis as a guide.

The third chapter in this section of the book expands the focus of international solidarity beyond relations with workers and unions in less developed countries. Written by Jeff Rechenbach and Larry Cohen, two leaders of the Communications Workers of America (CWA), it examines that union's attempts to progress beyond mere international exchanges of information or meetings of top union leaders to a more meaningful, rooted relationship of solidarity with unions abroad. Their analysis is based upon the intricate weave of relationships that telecommunications companies are developing worldwide. It conveys the urgency the CWA feels in its attempts to create international solidarity and the tentative nature of the union's initial endeavors in cross-border action and education. This union has been thinking strategically about how it needs to develop worldwide solidarity, and both this point and the seriousness of its goal of embedding solidarity down within the ranks are apparent from this chapter.

Opening Organizational Boundaries

Second, how well are unions "opening organizational boundaries"? In the decades between the end of World War II and the 1990s, U.S. unions became more bureaucratized and less open institutions than they had been in the 1935–1945 period. As the "movement" character of unions ebbed, the organizational boundaries of unions hardened. One consequence was an unwelcoming attitude toward all types of "outsiders." Coupled with this, unions put less and less of their resources into organizing the unorganized. At the same time, the suburbanization of capital and of living patterns weakened and fragmented working-class communities and consequently the labor movement (McLewin 1999). All told, unions became more isolated from communities, and they tended to lack the organizational flexibility to welcome new types of workers as members.

Organized labor's attitude toward immigrants fit the above pattern. The garment unions and the farm workers' union were partial exceptions because their workforces either were or became so overwhelmingly immigrant that the unions were forced to welcome immigrants and incorporate their concerns into the unions' functioning to at least some degree. But overall, the U.S. labor movement viewed immigrants as more of a threat than an opportunity in the second half of the twentieth century. Thus unions' attitudes toward—and relationships with—immigrants are good exemplars of their organizational openness in this period.

The two articles in this section examine unions' relationships with immigrants. Are unions now reaching out to immigrants, incorporating them as valued resources in the struggle for worker rights in this country? Or are they ignoring or, worse, shunning them? Ruth Milkman uses Los Angeles as a case to examine this question. Los Angeles has a heavily immigrant workforce, yet immigrant workers are less likely to be union members than are native-born workers. She finds that this is not because immigrants are "unorganizable" but because of their economic sectoral location. In fact, foreign-born workers may be more organizable in some respects than their nonimmigrant counterparts; they have displayed militancy and leadership characteristics useful to the entire labor movement. Milkman shows that recent successes with immigrant organizing in Los Angeles are qualitatively impressive but fragile. Furthermore, they have not appreciably changed the union density rate in the area.

In the following article Bruce Nissen and Guillermo Grenier examine the Miami, Florida, area to compare how four unions responded to mass immigration. Two subject unions are building trades craft unions with a long exclusionary history. The other two are industrially organized unions in a manufacturing and service industry. The authors find that the differing responses can be explained by differences in the unions' structure, their traditional membership and employer characteristics, their leadership's vision and ideology, and their internal cultural practices. The paper ends with nine things that unions could do to ensure that they more successfully open their organizations to immigrants and incorporate them as a strength, not an external threat.

Transforming Internal Goals and Operations

The final four chapters examine deeper questions of union purpose and type. If the labor movement needs to "reinvent" itself to become effective in the new environment, what would the "new unionism" look like? How should unions change, and is there evidence that they are indeed changing in the requisite manner? What ideological outlooks are animating the labor movement, and which are most adequate to the task of transforming them? What overall role could the labor movement play, that is, how could we theorize the labor movement as a coherent whole in the coming period? Fernando Gapasin and Edna Bonacich, Ian Robinson, and Paul Johnston address questions of this nature in the first three chapters in this final section.

Gapasin and Bonacich focus their chapter on manufacturing workers, a group that they believe the labor movement is wrongly abandoning because easier success is to be had in the public sector and service sector of the economy. They note that the new flexible global form of capitalism makes older forms of accommodation between labor and capital (the "social accord") obsolete. It also changes the nature of manufacturing work through the contracting out of work, offshore production, temporary/part time/independent contractor forms of flexibility, growing employment of marginalized people (immigrants, people of color, women), and employment instability. These conditions make organizing manufacturing workers extremely difficult, but Gapasin and Bonacich believe it is possible if the labor movement adopts a more leftist ideology and strategically either "moves up" or "moves down" from the workplace as a unit of organization. The authors strongly relate their prognosis of the labor movement's capacity for self-transformation to its ability to ideologically reorient itself to the left.

In the following chapter Ian Robinson develops a theoretical apparatus that allows us to categorize autonomous voluntary unions along the dimensions of their "inclusiveness" and their "radicalness." From this he comes up with four different types of unionism: business unionism, social unionism, social movement unionism, and sectarian unionism. He argues that the neoliberal restructuring of the past two decades has driven the U.S. labor movement in the direction of social movement unionism, even though the vast majority of U.S. unions are not yet of this type. Through an intricate set of arguments tracing multiple paths of causality on the leadership culture of a union, Robinson makes a strong case that many of the changes so detrimental to organized labor in the short run may actually be leading to a longer-term revival of the U.S. labor movement. This is because they force unions in the direction of social movement unionism, creating a more internally vibrant and externally powerful set of organizations. This intriguing and well-argued case deserves close attention from all who are concerned about the future of unions.

Paul Johnston likewise argues that social forces are driving the U.S. labor movement in the direction of social movement unionism. If this is true, he argues, a conceptual framework to guide and clarify the direction taken by the labor movement is needed. Although a wide variety of "social movement–like" activities have sprung up within multiple labor movements in recent years, there is a tremendous diversity of patterns and activities. How can all of the diverse movements be unified into a coherent whole, that is, within one "social movement frame"? Johnston argues that all movements "seek to defend, exercise, and extend the boundaries of citizenship." That is, labor can be conceptualized as a citizenship movement. By analyzing a wide variety of labor movements, he shows how the concept of citizenship provides a unifying agenda for a diverse movement. Johnston's article is simultaneously concrete in application while making a grand theoretical claim. It should provoke a great deal of reconsideration of our categories for conceptualizing organized labor in this country.

In the final chapter Bruce Nissen looks at one common theme running through most of the previous chapters: the need for unions to "transform" or "reinvent" themselves in some fundamental way. In a very preliminary analysis, he summarizes the arguments made by other chapter authors and notes the general contours of change to which they point: more inclusiveness, greater organizational flexibility, more rootedness in communities, less market orientation and more social orientation, more experimentation and risk taking, and ever-broadening conceptions of solidarity. Whether these changes are compatible and likely in the present environment remains to be seen from further innovation and analytic study.

References

Aronowitz, Stanley. 1998. *From the Ashes of the Old: American Labor and America's Future.* New York: Houghton Miffllin.

Bluestone, Barry, and Bennett Harrison. 1982. *The Deindustrialization of America.* New York: Basic Books.

Bluestone, Barry, Bennett Harrison, and Lawrence Baker. 1981. *Corporate Flight: The Causes and Consequences of Economic Dislocation.* Washington, DC: Progressive Alliance.

Bronfenbrenner, Kate. 1997. *Final Report: The Effects of Plant Closing or Threat of Plant Closing on the Right of Workers to Organize.* Dallas, TX: Secretariat of the North American Commission for Labor Cooperation.

Browne, Harry, and Beth Sims. 1993. *Runaway America: U.S. Jobs and Factories on the Move.* Albuquerque, NM: Resource Center Books.

Bruno, Robert. 2000. "Illinois Labor and the Return to Class Politics." *Working USA* 4, 1 (Summer): 92–126.

Craver, Charles B. 1995. *Can Unions Survive?* New York: New York University Press.

Craypo, Charles, and Bruce Nissen, eds. 1993. *Grand Designs: The Impact of Corporate Strategies on Workers, Unions, and Communities.* Ithaca, NY: ILR Press.

Eimer, Stuart, and Roland Zullo. 2000. "The 'Labor '96 Campaign: Testing the Effect of the Wisconsin AFL–CIO Political Outreach." *Working USA* 4, 1 (Summer): 73–91.

Fraser, Steve, and Joshua Freeman, eds. 1997. *Audacious Democracy: Labor, Intellectuals, and the Social Reconstruction of America.* New York: Houghton Mifflin.

Freeman, Richard. 1992. "Is Declining Unionization of the U.S. Good, Bad, or Irrelevant?" In *Unions and Economic Competitiveness,* eds. Larry Mishel and Paula Voos, pp. 143–169. Armonk, NY: M.E. Sharpe.

Garin, Geoffrey, and Guy Molyneux. 1998. "Informing and Empowering American Workers: Ten Rules for Union Political Action." In Mort., ed, pp. 113–126. New York: Verso.

Goddard, John, and John T. Delaney. 2000. "Reflections on the 'High Performance' Paradigm's Implications for Industrial Relations as a Field." *Industrial and Labor Relations Review* 53, 3 (April): 482–502.

Goldfield, Michael. 1987. *The Decline of Organized Labor in the United States.* Chicago: University of Chicago Press.

Kochan, Thomas, and Harry C. Katz, and Robert B. McKersie. 1986. *The Transformation of American Industrial Relations.* New York: Basic Books.

Kriesky, Jill, ed. 1998. *Working Together to Revitalize Labor in Our Communities: Case Studies of Labor Education–Central Labor Body Collaboration.* Orono,

ME: University and College Labor Education Association, University of Maine.

Lazes, Peter, and Jane Savage. 1997. "New Unionism and the Workplace of the Future." In Nissen, ed., pp. 181–207.

Mantsios, Greg, ed. 1998. *A New Labor Movement for the New Century*. New York: Garland Publishing.

McLewin, Philip J. 1999. "The Concerted Voice of Labor and the Surburbanization of Capital: Fragmentation of the Community Labor Council." In Nissen, ed., pp. 113–132.

——. 2001. "An Assessment of Union Cities: Where Is the Road Leading?" Paper presented to the United Association for Labor Education Conference, Boston, Massachusetts, April 26–28.

Meiksins-Wood, Ellen, Peter Meiksins, and Michael Yates, eds. 1999. *Rising from the Ashes: Labor in the Age of Global Capitalism*. New York: Monthly Review Press.

Moberg, David. 1989. "Hard Times for Labor." *Dissent*, Summer: 323–332.

Moody, Kim. 1988. *An Injury to All*. New York: Verso.

Mort, Jo-Ann, ed. 1998. *Not Your Father's Labor Movement: Inside the AFL–CIO*. New York: Verso.

Ness, Immanuel. 1998. "The Road to Union Cities: Labor Seeks to Transform the Culture and Structure of Central Labor Councils." *Working USA* 2, 4 (November–December): 78–86.

Nissen, Bruce. 1999. "Cross Border Alliances in the Era of Globalization." In Tillman and Cummings, eds., pp. 239–253.

——, ed. 1990. *U.S. Labor Relations 1945–1989: Accommodation and Conflict*. New York: Garland Publishing.

——, ed. 1997. *Unions and Workplace Reorganization*. Detroit: Wayne State University Press.

——, 1999. *Which Direction for Organized Labor? Essays on Organizing, Outreach, and Internal Transformations*. Detroit: Wayne State University Press.

Parker, Mike, and Jane Slaughter. 1997. "Advancing Unionism on the New Terrain." In Nissen, ed., pp. 208–225.

Robinson, J. Gregg. 1988. "American Unions in Decline: Problems and Prospects." *Critical Sociology* 15, 1 (Spring): 33–56.

Rosenthal, Steve. 1998. "Building to Win, Building to Last: The AFL–CIO Political Program." In Mort, ed., pp. 99–111.

Rothstein, Lawrence E. 1986. *Plant Closings: Power, Politics, and Workers*. Dover, MA: Auburn House Publishing.

Tillman, Ray, and Michael S. Cummings, eds. 1999. *The Transformation of U.S. Unions: Voices, Visions, and Strategies from the Grassroots*. Boulder, CO: Lynne Rienner.

PART I

CROSS-BORDER ORGANIZING AND SOLIDARITY

2

FREE TRADE AND WORKER SOLIDARITY IN THE NORTH AMERICAN AUTO INDUSTRY

STEVE BABSON

In many ways, the Ford assembly plants in Hermosillo, Sonora, and Wayne, Michigan, are remarkably similar. Both build the same car—the Escort until 1999, now the Focus. Both use nearly identical plant and equipment, featuring Kawasaki robots and Komatsu stamping presses. Both borrow selectively from a "lean production" model that includes work teams and just-in-time inventory. In both factories, union workers produce cars with competitive ratings for quality and cost (Babson 2000).

But there is one visible difference between the two plants that speaks directly to what U.S. and Canadian autoworkers fear most about globalization: the employee parking lots. At Wayne, they are full of late-model Ford, Chrysler, and GM products, most of them bigger, more expensive models than the subcompacts produced at the plant. At Hermosillo, on the other hand, the hourly lot is small, and there is not a single Focus behind the fence. As the best paid factory workers in the state, Hermosillo's Ford employees earned between $2 and $3 an hour in 2000 (*Contrato Colectivo de Trabajo 2000–2002:* 28)—more than double the rate in many of Sonora's border factories, but one-tenth the straight-time wages of Michigan's Ford workers. With the Focus selling for

The author would like to thank fellow members of the International Research Network on Autowork in the Americas (IRNAA) for their commentary and assistance, especially Huberto Juárez of the Autonomous University of Puebla.

$15,000 and up in Mexico, even this subcompact is a luxury item for most Mexicans. Consequently, Ford exports 95 percent of the Hermosillo plant's cars northward ("Producción Mensual"), leaving the parking lot to a fleet of white busses that every morning pick up workers who build cars for foreign customers.

These workers are not reconciled to their low wages, nor do they welcome their role as low-cost competitors of U.S. and Canadian autoworkers. Nevertheless, that is the role forced upon them in the global arena of free trade. A corresponding question is forced upon autoworkers across the continent: can the diverse labor movements of Mexico, the United States, and Canada overcome the competitive dynamic of free trade and establish a regional union movement based on cross-border solidarity? The answer to this question requires the posing of another: what is the economic and sociopolitical terrain of cross-border trade as it helps or hurts cross-border solidarity?

North American Auto

While auto labor in the new millennium remains fragmented and local, the auto companies are reorganizing on a continental basis. This dramatic shift in corporate strategy is highlighted by the contrasting dynamics in the United Auto Workers–General Motors (UAW-GM) strikes of 1970 and 1998.

In 1970, Mexico was an irrelevant footnote in the UAW's national strike against GM over issues of pay and retirement benefits. The company had just two factories in Mexico, employing a total of 4,300 workers: an aging truck plant in the Federal District, dating from the 1930s, and an engine plant in Toluca, opened in 1965. Both factories produced for Mexico's tiny domestic market, delivering a wide variety of models in relatively low volumes with little automation. It could be no other way—high tariffs and local-content requirements imposed by the country's nationalist government prevented GM from importing vehicles (Morris 1998, 115–116; Middlebrook 1995, 231; A. García and Lara 1998, 207–213). At a time when production totaled just 165,000 units in 1969 (less than 2 percent of the U.S. total), Mexico hardly mattered to the strike antagonists in the year that followed.

In 1998, however, GM's Mexican operations were a flash point in local strikes that shut down the company's North American operations. This was especially evident at Delphi's Flint East plant, the second of two factories in Flint, Michigan, where local strikes over work intensity and job security gradually starved GM's assembly plants of parts. Over the preceding twenty years, the Flint East workforce had fallen from 13,000 to fewer than 6,000 as the company installed new technology and expanded its Mexican production of instrument clusters and other small parts. "They just crated the equipment, hoisted it onto a tractor trailer, and sent it away to Mexico," as one local leader told the *New York Times*. "There's hardly anybody at this plant who hasn't seen machinery moving out in a crate with an address on it says 'Mexico'" (Dillon 1998).

Since the late 1970s, GM has been unloading these crates in Matamoros, Reynosa, Ciudad Juárez, and other factory towns on Mexico's northern border, a region known for its low wages and low levels of unionization. By 1998, GM's Delphi parts division had grown to fifty border factories employing 58,000 Mexican workers, nearly matching the 64,000 union members at its U.S. and Canadian parts plants (Delphi Automotive Systems 1998). In the meantime, GM was also opening new assembly plants in north and central Mexico, where workers produced 315,000 Cavaliers, Silverados, and Suburbans in 1998—two-thirds for export (Lira 2000). Significantly, of twenty-nine GM assembly plants in North America, the company's plant in Ramos Arizpe was one of only two that continued operating throughout the eight-week Flint strike, apparently supplied by parts made in Mexico and Brazil; among the few assembly plants able to reopen before the end of the Flint strikes, the first was the company's plant in Silao, Guanajuato ("GM to Resume Production at Mexican Plant Next Week" 1998).

In the scale and scope of its commitment to Mexico, GM has been at the cutting edge of wider changes transforming the southern tier of the North American auto industry. At each step in this transforming process, government policy on both sides of the border has provided the blueprint and the incentives for change. In this sense, "globalization" is not the spontaneous expression of market forces so often invoked by free trade proponents but is rather a product of public policy aligned—more often than not—with corporate planning. At the same time, globalization is not wholly determined by the policy goals of the corporate interests that profit by it. Certainly, U.S. corporations have reaped the bottom-line harvest of Mexico's low wages, but, ironically, it was the political success of the U.S. labor movement in 1965 that unintentionally opened the door for GM-Delphi.

In 1965 the AFL–CIO and the farmworkers union won repeal of the bracero program, a World War II–era policy that gave Mexican farmworkers temporary visas to travel north and work for U.S. agribusiness. Since this transient workforce undermined the organizing efforts of the farmworkers union, the labor movement lobbied the Johnson administration for repeal. Success created a new problem for Mexico, however, since it left Mexican farmworkers stranded along the border. In response, the Mexican government implemented a "border industrialization program" that would attract corporate investment to the northernmost edge of the country. Companies that built "maquiladora" (or "maquila") plants, as these border factories were called, could import parts duty-free and pay taxes only on the value added *so long as* the plant exported 100 percent of its output back to the United States (MacArthur 2000, 37; Kopinak 1996, 7–8).

The goal was to attract jobs to the economically depressed north without otherwise amending the policies of economic nationalism that dated back to the Mexican revolution of 1911–1917. That upheaval had been sparked by popular resentment of the Díaz dictatorship's close alliance with U.S. corporations and foreign landowners, who together owned 25 percent of the country's land and dominated Mexico's economy (Hart 1987, 276–326). To dismantle this original "free trade" regime, the revolution's leaders eventually (in the 1930s) nationalized key industries like oil and electricity while protecting Mexican business against foreign competition. The maquiladoras were to be the exception to rules that still opposed "Yankee imperialism" with high tariffs, local content requirements, and restrictions on foreign ownership (Morris 1998, 115–117).

In the 1970s, however, the government began to open additional loopholes for maquiladora employers, including a growing list of exemptions from federal labor law. By 1974 there were already 455 maquila factories along the border, employing 75,000 workers, most of them underpaid women rather than the male farmworkers originally targeted by the program. Investment accelerated yet again in the 1980s, when Mexico experienced a severe debt crisis and the government—at the urging of U.S. creditors and the International Monetary Fund—abandoned its previous strategy of economic nationalism. To pay its dollar-denominated debts, the Mexican government not only widened the incentives for U.S. corporations to invest in maquiladora production, but also began to open domestic markets to investment and trade. By the mid-1980s, currency devaluations had driven the dollar cost of Mexican labor below levels paid in South Korea and Taiwan, making Mexico all the more attractive to foreign capital (Bureau of Labor Statistics 1999). In this sense, the "maquilazation" of the economy was already well advanced by 1993, when the North American Free Trade Agreement (NAFTA) ratified Mexico's integration into a North American trading bloc dominated by the United States. Where before the opening of Mexico's economy to foreign investment depended on shifting government policy, now the changes were codified in treaty law (see Carrillo 2000; Kopinak 1996, 8–17; Morris 1998).

By the turn of the century, these policy-inspired transformations had dramatically realigned Mexico's industrial economy, with the auto industry (referred to also as "auto") taking the lead. Mexico's output of cars and light trucks had soared to 1.9 million units by the year 2000, a growth of 980 percent compared to 1970 and more than double the 755,000 units built in 1990 (Chappell 2001; "The Automotive Sectors of Latin America 1999," 292). The five largest manufacturers—Volkswagen, GM, Daimler–Chrysler, Ford, and Nissan—accounted for 99 percent of total production, with GM alone planning to double output to more than 600,000 units by 2007 (Karoub 1998; Lira 2000). A dramatic shift toward production for export was also gaining momentum. In 1970, Mexican vehicle exports were effectively zero; by 1986, they had inched upwards to 72,000 cars and light trucks, or 21 percent of total production; by 2000, exports had climbed to 1.4 million vehicles, representing 74 percent of total production. Domestic sales of cars and light trucks meanwhile climbed to 854,000 in 2000, nearly half of them imports (Chappell 2001). While this marked a new record, it represented a growth of just 21 percent since the previous record year of 1992; in the same period, production for export had grown 260 percent. This shift toward production for export entailed numerous changes in Mexican assembly plants, including a reduction in the number of models produced, a corresponding acceleration of production as model mix was simplified, an increase in automation, a shift toward certain lean production methods, and dramatic improvements in productivity and quality as these changes were implemented.

The growth in maquiladora factories continued as well. In March 2000, the industry magazine *Twin Plant News* counted a total of 3,384 maquila plants employing 1.2 million workers—a 1,500 percent growth in employment since 1974. Despite the low wages in the border plants, rural poverty and farm mechanization continued to drive new recruits north, swelling the overcrowded colonias near the factories. The fastest growing maquila sector in this hothouse economy was auto parts, with 228 plants employing 214,000 workers, trailing only the textile/clothing and electrical/electronic industries ("Maquila Scorecard 2000"). By the mid-1990s, Mexico's total employment in parts making (maquila as well as domestic firms) was already 2.5 times greater than Canada's and 45 percent of U.S. levels, with average hourly pay and benefits totaling just $3.32 an hour (Weintraub 1998, 235–237). In maquila plants on the northern border, total labor costs were lower still, estimated at $1.75 an hour in 1999 (MacArthur 2000, 332). In a significant departure from previous maquila investment, GM-Delphi in 1995 also began to transfer engineering work from Anderson, Indiana, to its research and development facility in Ciudad Juárez (Carrillo 2000).

In sum, Mexico's integration into a North American auto industry has followed an accelerating course over the last thirty years, guided and promoted by public policy initiatives on both sides of the border. The result, however, is not a uniform distribution of sales and production across the continent's three countries. Instead, Mexico and Canada have both become—for different reasons—low-cost export platforms to the U.S. market. Canadian labor costs expressed in U.S. dollars were roughly 26 percent lower in the mid-1990s than in the United States, with the $11 an hour (Canadian) differential attributable to Canada's devalued currency and lower health care costs (Kumar and Holmes 1998, 103). In contrast, Mexico's cost advantage has depended on public policies favoring low wages and suppression of labor rights.

It is in this uneven terrain that corporations find the leverage to exert downward pressure on wages and working conditions throughout the North American auto industry.

Downward Convergence

There is growing public awareness that Mexico's low wages and troubled unions are the fulcrum for downward pressure on pay and working conditions north of the border. While thousands of U.S. autoworkers have lost their jobs because the employer transferred operations to Mexico, the far larger number who remain have experienced a more pervasive form of "whipsawing"—the *threat* of transfer to Mexico or elsewhere unless workers moderate their wage demands and amend their work rules. What is less well known is that many Mexican autoworkers have also been victimized by whipsawing. In fact, the "southern strategy" of corporations moving to cheaper labor sites in the United States (and beyond) has been matched by an identical "northern strategy" in Mexico (Bensusán and Bayón 1998, 119–120).

The southward migration of employers is a well-established feature of U.S. labor relations, dating back to the nineteenth century. In the last twenty years, auto parts makers have extended this union-avoidance strategy beyond the southern United States to include Mexico, with a corresponding multiplication of whipsawing threats in the remaining plants of the north. Two examples will suffice, one involving an organizing drive, the other contract negotiations.

ITT Automotive

When workers at ITT Automotive in Michigan tried to organize a union and bargain for improvements in wages and working conditions, the company responded with a fear campaign focused on Mexico, as described by this report to the NAFTA labor commission:

> The company parked thirteen flat-bed tractor-trailers loaded with shrink-wrapped production equipment in front of the plant for the duration of the campaign with large hot-pink signs posted on the side which read "Mexico transfer job." The equipment came from a production line they had closed down over the weekend without warning. The same company also flew employees from their Mexican facility to videotape Michigan workers on a production line which supervisors claimed they were "considering moving to Mexico." (Bronfenbrenner 1996, 11)

This same report indicated that following the passage of NAFTA, employers were more likely to threaten to move production to avoid unionization, with 65 percent of manufacturing companies using this tactic against union organizing drives surveyed between 1993 and 1995. In 10 percent of the more than 500 campaigns surveyed, union organizers reported that companies like ITT openly threatened to move to Mexico, while in many others the threat was veiled or delivered in one-on-one meetings with supervisors (Bronfenbrenner 1996, 9–13).

GM-Delphi–Packard Electric

This company's Warren, Ohio, factory employed 13,500 workers in 1973 making the wire harnesses that distribute electrical signals throughout the car. GM began to move the most labor-intensive tasks south in the mid-1970s, first to Mississippi, then to Mexico. By 1998, virtually all of the assembly work was in northern Mexico, and the Warren plant employed fewer than 6,000. To stem the continuing job loss, the International Union of Electrical Workers (IUE) agreed to cut wages in half for new hires and postpone their movement to full pay until senior workers retired. "Every discussion or complaint," one worker said of her interactions with management, met the same response: "'We can always move your job to Mexico'" (cited in Helper 1998, 309–324). This whipsawing dynamic is especially powerful in the industry's more labor-intensive parts sector. While inflation-adjusted wages fell just 2 percent between 1988 and 1998 in U.S. assembly operations (pulled down by nonunion transplants), they fell 9 percent in the auto parts sector and 13 percent in engine electrical equipment (Herzenberg 1999, 6).

Wage indexes do not tell the whole story since they fail to capture the effects of a pervasive downward pressure on work rules that is spreading to the assembly plant sector. The potential for this kind of whipsawing grows as the companies build more car and truck models on both sides of the border, as indicated in Table 2.1. Multiple sourcing is currently the Big Three's preferred option since it distributes production across the continental market and makes the company less vulnerable to local disruptions. In Mexico, compact cars are more likely to find middle-class customers, while light trucks go to fleet sales and wealthy households; when these domestic markets slump, as in the mid-1990s, output can be exported to the north in even greater numbers ("The Automotive Sectors of Latin America, 1999" 270, 281–285, 292). Equally important, Mexican factories establish a low-cost benchmark for work organization and labor relations and with it, a heightened potential for whipsawing U.S./Canadian plants. This possibility has already been demonstrated in the case of GM Lordstown. With the aging of the J-car models produced in Ohio and Ramos Arizpe, the company proposed that the next generation Delta model be assembled in a new "modular" factory next to the old Lordstown plant—a move that would entail outsourcing of major components to lower-wage suppliers, with corresponding cuts in the assembly plant workforce. Local bargaining over the required work rule revisions began in 1998 amid headlines announcing that "GM Weighs Scrapping Ohio Plant, Building in Mexico" (1998). Based on company documents leaked to the media, these reports put additional pressure on local union leaders to meet at least some of the

Table 2.1

Cross-Border Vehicle Sourcing by the Big Three, 1998

Company and models	Mexican plant	U.S.–Canadian plant
Daimler–Chrysler		
Neon	Toluca	Belvedire
Cirrus, Stratus,	Toluca	Sterling Heights
Plymouth Breeze	Toluca	Bloomington[b]
Sebring, Avenger	Saltillo	St. Louis #2
Dodge Ram	Lago Alberto	Warren Truck
General Motors		
Cavalier, Sunbird	Ramos Arizpe	Lordstown, Lansing
Suburban, Silverado,	Silao[a]	Janesville, Arlington,[a]
Tahoe, Yukon, Sierra,		Oshawa, Fort Wayne, Flint
Chevrolet Pickup		Truck
Ford		
Escort, Tracer	Hermosillo	Wayne
Contour, Mystique	Cuautitlán	Kansas City
Ford F-Series	Cuautitlán	Kansas City, Kentucky Truck,
		Ontario, Norfolk

Source: Compiled from "North America 2000 Vehicle Production," *Automotive Industries*, October 1999, pullout; *Harbour Report 1999*, pp. 29–31.
[a]Trucks and SUVs.
[b]Mitsubishi, formerly jointly owned with Chrysler.

company's demands or risk losing the new model. Bargaining was suspended in 1999 pending national contract talks, and GM soon after postponed introduction of the Delta models, citing market forecasts and the shift to light trucks (Pryweller 1999). When local bargaining resumed, the union signed a "shelf agreement" that promised to reduce job classifications and trim the size of work teams if GM chose Lordstown to produce the next generation of small cars (Bureau of National Affairs 2001, A-3).

In the meantime, GM had already installed its modular manufacturing system in Ramos Arizpe, where assembly of the Pontiac Aztek began in 2000 in a new factory based on the same principals of outsourcing and radical downsizing of the workforce. "The Mexican plant," reported *Automotive News*, "provides the closest look at where GM wants to go with its new and renovated assembly plants in the United States" (cited in Miller 2000, 1).

As it happens, Ramos Arizpe also shows where the companies want to go with their new assembly plants *in Mexico*. In this case, the Aztek factory and other northern plants built since 1980 are the fulcrum for whipsawing that points southward, toward Mexican autoworkers in the older manufacturing centers around Mexico City and the Federal District. In fact, GM's initial move northward to Ramos Arizpe, where it broke ground for new assembly and engine plants in 1980, marked the opening round in the corporate campaign to renovate Mexican automaking. GM's target was the militant local union in the Federal District plant, where workers had conducted six strikes between 1965 and 1979, winning work rules and wages that put them in the forefront of Mexican auto unions. In 1980, however, GM refused to submit to contract terms granting bargaining jurisdiction to the Federal District union for any new GM plants in Mexico. The 106–day strike that followed ended in defeat for the Federal District union, leaving GM free to open the first Ramos Arizpe plant under contract with a rival labor organization (Bayón 1997, 90; Middlebrook 1995, 270, 273). Thereafter, the lower wages and weaker union traditions north of Mexico City attracted additional investment in assembly and engine plants: Chrysler Saltillo (engines and trucks), Ford Chihuahua (engines), Ford Hermosillo (cars), Nissan Aguascalientes (engines and cars), GM Silao (trucks), and Ramos Arizpe again (SUVs) (Bayón 1997, 62–65; Middlebrook 1995, 271–272). At the same time, Ford closed two plants in the Mexico City area and humbled the union at a third—Cuautitlán—in a series of bitter strikes and violent confrontations between 1987 and 1991. In 1995, GM capped its "northern" strategy by shutting the Federal District plant and shifting truck making to Silao, a greenfield plant with a fledgling union. Volkswagen—the only major company that did not move northward— otherwise conformed to events in 1992, firing the entire workforce to break a strike and enforce its model of lean production (Bayón 1997, 93–96; Juárez 1998, 173–205).

For many of Mexico's unionized autoworkers, the outcome of this process has been no less disastrous than it has been for UAW and Canadian Auto Workers (CAW) members victimized by whipsawing. While jobs have grown in the north and central regions, they have fallen in the south, where wages are higher and union traditions stronger. The mechanism for ratcheting pay downwards was the same as in Ohio, with the polarities reversed: workers at Ford's Cuautitlán assembly plant near Mexico City were told in 1987 that because their high wages made them uncompetitive, the company would not match the 23 percent raise it had already negotiated with Hermosillo's plant-based union. To end the

Cuautitlán union's sixty-one-day strike protesting this ultimatum, Ford fired the entire workforce, annulled the contract (paying a legally required severance), and selectively rehired 80 percent of the workforce under amended work rules and wages. Because the rehired workers had lost their seniority, Ford's payroll costs fell an estimated 40 percent (R. Garcia and Hills 1998, 146–150).

While whipsawing is primarily a north–south phenomenon in the assembly and engine-making sectors of Mexico's auto industry, it covers all points of the compass in the maquila sector, where employers can plausibly threaten to move labor-intensive operations to whatever location offers the cheapest labor. Even in Nogales, a border city with relatively low wages, nonunion auto parts workers report that complaints to supervisors elicit this all too common response: "They answered that we could complain all we wanted but that there was no other law than the maquila law and that no one can tell them anything, because if they do the plants will leave" (cited in Kopinak 1996, 142).

These constraints are wound all the tighter by government policies that hold wages below inflation while suppressing independent unions. Designed to attract further investment, this growth strategy has put Mexican workers on a wildly careening roller coaster since the late 1970s, with real wages falling dramatically during periods of economic crisis and peso devaluation—the late1970s to early 1980s, the mid-1980s, and the mid-1990s—and rising slowly during subsequent booms. From their record high in 1977, real manufacturing wages had fallen 33 percent by 1999—despite a doubling in labor productivity (Ramírez de la O 2000, 18).

Potential Allies

While many autoworkers in the United States and Canada assume that Mexicans must be benefiting from globalization to the same degree that northern workers are losing, the actual outcomes are mixed on both sides of the border. Jobs are up in most years, but real wages are stagnant or falling, bargaining leverage is weakened, and de-unionization is growing across the continent. On this basis alone, proponents of cross-border solidarity can find potential allies from Puebla to Oshawa.

Mobilizing that potential is difficult, however, when there are so few links among the labor movements of North America. Until the 1970s, U.S. labor generally favored policies that opened foreign markets to union made exports, and so long as import competition remained weak, this free-trade alliance with U.S. corporations went largely unopposed in union circles. When corporate America began to export jobs rather than goods, the initial response was protectionist, with most unions favoring "Buy American" campaigns that stressed patriotic feeling over cross-border solidarity. Efforts to find allies in foreign countries were also hampered by Cold War politics, which narrowed the range of acceptable allies to official, anticommunist organizations like the Confederation of Mexican Workers (CTM) (Nissen 1999, 44–45; Cowie 1997, 3–32).

For its part, Mexico's dominant labor organization neither welcomed nor promoted cross-border links through most of the 1980s and 1990s. The CTM's aversion, if not hostility, to international links with North American labor was rooted in that organization's unique ties to the Mexican state and the seventy-year reign of the Party of the Institutional Revolution (PRI). The CTM was forged in the 1930s, and its incorporation into the ruling party was part of a wider realignment of Mexican politics under President Lázaro Cárdenas (1934–1940). The Cárdenas government was moving leftward—nationalizing U.S. oil companies, initiating land reform, and supporting union organization—and the newly organized CTM, as it mobilized support for these initiatives, soon gained official status in the party's "labor sector." Subsequent presidential regimes were rarely so populist or labor-friendly, but PRI governments still delivered a widening stream of welfare benefits and social programs, including (in 1943) a national health care system organized under the Mexican Institute for Social Security (IMSS). As the dominant organizations in the PRI's official labor sector, the CTM's affiliated unions automatically counted their constituents as party members; the PRI, in turn, routinely appointed CTM leaders to the tripartite councils (labor, management, and government) of the IMSS and the Boards of Conciliation and Arbitration—the latter regulating union formation and labor relations. By the 1960s, the CTM's "official" status as the ruling party's labor arm had thoroughly politicized labor relations in auto and elsewhere, with collective bargaining often reduced to top-down deal-making between corporate and political elites (La Botz 1992, 64–74; Middlebrook 1995, 89–106).

This would change in the 1970s in ways that still define the labor relations system in auto, especially in the assembly sector. Until that decade, most autoworkers were subordinated to leaders appointed by the CTM's state federations. Many local unions had no regular elections, only occasional meetings, and no printed contracts. The CTM's political leverage meant that federal and local Boards of Conciliation and Arbitration favored the federation over rival unions, and the "exclusion clause" in most contracts required companies to fire any member—dissidents especially—expelled from the union. As the auto industry grew, however, these paternalistic structures came under increasing pressure from members protesting the lack of representation, and with President Luís Echeverría's equivocal support in the early 1970s, a movement to democratize union governance gained the upper hand. In addition to establishing regular elections and general assemblies in many local auto unions, movement leaders initiated an escalating strike wave that saw the number of walkouts jump from just two during the 1960s to at least twenty-five between 1972 and 1979. By the end of the 1970s, many unions in the assembly sector had won higher wages and improved work rules governing work intensity, seniority rights, transfers, promotions, and use of temporary workers (Middlebrook 1995, 222–254; Tuman 1998, 148–178).

As we have seen, events in the 1980s and 1990s reversed this trend with a series of union defeats at GM, Ford, and Volkswagen. Yet even as assembly plant locals had to accept flexible contracts with diminished work rules, some retained the democratic reforms of the 1970s and some—in the north—adopted their own democratic by laws (Babson 2000; Middlebrook 1995, 273–274). At the same time, the CTM's national leaders were endorsing (sometimes reluctantly) the PRI government's turn toward free trade (Bayón 1997, 36–37, 57), while corrupt leaders sold sweetheart "protection contracts" to companies as low-cost insurance against unrest (LaBotz 1992, 53–55). The result has been a continuing tension between local protests and official condemnation, as plant-based unions have contested low wages and diluted profit sharing while national leaders have supported government wage ceilings and productivity campaigns. This widening gap between union members and national leaders was underlined in 1996, when the national CTM canceled its traditional May Day march to forestall popular protests and hundreds of thousands of workers poured into the streets anyway. The CTM's dominant position eroded further after 1997, when several major unions joined with the Authentic Workers Front (FAT) to establish the National Workers Union (UNT) as an independent federation (Brooks and Carson 1998).

With John Sweeney's election to the AFL-CIO presidency in 1995, the U.S. labor movement began to reach beyond its continuing ties to the CTM and establish parallel links with these new formations. In the eyes of some CTM leaders, this simply confirmed their claim that U.S. and Canadian unionists were "foreign destabilizers" and protectionists in league with local dissidents. For independent unions and democratic currents within the CTM, on the other hand, the support of North American unionists was a welcome boost to the widening ferment in Mexico's labor movement. Even with the PRI's defeat in the presidential elections of 2000, however, the prospects for union growth and revitalization remain mixed. The pro-business National Action Party (PAN) won the election on a promise of reform and democratization, but local PAN governments in northern Mexico have been uniformly hostile to democratic and independent unions in the maquiladora plants. Local and federal Boards of Conciliation and Arbitration are still dominated by old-guard appointees linked to local elites and will likely continue to rule against plant-based dissidents and independent unions. Protection contracts barring independent organization are still in place across the maquiladora zone, and extra-legal arrest and official violence remain as the final bulwarks of the status quo (Garza 2000; La Botz 2000).

What clearly has changed in recent years is the dramatic widening of dialogue and debate, both within Mexico's labor movement and among union activists on all sides of the border. In assessing what this means for the North American auto industry, it is important to recognize that the presumption of a CTM monolith—however relevant in the past—no longer holds. The underlying structure of labor relations in the Mexican auto industry has always been decentralized and fragmented, a fact obscured by government efforts to rule by decree and by the national CTM's periodic interventions in local bargaining. Otherwise, there is far less uniformity in labor relations than is the case in the United States and Canada. While plant-by-plant variations have grown in all three countries, there are still national auto unions in the United States and Canada, with pattern agreements on wages, benefits, and other matters applying across assembly, power train, and Big Three parts making (the latter dwindling). In Mexico, on the other hand, there is no national autoworkers' union and, consequently, no industrywide pattern. For that matter, there is no companywide collective bargaining in any sector of the industry. Each assembly plant negotiates separately, with links to state and regional CTM federations usually outweighing the connection to national bodies (Bayón 1997, 53, 72–73). In the maquiladora/supplier sector, variation is equally evident, encompassing democratic movements within the CTM and independent unions fighting for recognition, as well as the more numerous company unions and protection contracts.

Consequently, the prospects for cross-border solidarity vary according to local conditions, a fact that widens the range of possible initiatives while also limiting the degree to which success in one location can be generalized to others. Consider the variation in the following cases.

Nogales

This production center on the Sonora–Arizona border is known for the lower level of unionization and the higher proportion of men in its maquiladora factories. "The only unions here," one U.S. plant manager has observed, "are ones which the company pays the dues for, and the workers don't even know they belong" (cited in Kopinak 1996, 169).

Matamoros

At the eastern end of the border, workers at least know they belong to a union. More than any other CTM affiliate in the maquila economy, the Union of Industrial Workers and Day Laborers (SJOI) has a reputation for contesting the terms and conditions of work and winning higher wages and shorter work hours. However, SJOI's capacity to win these improvements declined after a bruising confrontation in 1992, when the union's aging leader, Agapito Gonzalez, threatened to strike if employers did not agree to a 30 percent raise. On the eve of the walkout, federal police arrested Gonzalez and removed him to Mexico City, where he was placed under house arrest in the Hospital Los Angeles. The chastened union called off the strike and settled for a smaller raise (Adler 2000, 277–284).

Ford Hermosillo

Democratic ferment in this plant is measured by the number of caucuses—six—that have contested recent union elections. The CTM organized a national committee of Ford workers in the 1970s, but there has been no companywide bargaining since Ford closed its Federal District plants in the mid-1980s. In this context, the local has adopted a widening repertoire of collective actions to press for higher wages and profit sharing, including formal strikes, unofficial walkouts, plant-gate sitdowns, "collective absences," and slowdowns. After years of housing its offices inside the factory, the local has purchased land near the plant to build a union hall (Babson 2000).

GM Silao

There is no national bargaining for GM plants and, unlike Ford, no national CTM committee. Workers at the Silao truck plant are members of the Union of Workers in the Metal and Mechanical Industries (SITIMM), a regional CTM affiliate with thirty-six locals and 14,000 members, most of them in the state of Guanajuato. In addition to the Silao plant, SITIMM also represents several major companies in the nearby supplier park, including American Axle's new plant supplying rear axles for Silao. Since GM Silao opened in 1995, SITIMM's plant union has developed a vigorous internal democracy, with the 2000 elections going to a militant slate demanding—and winning—wage increases well above the government benchmark.[1]

Chrysler Toluca

The democracy movement of the 1970s never reached this assembly plant. A former production manager served as the union's general secretary between 1970 and 1993, initially appointed by the regional CTM and thereafter running unopposed in ritualistic elections. John Tuman describes his hold on power:

> With the help of the company and the CTM, he defeated emerging democracy movements in 1970 and 1975 by applying the exclusion clause against dissident workers. Because of his loyalty to the CTM, the general secretary of the Chrysler local was made a PRI labor sector representative in the Chamber of Deputies in the 1970s. Retiring from office in 1993, he appointed his son as the new general secretary. (Tuman 1998, 157–158)

VW Puebla

The largest plant union in Mexico's auto industry also has the most complicated organizational history. Workers voted in 1972 to leave the CTM and affiliate with the Independent Worker Unity (UOI); in 1981 they voted to leave the UOI and remain independent; in 1992, following defeat in the strike and lockout of that year, they affiliated with the Federation of Goods and Services Unions (FESEBES); in 1997, when FESEBES helped found the new national labor federation, the UNT, the VW union became one of its largest affiliates (Vanderbush 1998, 254–260). In the union's 2000 elections, a new leadership slate—one of twenty contesting the outcome in a plant workforce of nearly 13,000 workers—won control of the bargaining committee and launched a sustained drive for wage increases well beyond the 9 percent offered by VW and endorsed by the government. When the government declared the union's five-day strike to be illegal on technical grounds, union leaders mobilized a campaign of work-to-rule, refusal of overtime, plant-gate sit-ins, marches, rallies, and highway blockings that finally forced the company to agree to an 18 percent wage increase. Since 1999, as VW has outsourced major components to an ever-growing supplier park, the VW union has also begun to support strikes and organizing among parts workers.[2]

Cross-Border Solidarity

Given the fragmentation of Mexico's auto unions, the extreme decentralization of bargaining, and the varied organizational histories of plant unions, effective strategies for cross-border solidarity will have to adjust to local conditions on a case-by-case basis. Even in this varied terrain, however, there are some common features that can help, or hurt, the prospects for mobilization.

On the positive side, the North American integration of production has established a common "occupational idiom" familiar to autoworkers across the continent. As we have seen, workers are building the same parts and finished vehicles for the same market, and while this certainly widens the opportunities for whipsawing, it also demonstrates the potential for a countervailing solidarity. Efforts to support workers in diverse locations will also be aided by the shared nomenclature of transnational production. Mexican plants are still less automated than their northern counterparts, but the gap has narrowed dramatically in recent years. Work organization is likewise converging in assembly and first-tier supplier plants as companies borrow from the same lean production menu. Implementation varies according to the unique histories of each location, but the general terms (and the accompanying grievances) are becoming commonplace: "elimination of waste" (eroding workers' rest time), "quality in station" (adding responsibility without authority), "just-in-time inventory" (intensifying work stress), and "team-work" (promoting production-only goals). Whipsawing, as we have seen, victimizes workers in Mexico as well as in the United States and Canada, and it is accompanied by a second dynamic that most UAW and CAW members would not expect to find in Mexico: "outsourcing"—a word often used without translation—is increasingly on the minds of Mexican workers in the assembly sector, where companies bid out seats, instrument panels, and other components to suppliers paying lower wages.

At the same time, there are many barriers that stand in the way of a wider mobilization, none more obvious than the language barrier between Spanish- and English-speaking peoples. So long as this barrier blocks the way, routine communication will depend on specialists and translation media rather than the worker-to-worker interaction that builds a wider movement. This hurdle can be lowered: more people are learning a second language, simultaneous translation is becoming more available, and translation software makes written exchanges more feasible. But these remedies go only so far. Learning a second language is not for everyone, and translation services are not easily deployed beyond conferences and written communications. Many of these solutions also require up-front funding for classes, translators, and computers.

A second barrier is the heightened job insecurity felt in many corners of the auto industry. Shifting market shares, global mergers, and periodic downsizing all contribute to this anxious state, which continental whipsawing makes all the more intense, continuous, and potentially divisive for any cross-border union movement. Particularly in assembly and first-tier supplier plants, where pay and working conditions tend to be higher, union members and leaders in Mexico as well as in the United States and Canada naturally rally to the defense of their livelihood. Whipsawing may inspire some of them to acts of solidarity, but in the absence of countervailing union strategies, it can easily inspire a plant-based patriotism and a backlash against all competitors. The temptation to fall back on jingoistic or racist sloganeering is especially powerful when "the others" competing for jobs are foreign and remote—cast in stereotypical form as "gringo protectionists" or "wetbacks who work for nothing."

This chauvinistic potential can be countered only with campaigns that unite rather than divide workers. The shift from "Buy American" to "Buy Union" is a step in the right direction, as is any rallying cry that directs attention to the need for an *upward* convergence of pay and working conditions. The problem with Hermosillo, then, is not that Ford is investing in Mexican production, but that Ford is investing in Mexican production without *also* investing in Mexican consumption. Mexico's autoworkers (like their U.S. and Canadian counterparts) need good paying jobs, with real wages that are not only "good" compared to Mexico's falling standards, but "good" compared to their rising productivity. According to mainstream economists, this improvement in real earnings can happen only gradually—ignoring the fact that it did not happen *at all* through most of the 1980s and 1990s, while in our own history it has happened rather suddenly: in 1914, for example, when Henry Ford doubled wages in one stroke of the pen, and in 1946–1948, when the UAW and GM agreed to sizable wage increases protected by a cost-of-living escalator. In a context where Mexican workers need substantial and steady improvements in purchasing power to become customers for their own product, these remedies can find support among autoworkers on either side of the U.S–Mexico border.

The movement for such an upward convergence cannot be sustained, however, if collaboration is limited to the occasional summit meeting of top leaders. Important as these are, cross-border solidarity must also become a focal point of union-wide initiatives that counter the potential for a xenophobic backlash. Efforts in this direction have gained some momentum in recent years, and this accumulating experience suggests the possible future of a North American movement of autoworkers. Its elements would include the following.

Local-to-Local Meetings

The entry-level basis for cross-border solidarity is the face-to-face encounter among workers making the same product or working for the same company. Local-to-local meetings can begin with information exchanges that increase understanding and deepen the commitment to continued communication and proceed from there to more focused collaboration as opportunities arise.

Worker- to-Worker Meetings

Plant-based union meetings are not always possible, particularly in the maquiladora parts sector where union organization is sparse or is corrupted by protection contracts and company unions. On the U.S. and

Canadian side, the initiative may lie with citywide or regional bodies prepared to support the work of volunteers drawn from a variety of locals. UAW Region 1A on Detroit's west side has sponsored an International Labor Solidarity Network (ILSN) that periodically sends delegations to maquila cities and Big Three assembly plants in Mexico, with followup reports to regional and local meetings after they return. ILSN has also sponsored visits to Detroit by maquiladora workers reporting on their efforts to organize. Such initiatives have only a limited impact if divorced from a wider commitment to building a cross-border movement, but they are a necessary first step toward changing workers' perceptions. In 1998, the Central Labor Council of Northeast Indiana sent a mixed delegation to Reynosa that included workers from United Steering—a plant losing jobs to Mexico. "It's amazing that people survive under these circumstances," the president of Paperworkers Local 7452 later told his members at United Steering, reporting on the endemic poverty in Reynosa. "It sure helped us realize that the problem is not Mexican workers taking our jobs; it's corporate America and our own government" ("Indiana Labor Trip to Yield Results" 1998). This kind of collective experience can spur unionists to more concrete action.

Solidarity Funds

Hosting cross-border delegations and worker-to-worker meetings can be expensive, especially for the cash-starved groups that support maquiladora organizing. Organizations like the Coalition for Justice in the Maquiladoras (CJM) or the Border Committee of Women Workers (CFO) depend on dues and limited contributions from religious, environmental, labor, and women's groups on both sides of the border. To support their efforts, a growing (but still small) number of unions have established "Solidarity Funds" to help staff workers' centers and support the cost of organizers. The CAW's Social Justice fund is the largest of these, generating about $2.5 million annually through contract language obligating employers (about 100 in all) to pay a per capita amount into the fund—three cents an hour in the case of Big Three contracts, down to one cent an hour for smaller firms.[3] Several other unions have established a payroll checkoff ($1 per pay period in the case of United Electrical Workers [UE] contracts) to support cross-border initiatives (Wells 1998).[4] In the case of the Northeast Indiana Central Labor Council (CLC), local unions have pledged to support the CLC's solidarity fund with contributions and plant-gate collections, the money ear-marked for a CFO organizer in Reynosa ("Indiana Labor Trip to Yield Results" 1998).

Health and Safety Training

Because there is no national auto union in Mexico and because bargaining has so often been subordinated to political deal making, there is a corresponding underdevelopment of the technical skills and training that support broad-based union organization. Cross-border initiatives that help address this lack of infrastructure are especially visible in the area of workplace health and safety, with both union and activist groups like the Maquiladora Health and Safety Network providing training on hazard recognition and control. The CJM significantly expanded its training program in 2000 with regional meetings in Ciudad Juárez, Reynosa, and Nuevo Laredo, drawing local organizers and plant workers to train-the-trainer workshops conducted by UAW and CAW staff (Coalition for Justice in the Maquiladoras 2000; Kourous 1998).[5]

Crisis Support

The crucial role of cross-border solidarity has been underlined in the prolonged struggle to win recognition for the independent union at Han Young, a Korean-owned supplier of truck frames located in Tijuana. With the first strike in 1997 over low wages and dangerous shop conditions, community-based activists and unionists in the United States and Canada supported the Han Young workers against company firings and government suppression. A threatened boycott of Hyundai—Han Young's customer—and picketing of showrooms, loading docks, and Mexican consulates in twenty cities generated substantial publicity that helped restrain government suppression of the independents. While the outcome of this battle swung between defeat and victory and back again, with complicating divisions among the independent unionists, the Han Young struggle achieved a singular victory when government officials had to grant legal standing to the first official strike by an independent union in the maquiladora zone ("Victory in Tijuana" 1997; "As Han Young Strike Enters Third Month, Support Grows" 1998; "Han Young Strike Resurrected" 1999). Cross-border solidarity has also played a visible role in the case of Custom Trim, a formerly Canadian-based company that moved production of steering wheels to northern Mexico in the mid-1990s. Here too, a series of strikes and protests beginning in 1997 over wages and workplace safety led to illegal firings and official repression, countered by the solidarity efforts of U.S. and Canadian unions. This support grew out of previous cross-border links and information-sharing focused on chemical exposures. "The workers in Canada at first told us, 'We can't talk about solidarity when we're losing our jobs,'" recalled organizer Marta Ojeda. "But we said, 'You are going to lose your jobs anyway, at least lose them with dignity.'" The Canadian Steelworkers subsequently sponsored a speaking tour for the fired Mexican workers, generating substantial publicity ("Border Forum" 1998; "Ruling Keeps Custom Trim Struggle Alive" 1999).

NAO Submissions

Under NAFTA's labor side accords, citizen organizations can file "submissions" before the National Administrative Offices (NAOs) in Canada, Mexico, and the United States alleging that any one of these governments has failed to enforce its own labor laws. Even as a bureaucratic dead end with no enforcement power, the NAO process promotes cross-border solidarity by stipulating that citizens cannot file NAO complaints against their own government—the filing must be initiated in a second country. Consequently, labor and support groups have formed cross-border coalitions to submit cases that highlight illegal suppression of union organization in the United States and Canada, as well as Mexico. Of two dozen submissions in NAFTA's first seven years, three have focused on auto plants: Han Young, Custom Trim, and Echlin–Dana, the last a brake factory where FAT supporters contesting CTM control were beaten and fired. The submission process has helped bring together a widening coalition of unions and community-based groups, but as expected, the practical outcomes have been limited (Bognanno and Lu 2000). The official response to the NAO findings against Han Young and Echlin–Dana was to convene an informational meeting in Mexico in the summer of 2000 in which government administrators reminded official union leaders of the legal rights protecting workers and dissidents. When independent unionists from Han Young marched into the meeting, they were physically attacked by the official union leaders (Bacon 2000).

Union Councils

The Echlin–Dana NAO submission was the outgrowth of the first formal effort among auto unions to coordinate their efforts on a continental basis. Beginning as the Echlin Workers' Alliance in 1997 and continuing as the Dana Workers' Alliance after a change in plant ownership, the coalition eventually brought together every union representing Dana's organized factories in North America, including the UAW, CAW, FAT, UE, IUE, Teamsters, Steelworkers, Machinists, and Paperworkers. In April 1999, these unions organized a public rally in Fort Wayne, Indiana, and conducted plant-based leafleting of Dana workers across the continent, calling for the rehiring of workers illegally fired from the company's Mexican plant.[6]

The initiatives described above—local-to-local, and worker-to-worker meetings, solidarity funds, health and safety training, crisis support, NAO submissions, and union councils—represent the emerging elements of a North American movement of autoworkers. Cross-border solidarity has even demonstrated its capacity to alter the balance of power in collective bargaining, though the chief example concerns Canada rather than Mexico. During the Flint GM strikes of 1998, when the company moved crucial stamping dies out of a struck location, CAW president Buzz Hargrove announced that union members at GM's Oshawa plant would not accept the "runaway" stampings—even though such refusal was illegal under Canadian labor law. Recalling the UAW's support in 1996 when the Canadian union struck GM, Hargrove pledged "to repay that same kind of solidarity" (Akre 1998).

It is important to stress, however, that these initiatives have not yet coalesced into additional union councils, much less a North American federation of auto unions. The case of the Dana Workers' Alliance is telling: as the first formal council of auto unions, it is also the only such council, with little recent activity. The UE–FAT "Strategic Alliance" initiated in 1992 is still the only case where two unions have merged their cross-border activities to coordinate organizing and bargaining on a continental basis. Of special interest is their insistence that solidarity is a two-way street, with UE delegations traveling south to support organizing drives and a Workers' Center in Ciudad Juárez and FAT organizers traveling north to help UE organize Mexican American workers (Alexander 1998).

The UE–FAT culture of organizing is not easily reproduced across the larger scale and scope of union organization in North America. UE and FAT are relatively small unions with a combined membership of less than 100,000 and a long history of bottom-up organizing—the latter a survival mechanism during years of repression and (in the case of the UE) past "red scares." In this unique environment, the exceptional skills and personal ties of individual leaders can shape union strategy in ways that are not easily reproduced in larger, more diverse organizations, where proper channels are more deliberate and internal politics more complicated. There has been a widening recognition in recent years that worker-to-worker mobilization is a necessary survival mechanism for all unions in an era of official strike breaking and whipsawing. But application is uneven and uncertain, especially in a coalition effort like the Dana Workers' Alliance, where one or several unions can veto initiatives or withdraw support.

While these organizational dynamics can slow and even fracture cross-border solidarity, there is a political overlay to continental trade that also widens the field for coalition building. Cross-border trade is created and defined by government policy, and there is little doubt that union campaigns opposing NAFTA and blocking its extension have linked labor with a wider movement of students, environmentalists, and border-based community groups. In all likelihood, future campaigns will present a far more united labor front than in 1993, when Mexico's official unions endorsed NAFTA and only FAT and a handful of others opposed it. Since then, support for unfettered free trade has fallen dramatically in Mexico, with the UNT now publicly joining the AFL–CIO in calling for "a fundamental revision of NAFTA" ("AFL–CIO Deepens Ties with Latin American Unions" 1999). Public opinion in the United States has also swung behind the call for international labor rights, a shift demonstrated in 1999 and 2000 by the diversity of groups protesting the World Trade Organization (WTO) in Seattle and the China trade bill in Washington. Following these demonstrations, a national *Business Week*/Harris poll indicated that two-thirds of those surveyed believed free trade benefited consumers, but 69 percent also believed that trade agreements with low-wage countries undermined U.S. wages. Survey respondents placed the highest priority for future trade agreements on preserving the environment, avoiding job loss, and protecting workers' rights and expressed less concern for expanding exports or keeping prices low. Only 10 percent called themselves "free traders," compared to 51 percent who described themselves as "fair traders" and 37 percent who said they were "protectionist" ("Globalization: What Americans Are Worried About" 2000).

This sea change in public opinion bodes well for a labor movement still struggling to find its legs in the global economy. The organizational and political barriers to cross-border collaboration remain formidable, but the mental revolution that must precede programmatic change is underway. If nothing else, there is a growing recognition of the unique histories that define each nation's labor movement and the common grievances that link them all. The latter was demonstrated in the AFL–CIO's recent accords with Mexico's UNT and CTM, both of which call for measures protecting the workplace rights of millions of Mexicans working in the United States ("AFL–CIO Deepens Ties with Latin American Unions" 1999; "AFL, CTM Agree to Cooperate" 1999). Recognition that these immigrant workers come from a nation with a long and continuing history of workplace struggle has also gained ground in recent years, slowly supplanting the image of helpless victims deserving only sympathy or scorn. Mexican labor law, it turns out, is in many ways superior to labor law in the United States and Canada since many workplace rights are enshrined in the Constitution of 1917—a legacy of the Mexican revolution. "The problem is that these rights aren't enforced in Mexico; they are not even enforced in this country," UAW president Stephen Yokich observed in 2000. His remarks represented a significant advance over the protectionism of years past. "I wish we had the Mexican Constitution as far as workers' rights," he added. "It was born under a revolution, but I think it's dying under capitalism" ("UAW Organizing Continues in Vance, Mexico" 1999).

Notes

1. Interviews with leadership of SITIMM, May 21–24, 2000.

2. Interview with members of the VW union's bargaining committee (Revision Commission), September 29, 2000.

3. Phone interview with Ken Luckhart of the CAW's International Affairs department, August 14, 2000.

4. Phone interview with UE International Affairs Director Robin Alexander, August 11, 2000.

5. Interview with Frank Meirer and Pamela Vossenas, UAW Health and Safety Department, August 11, 2000.

6. Interview with Brad Markell, UAW Research Department, August 11, 2000.

References

Adler, William. 2000. *Mollie's Job: A Story of Life and Work on the Global Assembly Line*. New York: Scribner.

"AFL–CIO Deepens Ties with Latin American Unions." 1999. *Working Together: Labor Report on the Americas*, Fall. Minneapolis, MN: Resource Center for the Americas.

"AFL, CTM Agree to Cooperate." 1999. *Working Together: Labor Report on the Americas*, January-February. Minneapolis, MN: Resource Center for the Americas.

Akre, Brian. 1998. "Canadian UAW [sic] Vows to Shun Non-Flint Parts." *Oakland Press*, June 24.

Alexander, Robin. 1998. "The UE–FAT Strategic Organizing Alliance." In Juárez and Babson, eds., pp. 525–533.

"As Han Young Strike Enters Third Month, Support Grows." 1998. *Working Together: Labor Report on the Americas*, July–August. Minneapolis, MN: Resource Center for the Americas.

"The Automotive Sectors of Latin America." 1999. London: EIU—Economist Intelligence Unit.

Babson, Steve. 2000. "Dual Sourcing at Ford in the U.S. and Mexico: Implications for Labor Relations and Union Strategies." Paper presented at conference on "Multinational Companies and Emerging Workplace Issues." Douglas Fraser Center, Wayne State University, April 1–3.

Bacon, David. 2000. "Strikers Beaten at NAFTA Sponsored Hearing." *Mexican Labor News* 5, 4 (July). Web page, United Electrical Workers International Information and Action Site.

Bayón, María Cristina. 1997. *El sindicalismo automotriz mexicano frente a un nuevo escenario: Una perspectiva desde los liderazgos*. Mexico City: Facultad Latinoamericana de Ciencias Sociales.

Bensusán, Graciela, and Cristina Bayón. 1998. "Trabajadores y sindicatos ante la globalización: El caso del sector automotriz mexicano." In Juárez and Babson, eds., pp. 117–142.

Bognanno, Mario, and Jiangfeng Lu. 2000. "NAFTA's Labor Side Agreement: Withering as an Effective Labor Law Enforcement and MNC Compliance Strategy?" Paper presented at conference on "Multinational Companies and Emerging Workplace Issues." Douglas Fraser Center, Wayne State University, April 1–3.

"Border Forum." 1998. *Borderlines*, August.

Bronfenbrenner, Kate. 1996. "Final Report: The Effects of Plant Closing or Threat of Plant Closing on the Right of Workers to Organize." Submitted to the Labor Secretariat of the North American Commission for Labor Cooperation, September 30.

Brooks, David, and Jim Carson. 1998. "Mexican Unions: Will Turmoil Lead to Independence?" *Working USA*, March/April: 23–35, 88–91.

Bureau of Labor Statistics, U.S. 1999. "Hourly Compensation Costs for Production Workers, Index = U.S. 100, Transportation Equipment Manufacturing (US SIC 37), 1975–1996." May.

Bureau of National Affairs. 2001. "Auto Workers Approve Agreement with GM Allowing Lordstown, Ohio, Plant to Stay Open." January 16.

Carrillo, Jorge. 2000. "The Integration of the Mexican Automobile Industry to the U.S.A." In *Actes du GERPISA*, No. 28 (February).

Chappell, Lindsey. 2001 "Mexico Splinters Mark for New-Car, Truck Sales." *Automotive News*, January 29.

Coalition for Justice in the Maquiladoras. 2000. "Health and Safety Committee Report—Workshops in the Maquila Border." Annual meeting, May.

Contrato Colectivo de Trabajo, Planta de Estampado y Ensamble de Hermosillo, 2000–2002. Sindirato de Trabajadores de Ford Motor Company, CTM (Ford Motor Company Workers Union).

Cowie, Jefferson. 1997. "National Struggles in a Transnational Economy: A Critical Analysis of U.S. Labor's Campaign Against NAFTA." *Labor Studies Journal*, Winter.

Delphi Automotive Systems. 1998. SEC Form S-1, Amendment 1 (December 23), p. 94.

Dillon, Sam. 1998. "A 20–Year GM Parts Migration to Mexico." *New York Times*, June 24, p. B-4.

García, Alejandro, and Arturo Lara. 1998. "Cambio tecnológico y aprendizaje laboral en General Motors: Los casos del D.F. y Silao." In Juárez and Babson, eds., pp. 207–222.

Garcia, Roberto, and Stephen Hills. 1998. "Meeting 'Lean' Competitors: Ford de México's Industrial Relations Strategy." In Juárez and Babson, eds., pp. 143–154.

Garza, Enrique de la. 2000. "El sindicalismo mexicano frente a la transición política." *Trabajo y Democracia Hoy*, No. 58 (November–December): 6–20.

"Globalization: What Americans are Worried About." 2000. *Business Week*, April 24, p. 44.

"GM to Resume Production at Mexican Plant Next Week." 1998. Associated Press, July 22.

"GM Weighs Scrapping Ohio Plant, Building in Mexico." 1998. *Detroit Free Press*, June 11.

"Han Young Strike Resurrected." 1999. *Working Together: Labor Report on the Americas*, May–June. Minneapolis, MN: Resource Center for the Americas.

Hart, John Mason. 1987. *Revolutionary Mexico: The Coming and Process of the Mexican Revolution*. Berkeley: University of California Press.

Helper, Susan. 1998. "Lean Production and the Specter of Mexico." In Juárez and Babson, eds., pp. 303–324.

Herzenberg, Stephen. 1999. "Constructive vs. Destructive Competition: Statement of Stephen Herzenberg before the U.S. Trade Deficit Review Commission." Pittsburgh, PA, October 29, p. 6.

"Indiana Labor Trip to Yield Results." 1998. *Working Together: Labor Report on the Americas*, July–August. Minneapolis, MN: Resource Center for the Americas.

Juárez, Huberto. 1998. "La productividad y el trabajo en el contexto de la producción esbelta en VW de México." In Juárez and Babson, eds., pp. 173–205.

Juárez, Huberto, and Steve Babson, eds. 1998. *Confronting Change: Auto Labor and Lean Production in North America /Enfrentando el cambio: Obreros del automóvil y producción esbelta en América del Norte*. Puebla: Universidad Autónoma de Puebla.

Karoub, Jeff. 1998. "Mexican Workers Cautious." *Flint Journal*, July 19: A1.

Kopinak, Kathryn. 1996. *Desert Capitalism: Maquiladoras in North America's Western Industrial Corridor*. Tucson: University of Arizona Press.

Kourous, George. 1998. "Occupational Health and Safety in the Maquiladoras." *Borderlines*, August.

Kumar, Pradeep, and John Holmes. 1998. "The Impact of NAFTA on the Automobile Industry in Canada." In Weintraub and Sands, eds.

La Botz, Dan. 1992. *Mask of Democracy: Labor Suppression in Mexico Today.* Boston: South End Press.

————. 2000. "Vincent Fox Wins Mexican Presidency, Ends PRI Rule: Victory for Democracy or Neo-Liberalism?" *Mexican Labor News* 5, 4 (July). Web page, United Electrical Workers International Information and Action Site.

Lira, Guillermo. 2000. "Mexico Closes Century With a Bang." *Automotive News,* January 24, 20.

MacArthur, John R. 2000. *The Selling of "Free Trade": NAFTA, Washington, and the Subversion of American Democracy.* New York: Hill and Wang.

"Maquila Scorecard." 2000. *Twin Plant News,* March.

Middlebook, Kevin. 1995. *The Paradox of Revolution: Labor, the State, and Authoritarianism in Mexico.* Baltimore: Johns Hopkins University Press.

Miller, Joe. 2000. "Mexican Modules." *Automotive News,* June 5.

Morris, John T. 1998. "Economic Integration and the Transformation of Labor Relations in the Mexican Auto Industry." In Tuman and Morris, eds.

Nissen, Bruce. 1999. "Alliances Across the Border: U.S. Labor in the Era of Globilization." *Working USA,* May–June.

"Producción mensual de la planta Ford-Hermosillo, 1997–1998." Typescript in author's possession.

Pryweller, Joseph. 1999. "Delays Jolt GM Suppliers." *Automotive News,* June 21.

Ramírez de la O, Rogelio. 2000. "What Has Changed in the Performance of Employment and Wages in Mexico After NAFTA?" Third Seminar on Income and Productivity, NAFTA Commission for Labor Cooperation, Mexico City, February 25.

"Ruling Keeps Custom Trim Struggle Alive." 1999. *Working Together: Labor Report on the Americas,* January–February. Minneapolis, MN: Resource Center for the Americas.

Tuman, John. 1998. "The Political Economy of Restructuring in Mexico's 'Brownfield' Plants: A Comparative Analysis." In Tuman and Morris, eds.

Tuman, John, and John Morris, eds. 1998. *Transforming the Latin American Automobile Industry.* Armonk, NY: M.E. Sharpe.

"UAW Organizing Continues in Vance, Mexico." 1999. *Ward's Automotive Reports,* February 7, p. 5.

Vanderbush, Walt. 1998. "An Uphill Struggle to Resist Downward Harmonization in Puebla, Mexico: The Case of Volkswagon Workers." *Economic Development Quarterly,* August.

"Victory in Tijuana." 1997. Campaign for Labor Rights web page, December 17.

"Volkswagen Workers." *Economic Development Quarterly,* August.

Weintraub, Sidney. 1998. "Incomes and Productivity in the Auto Industry in North America." In Weintraub and Sands, eds.

Weintraub, Sidney, and Christopher Sands, eds. 1998. *The North American Auto Industry Under NAFTA.* Washington, DC: Center for Strategic and International Studies.

Wells, Don. 1998. "Building Transnational Coordinative Unionism." In Juárez and Babson, eds., pp. 487–505.

3

FOUR MODELS OF CROSS-BORDER MAQUILA ORGANIZING

HENRY J. FRUNDT

As corporate globalization has progressed in the past decade, U.S. unions have stepped up cross-border organizing. They have tested a variety of fresh methods and models, most notably in Central America, Mexico, and the Caribbean. After some historical and definitional comments, this essay will explore the benefits and drawbacks of four models of "North–South" cross-border organizing in the maquila industry: (1) coalitional organizing; (2) federation-to-federation organizing; (3) international campaign organizing; and (4) clandestine targeting. It will then discuss certain challenges that models of cross-border approaches commonly encounter, including how to expand the leadership of women and determine the responsibilities of outside monitors. It will examine how elements of the four models have been combined in two recent cross-border successes; and it will conclude by suggesting how the four models might operate bidirectionally in the maquila and other sectors.

Historical and Definitional Comments

Cross-border organizing expands beyond cross-border communication and solidarity to involve very specific labor action. For activists and scholars who view corporate globalization in class terms, organizing across borders is a requirement for the effective protection of working people everywhere. As transnational companies and imperialist states expand, Marxist and conflict analysts have stressed the importance of subordinating national interests to a world perspective (e.g., Boswell

45

and Stevis 1997; Howard 1995). As international social forces become pronounced, even Durkheimian and functional approaches adopt world-applicable concepts for union replication and maintenance (Sturmthal 1973). Specific writers about the sociology of work urge unions to cultivate an international strategy (Figueroa 1998; Levinson 1972; Waterman 1998).

Yet no matter how compelling the theoretical postulates, it is only recently that U.S. unions have become genuinely interested in conducting joint organizational efforts with counterpart unions abroad. Fear of communism along with perceived advantages from U.S. corporate expansion reinforced the nationalistic and protectionist rationales promulgated by U.S. labor leaders (Nissen 1998). Of course early in the twentieth century, U.S. unions at least nominally participated in European and Latin American conferences that emphasized cross-border exchange and the expansion of International Trade Secretariats (ITSs) for each sector. They proclaimed the right of unions to affiliate internationally as endorsed by the International Labour Organisation (ILO) and then the International Confederation of Free Trade Unions. Yet the early cross-border contacts did not imply that U.S. federations directly engaged in such organizing (i.e., the creation of new unions or the negotiation of contracts). They usually restricted their linkages to sharing information, passing resolutions, and writing supportive letters.[1] It is true that certain union "internationals" like the United Auto Workers (UAW) did cultivate trade union development elsewhere in North and South America (Windmuller 1954). Nevertheless, most U.S.-based unions relinquished overseas organizing efforts to grossly politicized entities, especially the AFL–CIO international affairs department and its four regional institutes exemplified by the American Institute for Free Labor Development (AIFLD). While these entities occasionally aided specific genuine labor struggles (e.g., in Paraguay and Honduras; see Greenfield and Maram, eds. 1987), they certainly did not represent an overall coordinated approach to cross-border organizing. Rather, AFL international organizers such as Serafino Romualdi preferred to create alternative union organizations designed to undermine, not enhance, local confederations, as happened in Brazil, Mexico, El Salvador, and Guatemala following the U.S.-engineered coup against the Arbenz regime (Armstrong 1987 et al.; Barry 1996; Barry and Preusch 1990; Weinrub and Bollinger 1987; Sims 1992;

Spalding 1988a, 1988b, 1993). All in all, official U.S. labor efforts have been correctly dismissed as primarily serving national foreign policy, not international union interests. In the 1990s, when U.S. unions awoke to the need for cross-border collaboration to fend off unrestricted free trade initiatives such as the North American Free Trade Agreement (NAFTA), they did so primarily to protect U.S. jobs, not to cultivate class-based international solidarity (Nissen 1999).

What Is Genuine Cross-Border Organizing?

The "nationalistic" tenor of the U.S. labor movement offers a clue as to why it has been slow to adapt cross-border organizing. It also affects a more fundamental organizational rationale that sociologists have entitled resource mobilization. For example, Jo Freeman (1983) believes that a viable social movement (in this case across a border) first requires a cooptable network. Such a network could be community- as well as labor-based. Due to nationalistic inhibitions, U.S. unions have lacked (or have not exploited) preexisting networks, and this has retarded joint action. Even in the 1980s, when insurgent labor members protested AFL–CIO positions on Central America and crisscrossed North America with Latino delegations, these unionists did not systematically cultivate cross-border social linkages. They did establish a "transnational activist network" (see Keck and Sikkink 1998), which local unionists could call upon to remedy specific abuses such as obtaining freedom for imprisoned union leaders. However, they were less able to mobilize resources for long-term organizational development.

In addition to network exploitation is the question of network sustainability. During the 1980s, despite the decline of National Labor Relations Board (NLRB) victories, U.S. organizers achieved some success in building an activist network via media publicity and corporate campaigns. In another venue under conditions of repression, so did Latin American organizers. But conditions of globalization propelled corporate sophistication and subdivision, forcing activists everywhere to adopt more nuanced and legally savvy approaches. In their survey of union tactics in NLRB elections, Bronfenbrenner and Juravich (1998) empirically verify more than ten successful union approaches.[2] Responsive activists trained at the AFL–CIO Organizing Institute (OI) stressed the importance of careful leadership training and membership organizing utilizing these tactics.[3] Another ingredient for success across borders is significant involvement of participants in both countries.

Considering these factors, we come to a rough definition of what cross-border organizing ought to involve, at least on a minimal level:

1. Organizers from one country become actively engaged in a union's struggle for recognition and contract rights in another country.
2. In approaching the struggle, they build on preexisting networks and stress membership organizing.
3. As well as direct material assistance, active engagement involves sustained leadership training for worker-related mobilization.
4. Organizing also includes a legal component and the generation of local support. (There is a fine line in distinguishing certain forms of organizing and certain forms of support assistance that I hope to clarify).
5. Organizing across borders cultivates international support via a transnational activist network.
6. True cross-border organizing is bidirectional at least to some degree.
7. To the extent that it is successful, organizing achieves not only core labor rights, but also a sustained union structure.

In all, cross-border organizing is a very specific type of international union collaboration that involves direct action to form unions and win collective bargaining contracts.

In the past decade, scholars and union participants have begun to describe cross-border organizing efforts, and groups like the Campaign for Labor Rights (CLR) have arisen to publicize them. U.S. and Mexican trade unions have learned that frontier organizing with counterpart labor coalitions and federations brings success (Alexander and Gilmore 1994, 1999; Babson in this volume; Hathaway 2000b; Kamel and Hoffman, eds. 1999). For Central America and the Caribbean, some relatively precise accounts describe how specific cross-border efforts were employed in the apparel sector (see Anner 1998; Armbruster 1995, 1999; Brooks and Tate 1999; Coats 1991, 1993, 1996; Frundt 1999; Reed and Brandow 1996). In the Latin American maquila sector overall, at least four approaches to what we define as cross-border organizing have emerged, and we discuss them below.

Four Models of Organizing

Coalitional Organizing

In the United States, the first model of cross-border organizing to emerge on a broad scale involved a variety of organizations in addition to unions—in what we call *coalitional organizing*. In this approach, the construction of alliances on the basis of preexisting networks is especially pronounced. The best example of coalitional organizing is associated with the Coalition for Justice in the Maquilas (CJM), which was formed in the late 1980s by religious, labor, and community groups, including the AFL–CIO, which atypically offered financial support. Moody (1997) found it refreshing that the AFL–CIO even worked with religious and community-based alliances that included non-AFL unions (the United Electrical Workers [UE]/Frente Auténtico de Trabajadores [FAT]; and the Canadian Labour Congress [CLC]). The CJM faced a formidable task in Mexico since the powerful state-affiliated union federation, the Confederación de Trabajadores Mexicanos (CTM), had often made arrangements with local companies to establish "white" unions that would keep labor peace but otherwise prevent an independent worker voice in union and contract activities (see La Botz 1995). While the CJM originally emphasized corporate codes, its primary organizing impetus became the convening of border meetings to offer instruction regarding legal rights and to aid the formation of protective associations and unions in the maquilas. It also extended strike support (see Kamel and Hoffman, eds. 1999).

The CJM coalition has allowed a diversity of organizing approaches. In the mid-1980s, one (to be) CJM affiliate, the Comité Fronterizo de Obreras (CFO) of women maquila workers formed a special alliance with the American Friends Service Committee's (AFSC's) Maquiladora Project that occasionally even operated within organizations affiliated with the CTM. The CFO would hold weekly meetings, design educational training, and recruit action volunteers to work inside plants. The volunteers would instruct coworkers on the protections of Mexican law regarding base and overtime pay, eight-hour days, maternity leave, and retirement (among other things). Their method was to develop a self-defense position that operated in a gradual, nonthreatening but consistent way. Working with the CJM, they promoted company publication of their standards of conduct, which included environmental protections and basic labor rights, to which workers could appeal (Kamel and Hoffman, eds. 1999).

The CFO was also bidirectional. In the early 1990s, it exchanged visits with the Tennessee Renewal Network. The exchange informed disgruntled Tennessee workers and enabled laid-off women in Matamoros to win indemnity and file a court claim when they were unjustly fired. CFO counselors advised against early settlements and strategized on work stoppages to publicize health violations. In addition to solidifying understanding and moral support, their efforts gained plant cleanups (Tong 1993). The CFO also helped pressure the local CTM's Sindicato de Journaleros y Obreros Industriales (SJOI) to gain higher wages for the Matamoros area.[4]

In another CJM-related action examined by Hathaway (2000a, 8ff), Matamoros Working Class Youth (PJO) encountered severe health problems and anencephalic children traceable to an autotrim plant (see also CJM 1999). The PJO's CJM contacts led it to an Ontario, Canada, steelworkers' local confronting a phaseout of its own. The two groups formed an alliance that in turn demanded health and safety changes in the official Custom Trim 1997 contract. When the company refused to negotiate, the PJO workers walked. However, the plant's corrupt CTM union signed the new contract anyway, enabling the company to fire twenty-eight PJO activists and physically threaten their families. Just as the PJO/steelworker alliance won labor board ruling on reinstatement, Custom Trim was sold. However, workers filed a successful complaint on health issues with the NAFTA supervising board that required U.S.–Mexican ministerial consultations.

Cross-border coalition organizing also exploits transnational activist networks. In 1997, following two weeks of organized work stoppages at a GM plant, a CJM participant, the Interfaith Center for Corporate Responsibility (ICCR) and the AFSC brought worker representatives to GM's annual meeting to urge distribution of profit-sharing payments. Previously, ICCR advocacy had forced GM to set up a housing program for workers. It also pressed for a living wage initiative (Kamel and Hoffman, eds. 1999).

Coalition organizing retains certain advantages. It broadens the struggle of workers to include salient community and environmental issues; it also mobilizes support from a larger constituency and aids ordinary people in connecting their concerns to a class-based movement. At the same time, it operates with particular effectiveness in an anti-union, or white-union environment. In examining "outcomes" of thirty CJM campaigns, Williams 1999 demonstrated that high levels of collaboration among coalition members have won high results, such as better wages and working conditions. These are significant accomplishments. Nevertheless, while coalition organizing improves conditions for workers, it does not in and of itself necessarily result in a sustainable union. Such a union can form under these conditions, but to survive, it often requires the backing of a militant labor federation.

Federation-to-Federation Organizing

In the second organizing model, coalitional relationships continue, but the primary organizing impetus comes directly from unions. However, more than simply cooperating across a border, unions on both frontiers formalize their association in order to address legal formations and bargaining issues. Their approach is to develop a trust relationship that solidifies members across the divide. The model also bases its relations on preexisting networks that have originally been "exploited" by each union federation independently. This leads to the formulation of joint strategies for organizing new unions and contracts that benefit both interests.

The first federation-to-federation effort began in agriculture with the Farm Labor Organizing Committee (FLOC) in the 1980s,[5] and was repeated by the Communications Workers of America (CWA).[6] In the maquila sector, the UE/FAT collaboration became the most well-known and engaging example, as Alexander and Gilmore (1999) and Hathaway (2000b) have described. These two federations were not affiliated with the major national union confederations, leaving them freer of nationalistic and bureaucratic constraints. They also shared a goal of social movement unionism.[7]

The UE/FAT collaboration began in joint efforts to prevent the passage of NAFTA in the early 1990s. The two federations decided to cooperatively address Mexican companies that the UE had organized in the United States, notably General Electric (GE). With UE guidance, FAT won local representational elections at GE's Juárez plant. However, the alliance faced a counterforce that would be less evident in post-AIFLD Central America: not only did the state inhibit the recognition of independent unions, but also the state-affiliated CTM intervened with trumped up rationales to have the Mexican labor board disqualify worker elections that the alliance had won![8]

In the face of such challenges, UE/FAT's GE collaboration "gained some important border organizing experience and developed a strong relationship" based on mutual respect. It achieved the first secret ballot election in Mexican labor history (Hathaway 2000a, 3). Despite the many worker firings and failure to reach union status, the alliance's social movement orientation caused UE/ FAT members to "renew our dedication toward the struggle." The alliance established the Workers' Center of Juárez to cultivate union organizing and leadership. Workers migrated to Juárez with little knowledge of economic opportunities, so education in workers' rights, organizing, attorney support, and community programs on health proved essential. The center also provided a place for culture, where workers shared information, mutual support, and ways to improve their lives (Hathaway and Robles 1996, 11ff.).

In 1995, UE/FAT shifted its organizing energies toward the less union-resistant environment of Mexico City. It inaugurated a series of noteworthy efforts in the metal industry. At one infamous plant, the Echlin foundry at Itapsa, asbestos; dangerous solvents; faulty machinery; and a lack of protective equipment, labeling, and training caused the workers to demand the right to organize. UE/FAT engaged a coalition of seven unions that pledged "to organize the thousands of unorganized Echlin workers . . . to bring justice to their workplaces and increase our collective strength" (official statement; cited in Hathaway 2000a, 3–4). At the Itapsa plant, the alliance supported a drive by three young organizers that culminated in a large demonstration on election day. Immediately, the CTM engineered an election postponement and convinced Echlin to fire fifty unionists. Many accepted severance. Yet the alliance offered strike pay for those resisting. On the new election day, an armed goon squad guaranteed a vote overwhelmingly favorable to the CTM, and the company threatened and fired remnant workers. One organizer whom the labor board reinstated was fired a second time because of CTM intervention (Alexander 1999, 152).

The UE/FAT alliance then invoked an international campaign, but it did so in conjunction with a legal strategy to test the NAFTA labor side accords, a multilateral remedy unavailable to unions in Central America.[9] As many have pointed out, the NAFTA remedies are weak; most decisions are advisory, except for those affecting health and child labor (see Alexander 1999; Alexander and Gilmore 1994; Cook 1999; Stillerman 2000). Even the latter resulted only in ministerial consultation. However, the alliance's hope was to gain trinational consultations over the gross violations of Mexico's labor law. It was the second time that UE/FAT had employed this approach, the first having ended in dismal failure. This time, the alliance mobilized eleven unions which exchanged information about problems with Echlin asbestos. They filed a complaint with the NAFTA supervising board in all three countries.

The UE/FAT's federation-to-federation approach was also uniquely bidirectional. The UE/FAT emphasized worker-to-worker exchanges "to deepen understanding and undercut stereotypes...." Rank and file have toured plants . . . walked picket lines, assisted organizing drives (Alexander 1999, 141). Visitations by FAT organizers and artists to UE election sites in the Midwest helped stimulate local workers to vote. In 1995, FAT organizer Robert Valerio, who had been fired from GE Juárez, arrived in Milwaukee to assist an UE organizing drive among Mexican workers at Ace/Co foundry. Valerio calmed workers and responded to management's anti-union propaganda (Hathaway 2000a, 7).[10]

Given the lack of bona fide unions in Mexican maquilas, certainly the UE/FAT's approach to building a trust relationship for the longer term makes sense. True, the federation alliance has not demonstrated major success at any specific plant. Despite solid organizing, it has faced criticism that it champions unwinable causes or is late in selecting targets.[11] However, in constructing itself through preexisting labor and community networks, the alliance has formed a sustainable organizational base that is poised to take advantage of Mexico's potential openness to independent labor federations under the Fox government, which defeated the CTM-linked Partido Revolucionario Institucional (PRI). Also, the UE/FAT did combine organizing with its use of the NAFTA side agreement to file cases documenting the grossest inequities. After its lost election at Echlin, the alliance was much more sophisticated in mobilizing outside support for its second NAFTA appeal and achieved some beneficial rulings (Alexander 1999). Kay (2000, 5) found a silver lining in NAFTA's facilitation of cross-border union alliances. UE international affairs director Robin Alexander believed it ironic that NAFTA's only positive contribution "is our relationship with FAT . . . the UE–FAT Strategic Organizing Alliance, an effort to build a new kind of international relationship focused on organizing and also on rank and file solidarity . . . a binational partnership (1999,141). The two federations "coopted" an existing network in a way that sustained both federation partners in preparation for the "new" Mexico (see Compa 1999).

International Campaign Organizing

The third U.S. approach to maquila organizing is the international campaign. This approach has been characteristically adopted by the National Labor Committee (NLC), which established a valiant record of Central American union support work during the 1980s. In the 1990s, the NLC made astute use of the technique elucidated by Keck and Sikkink's (1998) model of transnational activist solidarity known as the "boomerang" effect. Blocked from reasonable redress by their own governments, local grievants can toss a boomerang by contacting activists abroad who employ various resources to pressure the same governments (or local corporate affiliates). The authors explore how transnational activists employ a range of responses that take advantage of the structural vulnerability of name brand recognition to benefit local constituencies (see also Anner 1998). Acting on the basis of a local workers' struggle over firings or barriers to union formation, the NLC tapped several of these methods when it mobilized U.S. students, consumers, and trade unionists to boomerang the parent company of protesting workers (see Barlow and Clark 2001; Ching Yoon Louie 2001; Klein 2000; Ross, ed. 1997). The results have stopped firings and brought union recognition, for example, in El Salvador at Mandarin, a GAP contractor, and DoAll, a producer for Liz Claiborne.

It was the embarrassment caused by NLC-led demonstrations in front of the GAP stores in 1995 that forced the company to live up to its code of conduct and agree to independent monitoring (Pattee 1996). The victory also brought a commitment to gradually rehire fired workers who had gone out on strike. However, the workers were not fully informed about the settlement until after it occurred, and a number of activists accepted severance. The action gained recognition for the workers and protected their jobs, an important accomplishment; but it did not leave intact a strong union. Indeed, Mandarin even set up an alternate white union that remains in place (Anner 1998; Brooks and Tate 1999).

In the DoAll case, the NLC conducted its boomerang campaign more attentively. Since 1992, when the 2,000–strong Korean-owned DoAll had begun producing for Liz Claiborne, workers had engaged in five unsuccessful attempts to organize a union in order to counter abusive practices.[12] Despite Liz Claiborne's promises, each time DoAll would quickly fire potential union leaders.[13] During 1999, the NLC allied with the United Students Against Sweatshops (USAS), a then emerging group concerned about campus purchasing (see below), to visit DoAll workers. True to form, management abruptly fired about fifteen workers simply for speaking to the students (USAS/NLC 1999). Consulting with CENTRA, a Salvadoran labor research institute, the Central de Trabajadores Salvadorenos (Salvadoran Workers Central) (CTS) labor federation, and the Independent Monitoring Group of El Salvador Grupo Monetor Independiente de El Salvador (GMIES), USAS/NLC gathered and forwarded worker testimonies to Liz Claiborne. In October, it arranged for several DoAll workers to tour U.S. campuses. In November, thirty-eight workers clandestinely agreed to a union and submitted documentation to the Labor Ministry. Over the subsequent ten days, DoAll terminated all workers it suspected had some involvement. Immediately, USAS/NLC inaugurated a massive campaign that inspired student fasts and sit-ins across the United States and Canada. Liz Claiborne publicly committed itself to respect freedom of association and to so notify DoAll. Student occupations, such as at the University of Pennsylvania administration building, "meant a lot" to the workers. "They went into negotiations feeling stronger" (USAS/NLC 1999, 2). By the second week of December, NLC called off further escalation and a planned delegation. In February 2000 the local union won reinstatement of thirty-one workers with 100 percent back pay, no reprisals, and independent monitoring by GMIES. Yet in such a large factory, the campaign for union recognition may have been premature, thereby preventing formation of an organization with sufficient clout to negotiate a contract.

The international campaign model meets our definition of cross-border organizing. A local group of workers that encounters difficulties obtaining union recognition requests aid from a union-connected transnational actor to pressure international companies. In turn, these companies force local contractors to respect labor laws. While this approach is weak on local on-ground leadership development, it does involve worker networks. The campaign model extends beyond international solidarity assistance to offer advice about local strategies and legal approaches. To an extent, the campaign is bidirectional, as workers from the local area of conflict tour the United States and speak at local union rallies. However, the emphasis is on the international network, not on fortifying local structures. Organizing impetus largely depends on the pressure exerted by transnational actors, more than on what occurs on the ground. The campaign's focus is to cultivate international linkages *de nuevo* that are directed toward crisis response. When this network is mobilized too quickly—in what has been characterized as the North American "cowboy" approach[14]—it may actually undermine long-term local membership organizing.

Labor groups are hardly the only ones to adopt the campaign approach. Keck and Sikkink (1998) analyze a number of other efforts.[15] Yet as Armbruster (2000) points out, none of the pressure methods outlined by the authors involve on-ground organizing. This is because organizing, if it is to be successful, must take primary impetus from the local situation, that is, in this case, the in-plant and community experiences of workers. When it is not used in combination with other models, international campaign organizing can lead to misunderstandings and a weakly organized local union.

Clandestine Targeting

The fourth approach to cross-border organizing places much more weight on local mobilization. The vision of those selecting the target is to first organize one plant as a model and then expand that example to other factories in the sector.[16] This approach often begins by partnering with a local federation; it then devotes more attention than the international campaign approach to creating teams that engage in clandestine on-ground leadership development and the quiet fortification of a workers' local. The strategy is to develop a cadre of sufficient size not only to form a union, usually not a high numerical threshold, but also to successfully demand contract negotiations, a much higher threshold. Although it is not always strategically identified, the target approach does depend on preexisting social networks among workers, who themselves tap into community and blood relations to expand their trust-based associations.[17] An ITS, the International Textile, Garment, and Leather Workers Federation (ITGLWF, or its Latin arm, FITTIV), has recently adopted this approach, often with assistance from the U.S. Labor Education in the Americas Project (US/LEAP). So has the AFL–CIO-sponsored center that replaced AIFLD after the federation's leadership shake-up in 1995—the American Center for International Labor Solidarity (ACILS).

The first notable cases of target organizing were at Phillips–Van Heusen (PVH) in Guatemala, Bonang/Bonahan in the Dominican Republic, and Kimi in Honduras, as I have illustrated elsewhere (Frundt 1999). All three textile plants had some contact with a major national confederation, but that confederation did not have the resources (or subculture) to begin an all-out organizing effort in the maquila sector. In addition, the organizing approach to which the confederation had become accustomed was a "blitz" of noisy demonstrations designed to court public opinion and prevent repression in times of exceeding danger. ITS organizers, who had received their training at the AFL–CIO OI, advocated a more subtle approach. They coached leaders to unobtrusively move from house to house to identify and contact potential members and to gradually increase membership numbers to appropriate strength for negotiations (see Armbruster 1999; Johns 1998 on PVH).

ITS targeting also employed international pressure that US/LEAP coordinated with on-ground action. Corporate and government intransigence motivated local union members to seek assistance from this transnational network—for example, when the Guatemalan labor minister refused to rule on a union petition at PVH/Camisas Modernas. Leafletters fanned out across the United States to educate consumers of the Guatemalan and PVH double standard. But the target strategy subordinated the international campaign to the activities on the ground.

The clandestine targeting approach also brought some success in the Dominican Republic and Honduras. In the Dominican Republic, effective target strategies by the Federación Nacional de Trabajadores de Zonas (FENATRAZONAS), the Union of Needletrades, Industrial, and Textile Employees (UNITE), and the ITGLWF in the Dominican Republic during the 1990s established a basis for sector organizing (Frundt 1998, 1999). In 2000, four factory unions in the Bonao free zone combined forces to win the first zonewide bargaining agreement. Aided by ACILS, FENATRAZONAS trained its entire leadership and hired seven full-time organizers to pursue similar agreements in other free trade zones.

Following unionization at Kimi in Honduras, Yoo Yang became the next textile union to win recognition in the antilabor Continental Park Trade Zone. Organizers approached Yoo Yang utilizing similar clandestine techniques as they had at Kimi, quietly cultivating well-trained leaders and a supportive cadre. However, after union elections in August 1999, management fired the executive committee. Workers then refused to work, demanding that the leaders be rehired. Finally, after another strike, the company relented. In March 2000, Yoo Yang recognized the union and made a commitment to negotiate.

The ITS organizing effort went a step further, demanding that Yoo Yang workers be part of an industrial or sector union.[18] The Honduran Labor Ministry denied this request. When workers applied for protective factory union status, members of the union executive committee were reportedly bribed to resign. The resilient workers chose new leadership and negotiated a sequel agreement with management. It took further international pressure to assure government recognition (US/LEAP 2000c), and negotiations moved forward in spring 2001.

Thus the clandestine targeting approach has achieved success. In each case, workers gained union recognition and also won a contract. However, ITS organizers did encounter a major snag in the target model: after about eighteen months, larger corporate maneuvers often abruptly halted key victories. In Guatemala and Honduras, the parent companies terminated orders and subcontracted their work elsewhere. Armbruster (2000) attributes part of the failure at PVH to insufficient union leadership development and the lack of ongoing organizing within the local. However, the power of corporations to undermine union structures at a single plant remains the primary factor. Evidence suggests that in the PVH/Camisas case, the shift of production to nonunionized plants nearby had been preconceived by PVH and the Guatemalan maquila sector leadership (see also US/LEAP 2000b). In the Kimi case, following several widely publicized local disputes, the Korean management decided to close and shift production to a nonunion Guatemalan plant even though J.C. Penney had agreed to maintain orders in Honduras (US/LEAP 2000a). Thirteen U.S. and Canadian unions and nonprofit organizations committed themselves to "follow Kimi to Guatemala" and to "work vigorously to persuade Kimi to re-open its unionized factory in Honduras" (US/LEAP 2000b). However, Kimi changed its name to Duke Company, Inc., and the pursuit of its university apparel contracts proved illusive (see US/LEAP 2001).

The ITS target model has achieved greater success in creating a solid local union than has the international campaign model. In Guatemala, the Dominican Republic, and Honduras, workers experienced the reality of their power, a memory that does not lightly disappear. Perhaps for that reason, however, the model is more vulnerable in the short term to companies canceling their production contracts to prevent the model's expansion. The approach may pay off, as in the Dominican Republic, where its trained organizers move among other maquilas and select more targets. Nevertheless, the target approach raises questions for those who seek to protect employee jobs. It leaves begging certain answers for what else is required for organizing success.

Each of the four models of cross-border organizing we have considered has strengths and weaknesses. The coalitional approach takes best advantage of preexisting, broader networks that give it a staying power even when official union structures cannot function, but it does not always have the legal clout to accomplish organizational objectives. Federation collaboration better achieves such objectives but may lack the breadth of community support. It can sustain setbacks in individual struggles and is the most bidirectional of all the models but so far has not yet won many contracts. The international campaign is most effective at pressuring name brand companies and thereby providing workers with some remedy, but it does not necessarily strengthen local structures. The target approach has a much more developed strategy for leadership development and cadre maintenance, but it is more vulnerable to the maneuverings of corporate power.

Of course, as I have implied elsewhere (Frundt 1999), the most effective cross-border organizing requires a combination of these aspects. But before we consider how they can effectively interact, we need to consider two dilemmas that all four models face: appropriate use of independent monitoring and sensitivity to considerations of gender.

Common Challenges and Examples of Model Integration

In addition to their strengths and weaknesses, organizing models all share certain challenges. Of those considered here, the role of outside monitors has received increasing attention due to the exciting revival of student interest in labor issues. Maquila hiring patterns have also forced trade unionists to become more attentive to the role of women in the organizing process.

Independent Monitoring

As indicated above, the concept of outside or independent monitoring first gained prominence in conjunction with the NLC–GAP accord on Mandarin in 1995. The NLC insisted that company compliance with its own employee code required the transparency of independent monitoring. Typically, an independent monitoring group would be constituted by human rights representatives, university officials, religious and community leaders, and so forth. When GAP agreed to this, NLC director Charles Kernighan proclaimed a "sea change" in company–maquila relations. In El Salvador, the GAP agreement led to the creation of the outside monitoring group GEMHI. For the Kimi plant in Houndras, a similar group was formed out of the Commission for Human Rights (CODEH). COVERCO monitored Liz Claiborne plants in Guatemala. In Mexico outside monitoring was often done informally by community groups such as the CFO.

After the emergence of the White House–initiated Fair Labor Association (FLA) in 1997, industry officials quickly set up their own outside monitoring systems, employing for-profit firms like Price Waterhouse (Greenhouse 2000). In addition to their particular biases and secrecy, these accounting firm representatives often had little idea about what constituted worker rights, much less how to measure them, and routinely delivered local plants a clean bill of health. However, beginning in 1998, college students became increasingly interested in verifying that university-licensed products were "sweatshop free." As college delegations discovered gross discrepancies between company codes and contractor compliance, the mushrooming USAS protested on many campuses against industry-controlled FLA monitoring. It urged adoption of more rigorous monitoring procedures and created the Workers Rights Consortium (WRC) to achieve this. The student-led WRC forced companies selling to the collegiate market to disclose the location of their suppliers. In turn, this enabled organizers to quickly contact local worker networks facing incipient struggles.

Community-based independent monitors can certainly play a positive role because they offer a more objective appraisal of actual working conditions, as well as pertinent legal issues. Nevertheless, whether they are community- or corporate-based, independent monitors leave certain theoretical and practical problems unresolved. If independent monitors replace what unions are conceptually designed to be—workers negotiating their terms and conditions—what does that imply for the collective bargaining process? On the one hand, as the model of coalitional organizing demonstrates, other organizational forms can arise to mediate worker–employer relations. But on the other hand, as a practical matter, independent monitors must specify who will be the final determinant of certain local conditions. If ILO conventions are to be honored, this must be the local union.

Women as Unionists

A second issue revolves around appropriate adaptations for gender in the design of cross-border organizing. Gender relations play a hidden role in each of the four models of organizing considered above (see Bonacich et al., eds. 1994; Dunn 1996; Needleman 1998; Safa 1995). First, consider that in maquilas, women constitute the majority of the workforce. This means that organizers must devote more attention to women's concerns. In the past, women could gain only temporary work status due to family obligations, making them less likely to form unions. They also received less education about their rights and capabilities. However, this is changing, as ITS, ACILS, and local organizers have recognized. Clandestine models of organizing are often more women-friendly and build on women-molded networks. Coalition organizers also understand the advantages of gender-grounded collaborations, such as along the Rio Grande, that do not result in immediate union formations. In advocating feminist-based organizing, Kamel (1990) explored how *La Mujer Obrera* (a border organization for working women) was instrumental in training women to demand that local companies post personnel policies to which they could then appeal, even though they feared organizing a direct union. Kamel and Hoffman's 1999 volume and the AFSC efforts offer more examples. Hill (1997) describes how the Support Team International for Textilers (STITCH) created a maquila support network among Guatemalan women. In the models above, federation and target organizing became notably sensitive to gender considerations.

Model Combinations

Keeping in mind the nuances of independent monitoring and gender-related organizing approaches, let us now consider how the four organizing models might be effectively combined. Here, we have lessons to learn as revealed by two illustrative examples. The first is that of the Nicaraguan Confederation of Textile Workers (CTC), an ITGLWF affiliate that adopted a coalitional approach to organizing but included elements from targeting and the international campaign. The second is that of the Sindicato de Trabajadores de Empresa Mexmode Internacional de México (SITEMIM), a union from Atlixco, Puebla, that combined on-ground action with USAS support.

CTC

Details of the CTC struggle illustrate the tensions of cross-border model elements overcoming obdurate corporate and state cultures. The CTC originated under Sandinista rule, which promoted trade unionism, and the confederation was closely allied to the state. After the Sandinista defeat in 1990, Sandinista-related unions experienced external and internal turmoil as they sought an independent role (see O'Kane 1994; Stahler-Sholk 1995). Following trade union divisions in 1996, Pedro Ortega remained a strong Sandinista textile union leader. Ortega's leadership offers insight on how specific plant organizing depends on both a strong federation and international action. Ortega maintained a clear position about independent clandestine organizing, which helped the *16 de agosto* union at Fortex become Nicaragua's first Free Trade Zone union in 1992. However, legal recognition did not come easily. The trade union leader cultivated international network support, gaining a 1995 *Dateline* exposé through the NLC. Nevertheless, under the increasingly neoliberal Nicaraguan Labor Ministry, it took until 1996 for the Fortex union to win legal recognition. To achieve a contract required a substantial international boomerang effect, largely organized by Witness for Peace (see Witness for Peace 1998).

As in the Dominican Republic, such a victory stimulated the formation of other free trade zone unions. By 1999, Nicaragua had eight functioning maquila unions, earning the prize for the most highly unionized industrial park in the region. Most efforts were not directly attributable to cross-border organizing. However, 2000 brought a government and business-oriented labor minister increasingly beholden to Taiwanese investors. Free zone company managers stumbled over themselves to fire union leaders. Workers exhausted legal remedies to stop or reverse the terminations. At this point, Ortega petitioned Witness for Peace and other international union activist groups for essential cross-border support.[19] The CTC and its U.S. allies viewed the behavior of Mil Colores, which terminated 200 union activists, and the 1,800–strong Chentex, which fired 700, including the union executive committee, as especially egregious. Both produced clothing for two noted U.S. retailers, Kohl's and Target. Chentex paid workers $.20 each for a daily output of 25,000 jeans that retailed for $30 apiece. In 1998, the workers had negotiated a year's wage postponement. When the company refused the reopener in 1999, they ultimately struck for two days. Nearly half were fired (Pitkin 2001). Ortega and fired worker Rosa Ocampo González arrived in the United States for a tour and dramatic appearance at the Kohl's shareholder meeting (St. Louis 2000). The companies refused to listen to Ortega, who then joined the advisory council and founding convention of the student-created WRC. By September 2000, the U.S. owner of Mil Colores was ready to recognize the union and engage in good faith negotiations despite contrary pressure from Las Mercedes zone owners. However, Chentex proved intractable.

In an unusually coordinated response, the CLR, the ITGLWF, Nicaragua Network, Witness for Peace, NLC, Resource Center for the Americas, USAS, and US/LEAP inaugurated an action plan and supportive leaflet campaign. The NLC did presswork; CLR and USAS mobilized pickets; various unions helped with resources; US/LEAP facilitated strategy discussions with U.S. unions, researched Chentex's owner (the Nien Hsing conglomerate), and contacted other Nien Hsing customers. This won cooperation from Taiwanese activists, who organized as the Taiwanese Solidarity with Nicaraguan Workers (TSNW). The ITGLWF and TSNW pressured Nein Hsing and the Taiwanese government that had subsidized the conglomerate. Chentex began to negotiate. However, Nien Hsing, which owns factories throughout the region, *increased* its efforts to "criminalize" trade union activity. Having filed countercharges against union leaders for destroying property and impeding international commerce, it then demanded that the Nicaraguan Labor Ministry cancel the union altogether. Ortega and the U.S. coalition called for a year-end holiday mobilization at Kohl's and Target. Supporters conducted more than five hundred actions and educational leaflettings at stores, assembled letter-writing drives, created human billboards and banner drops, and enacted civil disobedience. Labor delegations visited Taiwanese offices throughout the United States. Congresswoman Cynthia McKinney and the General Accounting Office probed into why the U.S. Army and Airforce Exchange Service was buying Chentex jeans.[20] With AFL–CIO assistance, a Nien Hsing labor leader from Lesotho visited Nicaragua.

The CTC also requested trade pressure on Nicaragua directly. The AFL–CIO, ACILS and ITGLWF stepped in to invoke Caribbean Basin trade rules and petition the ILO, motivating the U.S. trade representative to qualify implementation of the Caribbean Basin Trade Partnership Act in October 2000. She "expressed particular concern with respect to anti-union activity at two apparel factories in the Las Mercedes Free Trade Zone and successfully sought the government's assurances that workers at those factories would be informed of their rights" (USTR 2000). Such outpourings prompted Chentex union leader Zenayda Torres to "come to realize that we need international support [which] has filled us with hope" (CLR 2001b).

By January 2001, the CTC had reached an agreement with Nien Hsing representative Lucas Huana to reinstate two fired union leaders (out of nine), distribute severance to the others, and rehire about eighty of the fired workers over a two-month period. However, the eighty union-selected workers proved unacceptable to Chentex, which countered with a factory protest against the agreement (CLR 2001a). The Nicaraguan government was more vulnerable. In April the supreme court ruled on an appeal sponsored by the Nicaraguan Center for Human Rights that Chentex must rehire all nine union officials with back pay since the law prohibited leader firings during negotiations. It was an unprecedented victory. Yet Chentex still flouted the court, forcing union leader Gladys Manzanares to reconsider how to achieve her first goal, "to get the hundreds of other union workers . . . rehired" permanently without more firings and appeals (CLR 2001c, 2001d). Finally in May, union and company agreed to a plan that rehired four union officials and seventeen other workers. The remaining union leaders received back pay, double severance, and a $1,135 bonus. Nevertheless, in the month that followed, management ostracized the unionists and fired any workers who talked to them, forcing the remaining leaders to resign.

The CTC example combines elements of the four organizing models: it began with target organizing of Fortex, and this expanded to other maquila textile plants. To assure contract victories, it also mobilized an international campaign that included nongovernmental organization (NGO) coalitional relationships. When firings increased in 1999, the CTC again tossed the international boomerang, and NGOs worked to coordinate actions. While it did not achieve a federation-to-federation alliance, the CTC solidified its connections to the AFL–CIO through ACILS. Yet the combination brought campaign lessons. In Nicaragua, maquila unions declined from eight to two in two years. At Chentex, a 700–strong union was reduced to twenty-one leaders, all of whom eventually had to leave, although they promised to organize elsewhere. Tensions developed within the CTC, partly because the publicity-oriented approach absorbed local energy . "This is an international campaign," Ortega said at one point. "We'll pick up the organizing later." In addition, while U.S. campaign coordination was effective, it was not always smooth or timely. While Kohl's proved far more stubborn as a U.S. focus than leafletters had anticipated, the campaign also did not articulate a coherent plan for corporate communication. Nien Hsing was a better target, but it took too long for supporters to pursue this. In addition to allowing publicity to trump organizing, the campaign did not clearly delineate responsibilities for research and legal action. The example's last phase overly relied on the international campaign model, yet its organizing base persisted. Despite many obstacles, the model combination brought a remarkable victory against vehemently asserted corporate control.

SITEMIM

The second example of a model combination was the struggle to form an independent union at Mexmode, a Korean-owned Mexican maquila that produced Nike and Reebok sweatshirts sold at U.S. colleges and universities. In this case, the combination of organizing and international support was more balanced. Learning from the difficulties that independent federations had with the CTM noted above, local leaders were notably adroit in handling the local FROC–CROC affiliate despite considerable intimidation. In January 2001, 800 of Mexmode's 900 employees conducted a wildcat strike in support of five coworkers fired for attempting to form an independent union. The company had arranged a labor contract with FROC–CROC that neither provided required benefits nor prevented forced overtime and abuse—a clear case of a protection contract. Its purpose had come to a head the previous month, when the company had unabashedly terminated 25 workers who complained about poor pay and rancid cafeteria food, precipitating the union organizing drive. When the January strikers occupied the factory perimeter, the company summoned police with the reported assistance of the FROC–CROC. The 200–strong riot squad arrived, beating the strikers and sending 15 to the hospital. Despite a nonreprisal agreement, guards halted returning workers at the gates, fired many, and forced others to resign or declare written loyalty to FROC–CROC, in addition to losing seniority and pay status.

Immediate campaigns mobilized on the ground and within the U.S. student movement. At the plant, locked out workers coordinated with assistance from the Comite de Apoyo al Trabajador and other support groups in Puebla and ACILS. Student protests and the International Labor Rights Fund (ILRF), a member of the FLA, convinced Nike to commission a noted Mexican labor lawyer, who confirmed FROC–CROC's company union status, contract irregularities, unpaid benefits, and lack of trust. He recommended immediate rehiring of all terminated and warned of FROC–CROC intimidation (Alcalde 2001; see also ILRF 2001). USAS and the WRC also sent delegations that verified conditions, including food sickness and beatings (Usenmez 2001). To be sure, Nike then retained the FLA-approved independent monitoring firm Verité, which reached similar conclusions and recommended a secret ballot election. Nike and Mexmode management agreed to rehire all leaders and strikers. However, the CTM, with its strong Puebla base, had much to lose, creating a situation similar to the standowns often faced by the UE/FAT. A phalanx of sympathetic police still guarded the plant. Strike leaders admitted past the gates were kept in isolation (de Erick 2001). FROC–CROC solicited workers to buy off in-plant supporters of the now locked out workers at $50 a head (Perez 2001). It insisted that all returnees affiliate with the only "legal union." When a significant number mustered the courage to cross the gates and form their own union (SITEMIM 2001), FROC–CROC threats accelerated. It filed twenty-one charges of labor violations against the incipient group.

At each intimidation, however, USAS observers would e-mail campuses, and students would deluge administrations and the local press.[21] University presidents and many others quickly petitioned Nike and Reebok to intervene. Both responded, Nike with a remediation plan and Reebok with direct representation to remove the plant's worst managerial intimidators. By March 2001, 400 workers had returned, and SITEMIM had begun to function unofficially. Women were notably in the leadership. Five union leaders communicated to their U.S. allies: "We are conscious that without your support, this would not have been accomplished. . . . We need that you do not leave us alone" until we gain government recognition (SITEMIM 2001). In summer 2001, the CLR mobilized U.S. supporters to visit the country's forty-two Mexican consulates to petition acceptance of SITEMIM's union registration by the CTM-influenced local government in Puebla. ACILS also helped convince Mexmode management that a bona fide union would bring labor peace. By September, SITEMIM became official, and signed up 80 percent of the plant's workers.

With a solid base, the independent union is in a position to win future elections and avoid protection contracts.

The Puebla organizing effort combined with student-led actions in the United States that involved elements of all four organizing models (coalitions with groups in Puebla, federation support via ACILS, and a coordinated campaign that amazingly brought together both the WRC and the FLA, as well as USAS, CLR, Canadian Maquila Solidarity Network, US/LEAP, and others). One lesson from the combination of models is that to be lasting, the mixture must forcefully link member organizing efforts on the ground with any international action. "I hope we've seen the last of publicity-driven campaigns," stated ACILS Mexican field representative Jeff Hermanson. "They reveal the folly of single plant approaches, of not having an organizing effort on the ground, of not doing research up front, and of waiting too long after worker firings to gear up action in the North. Kuk Dong was a campaign which coordinated publicity with organization" (comments to labor advisory group, June 4, 2001).

Reflections

How might these four models and/or their combination be extended to other sectors? A key aspect revolves around the question of bidirectionality, that is, the extent to which organizing truly moves in both directions across frontiers (see Davis 1995; also see Milkman, Grenier, and Nissen chapters in this volume). This becomes increasingly important under new AFL-CIO immigration policy as Latin immigration expands (Stalker 2000). As we saw, a weakness of cross-border work in Central America has been its largely one-way process. While delegations of Central American unions have visited the United States to describe their repression and this has sometimes been employed to stimulate local activities, nearly all the organizing has been done in Central America. The UE/FAT alliance offers a clearer way in which organizers can overcome cultural barriers to union membership on both sides of the border. No doubt as well, visiting USAS students, inspired by their Chentex and Kuk Dong experiences, will not only contribute to organizing campaigns within the United States, but also will invite southern organizers to come here to assist.

Bidirectionality has also been utilized in other sectors.[22] Difficulties can emerge, as when FAT sent organizers to Washington state to help Teamsters in a food sector organizing drive. It was a challenge for the Mexican activists to accept certain leadership decisions.[23] Unions must face and resolve these kinds of cultural and structural inhibiters as they strive for more effective bidirectional efforts in the future. US/LEAP director Stephen Coats argues that "Cross border work must be grounded in partnership with organized labor on the ground in the south." However, he also recognizes that such partnerships are "extremely difficult to develop and maintain." He cites among the obstacles the language, culture, trust, weak communication structure, differing priorities, and internal divisions (in north and south). "The apparel sector, with its highly mobile capital" is also "notoriously difficult to organize." This will be achieved only by a sustained bidirectional commitment over the long term that brings together the many groups involved.

In addition to bidirectionality, other aspects of the four models can certainly be applied to auto manufacturing, food processing, metalworking, and telecommunications (among other areas). In the twenty-first century, the United Food and Commercial Workers has stepped up its cross-border contacts in Latin America, just as the United Auto Workers (UAW), CWA, the United Mineworkers, and FLOC have done. Each sector will also confront tensions about when to build on the international campaign and when to wait for clandestine target organizing to take hold to assure a contract. Each sector must also explore relations with community groups, especially as they involve environmental and women's issues. Some may daringly venture to formalize a federation-to-federation organizing alliance, taking lessons from UE/FAT. In all sectors, workers must be trained on how to understand and use corporate codes. One new cross-border strategy that emerged from the combination of models in Nicaragua, Honduras, and Guatemala is a common effort to convince North American jobber clients to produce or put work into unionized factories in Mexico and Central America. This could lead to a worker-supervised global "union" label that would have profound implications for international campaigns.

We have examined four models of cross-border organizing and their combinations that are being tested in the Latin American maquila sector. Each model has strengths and weaknesses that can be complementary when grounded in on-ground worker struggle. If unions are to mount a forceful response to unrestrained corporate globalization, they must further pursue these models in other sectors and develop greater skill in handling independent monitoring, gender relations, and bidirectionality.

Notes

1. Eduardo Diaz of the U.S. Postal, Telegraph, and Telephone ITS, hopes to "refocus secretariats away from meetings and resolutions" (cited in Alexander and Gilmore 1994, 47). In the 1970s, some food sector and metalworker unions formed joint councils for specific companies (Unilever, Nestle), but these were exceptions

and in any case did not involve direct cross-border work (see Levinson 1972).

2. These include formation of a representative committee (and percentage of workers on the committee), percentage receiving house calls (and whether rank and file did them), number of small-group meetings, percentage surveyed one-on-one, establishment of a bargaining committee before election, solidarity days, rallies, job actions, community coalitions, and media.

3. Despite legitimate criticisms of OI approaches (see Early 1998), institute graduates did learn the principles of membership-based organizing as summarized by Nissen (1998).

4. Cravey (1998, 48) demonstrates the border's large historical differences in unionization rates and wages, with Matamoros and Reynosa doing the best.

5. In 1986, when the FLOC was negotiating with Campbell's Soup, the company warned it would shift growing operations to Mexico. FLOC leader Baldemar Velasquez contacted the Mexican union representing Campbell's workers and formed a bargaining alliance that at minimum led to a phase-in wage parity agreement and an immigration sponsorship program (Alexander and Gilmore 1994).

6. The CWA was actually inspired to begin cross-border federation organizing by its Canadian counterpart in the CLC concerned about Air Canada's threat to shift its ticket reservation phone system to New Jersey. A few years later, U.S. airlines sought to send U.S. reservation activities to Canada. The CWA, Teamsters, and Transport and General Workers Union–UK (TGWU) in Britain established a work-sharing agreement: reservations made in each country were considered the work of the unionized workers in that country. Members would refuse calls from each other's countries in case of rerouting. In 1989, the CWA and CLC also formed a broad international coalition that included the Mexican Telecommunications Union. CWA set up a cross-border organizing school. But when U.S. Sprint's Spanish-language workers attempted to join CWA, the company shut down its Spanish service. The Telecom workers filed a complaint in Mexico under the NAFTA side accords that ultimately gained ministerial consultations. Telecom pressured to keep Sprint out of Mexico (Cohen and Early 1999; Moody 1997).

7. FAT, which began in 1960 under Catholic sponsorship, found its network among a working-class Christian youth group in León. The UE grew as a radical CIO union in the 1930s. Besides stressing the freedom to organize and self-manage (*autogestión*), both groups are fiercely independent from political parties and corporations. The two "federations" are also relatively small and iconoclastic, wielding power and influence greater than their numbers (Hathaway and Robles 1996). They also exemplify "social movement unionism," as Robinson explores in this volume.

8. The CTM has often worked against genuine union interests, such as signing management "protection contracts" to prevent worker dissent (see La Botz 1995). One major example was the CTM's intervention to prevent recognition by Hyundai and the Mexican labor board of a twice-elected FAT affiliate (Alexander and Gilmore 1999).

9. The African/Caribbean trade initiative does contain certain labor rights provisions, but they are still unilateral, in line with mechanisms in the General System of Preferences (see Frundt 1998).

10. The Teamsters asked FAT organizer Jorge Robles to mobilize the mainly Mexican fruit pickers and packers in Washington state. Robles found Teamster strategy and vertical decision-making confusing, but he stuck with it (Hathaway 2000a).

11. One case that deserves a full and careful analysis is the lost mid-2000 election at the Duro paperbag company in Tamaulipas, a privately-owned U.S. firm that produces for Hallmark and Neiman Marcus (see CJM Alert, "Gangster Union Wins in Rio Bravo," March 6, 2001).

12. After a 1996 documentary by the Canadian Broadcasting Corporation's Fifth Estate, the company had pledged an end to abuses.

13. Liz Claiborne is cochair of the Fair Labor Association, which ostensibly recognizes the right to unionize. The company publicizes an employee code of conduct, but few Salvadoran workers have any knowledge of it (USAS/NLC 1999, 6).

14. As discussed at the Clean Clothes Campaign conference, Barcelona, Spain, March 2001.

15. Despite the authors' familiarity with unions, they do not closely analyze local union attempts to toss boomerangs at resistant state agencies or corporate affiliates.

16. There may be parallels here to "hot shop" organizing, criticized by Lerner (1998) as insufficiently broad; but in nonunionized repressive conditions, some organizers believe that identifying a target is the best approach to that goal (Fieldman 1999).

17. In addition to membership-based organizing, discussed by Early (1998) and Nissen (1998), anthropologists have identified the significance of community networks in other contexts, for example, Green (1999) in Guatemala.

18. Since it takes two unions to request industrial union status, the Kimi union created a separate entity to join the request. In March 2000 the Honduran labor minister ruled this strategy illegal. The union appealed this decision, as it also pursued factory union status.

19. Between January and June 2000, Mil Colores fired 200; Chentex fired 9 union leaders in addition to 700 workers; Jem III fired 100; Chi Hsing fired 2 union leaders and canceled the union's registration. The local textile federation drew on a transnational activist network that encompassed the CLR, NLC, Nicaragua Network, Quixote Center/Quest for Peace, Tecnica, Upper West Side/Tipitapa Sister City Project, US/LEAP, and others.

20. Inspired by a *New York Times* report, December 3, 2000 (see CLR 2001a).

21. On January 25 and 26, 2001, USAS circulated University Wire press accounts from the University of Washington, Georgetown, University of Wisconsin, University of Michigan, University of Iowa, University of North Carolina, Brown University, Oklahoma State, and the University of California, Los Angeles, among others.

22. The UE/FAT alliance teamed with CJM and the CLR to demand recognition for the union at Congleadora del Rio, which ships to Smucker's. US/LEAP arranged for Guatemalan unionists to organize Central American poultry workers in the United States under Retail, Wholesale, and Department Store Workers Union (RWDSU) and United Food and Commercial Workers Union (UFCW) auspices.

23. Community-based organizing can also exhibit bidirectionality such as Hathaway (2000a) demonstrated in the environmental outcomes surrounding the lost strike at Cananea copper.

References

Alcalde Justiniani, Arturo. 2001. "Opinion Regarding the Case of Kuk Dong International." January 30.

Alexander, Robin. 1999. "Experience and Reflections on the Use of the NAALC."
   Memorias: Encuentro trinacional de laboralistas democráticos. Mexico, D.F.:
   Universidad Nacional Autónoma de México.
Alexander, Robin, and Peter Gilmore. 1994. "The Emergence of Cross-Border Soli-
   darity." *NAACLA Report on the Americas* 28, 1 (January–February): 42–48.
————. 1999. "A Strategic Organizing Alliance Across Borders." In Tillman and
   Cummings, eds., pp. 267–275.
Anner, Mark. 1998. "Transnational Campaigns to Defend Labor Rights in Export
   Processing Plants in El Salvador, Honduras, Guatemala and Haiti." Paper pre-
   sented at the Latin American Studies Association Twenty-First International
   Congress, Chicago, September 24–26.
Armbruster, Ralph. 1995. "Cross-National Labor Organizing Strategies." *Critical
   Sociology* 21, 2: 75–89.
————.1999. "Globalization and Cross-Border Labor Organizing: The Guatema-
   lan Maquiladora Industry and the Phillips–Van Heusen Workers' Movement."
   Latin American Perspectives 26, 2: 108–128.
————. 2000. "Globalization and Cross-Border Labor: Organizing in the Ameri-
   cas: The Phillips–Van Heusen Campaign, the Battle in Seattle, and Beyond."
   Paper presented at the Latin American Studies Association Twenty-Second In-
   ternational Congress, Miami, March 16–18.
Armstrong, Robert, Hank Frundt, Hobart Spalding, and Sean Sweeney. 1987. "Work-
   ing Against Us: AIFLD and the International Policy of the AFL–CIO." New
   York: NAACLA.
Barlow, Maude, and Tony Clark. 2001. *Global Showdown.* Toronto: Stoddart.
Barry, Tom. 1996. "Labor Bosses on Foreign Turf." *Democracy Backgrounder* 2, 1
   (February).
Barry, Tom, and Deb Preusch. 1990. *AIFLD in Latin America: Agents as Organiz-
   ers.* Albuquerque, NM: Resource Center.
Bonacich, Edna et al., eds. 1994. *Global Production: The Apparel Industry in the
   Pacific Rim.* Philadelphia: Temple University Press.
Boswell, Terry, and Dimitris Stevis. 1997. "Globalization and International Labor
   Organizing: A World-System Perspective." *Work and Occupations* 24, 3.
Bronfenbrenner, Kate, et al., eds. 1998. *Organizing to Win.* Ithaca, NY: Cornell
   University Press.
Bronfenbrenner, Kate, and Tom Juravich. 1998. "It Takes More than House Calls:
   Organizing to Win with a Comprehensive Union-Building Strategy." In
   Bronfenbrenner et al., eds., pp. 19–36.
Brooks, Ethel, and Winifred Tate. 1999. "After the Wars: Cross-Border Organizing
   in Central America." *NAACLA Report on the Americas* 32, 4 (January–Febru-
   ary): 32–37.
Ching Yoon Louie, Miriam. 2001. *Sweatshop Warriors.* Boston: South End Press.
CJM (Coalition for Justice in the Maquiladoras). 1999. "'Someone Has to Stop
   This': Testimony of an Autotrim Worker in Matamoros." In Kamel and Hoffman,
   eds., pp. 45–47.
CLR (Campaign for Labor Rights). 2001a. *Rapid Action Network Alert.* February 9.
————. 2001b. *Rapid Action Network Alert.* March 1.
————. 2001c. *Labor Alert.* April 6.
————. 2001d. *Labor Alert.* May 11.

Coats, Stephen. 1991. "Phillips–Van Heusen Workers Organize." *Report on Guatemala* 12, 4 (Winter).

———. 1993. "Maquila Workers Campaign: Success Raises Questions." *Report on Guatemala* 14, 2 (Summer).

———. 1996. "Taking on Phillips–Van Heusen: Maquila Workers Fight for a Contract." *Report on Guatemala* 17, 4 (Winter).

———. 1998. "Reflections on the Issue of Independent Monitoring." Washington, DC: Campaign for Labor Rights.

———. Forthcoming. "Central America Labor Solidarity: Lessons for Activists?" In *Organizing for Globalization*, ed. United for a Fair Economy.

Cohen, Larry, and Steve Early. 1999. "Defending Workers' Rights in the New Global Economy: The CWA Experience." In Nissen, ed.

Compa, Lance. 1999. "The North American Agreement on Labor Cooperation and International Labor Solidarity." *Memorias: Encuentro trinacional de laboralistas democráticos*. Mexico, D.F.: Universidad Nacional Autónoma de México.

Compa, Lance, and Stephen F. Diamond. 1996. *Human Rights, Labor Rights and International Trade*. Philadelphia: University of Pennsylvania Press.

Cook, Maria Lorena. 1999. "Trends in Research on Latin American Labor and Industrial Relations." *Latin American Research Review* 34, 1: 237–255.

Cravey, Altha J. 1998. *Women and Work in Mexico's Maquiladoras*. Lanham, MD: Rowman and Littlefield.

Davis, Terry. 1995. "Cross-Border Labor Organizing Comes Home." *Labor Research Review* 23: 23–29.

De Erick, Diaz Xolo, Ivan Kuh Dong (Mexmode strike leader). 2001. Signed statement, reproduced by Eric Brackken, United Students Against Sweatshops (USAS) listserve. February 16.

Dunn, Leith L. 1996. "Women Organizing for Change in Caribbean Free Zones." In *Confronting State, Capital and Patriarchy*, ed. Amrita Chhachhi and Renee Pittin. New York: St. Martin's Press.

Early, Steve. 1998. "Membership-Based Organizing." In Mantsios, ed., pp. 82–103.

Fieldman, Bruce (organizer with ITGLWF). 1999. Interview with author.

Figueroa, Hector J. 1998. "International Labor Solidarity in an Era of Global Competition." In Mantsios, ed., pp. 305–319.

Freeman, Jo. 1983. *Social Movements of the Sixties and Seventies*. New York: Longman's.

Frundt, Henry J. 1996. "Trade and Cross-Border Labor Strategies in the Americas." *Economic and Industrial Democracy* 17, 3 (August).

———. 1998. *Trade Conditions and Labor Rights: U.S. Initiatives, Dominican and Central American Responses*. Gainesville: University Press of Florida.

———. 1999. "Cross Border Organizing in Apparel: Lessons from the Caribbean and Central America. *Labor Studies Journal* 24, 1 (Spring): 89–106.

Green, Linda. 1999. *Fear as a Way of Life*. New York: Columbia University Press.

Greenfield, Gerald, and Sheldon Maram, eds. 1987. *Latin American Labor Organizations*. Westport, CT: Greenwood Press.

Greenhouse, Steven. 2000. "Nike's Chief Cancels a Gift over Monitor of Sweatshops." *New York Times*, April 25, p. A16.

Hathaway, Dale A. 2000a. "Transnational Support of Labor Organizing in Mexico:

Comparative Cases." Paper presented at the Latin American Studies Association Twenty-Second International Congress, Miami, March 16–18.

———. 2000b. *Allies Across the Border: Mexico's Authentic Labor Front.* Cambridge, MA: South End Press.

Hathaway, Dale A., and Jorge Robles. 1996. "The FAT and the Workers' Center of Juárez." Pittsburgh: United Electrical Workers.

Hill, Jennifer. 1997. "Guatemala: Stitching Solidarity." *Off Our Backs* 27, 3 (March): 10–11.

Howard, Andrew. 1995. "Global Capital and Labor Internationalism in Comparative Historical Perspective: A Marxist Analysis." *Sociological Inquiry* 64, 3/4: 365–394.

ILRF. 2001. "Report to Universities Affiliated with FLA Regarding the Kuk Dong International Conflict in Axtlico, Puebla, Mexico." January 25.

Johns, Rebecca A. 1998. "Bridging the Gap Between Class and Space: U.S. Worker Solidarity with Guatemala." *Economic Geography* 74, 3 (July): 252ff.

Kamel, Rachael. 1990. *The Global Factory.* Philadelphia: American Friends Service Committee.

Kamel, Rachael, and Anya Hoffman, eds. 1999. *The Maquiladora Reader: Cross-Border Organizing Since NAFTA.* Philadelphia: American Friends Service Committee.

Kay, Tamara. 2000. "A Conceptual Framework for Analyzing 'Labor Relations' in a Post-NAFTA Era." Paper presented at the Latin American Studies Association Twenty-Second International Congress, Miami, March 16–18.

Keck, Margaret, and Kathryn Sikkink. 1998. *Activists Beyond Borders.* Ithaca, NY: Cornell University Press.

Klein, Naomi. 2000. *No Space, No Choice, No Jobs, No Logo.* New York: Picador.

La Botz, Dan. 1995. *Democracy in Mexico: Peasant Rebellion and Political Reform.* Boston: South End Press.

Lerner, Steven. 1998. "Taking the Offensive, Turning the Tide." In Mantsios, ed., pp. 69–81.

Levinson, Charles. 1972. *International Trade Unionism.* London: Allen and Unwin.

Mantsios, Gregory, ed. 1998. *A New Labor Movement for the New Century.* New York: Monthly Review Press.

Moody, Kim. 1997. *Workers in a Lean World.* London: Verso.

Needleman, Ruth. 1998. "Building Relationships for the Long Haul: Unions and Community-Based Groups Working Together to Organize Low-Wage Workers." In Bronfenbrenner et al., eds., pp. 71–86.

Nissen, Bruce. 1998. "Utilizing the Membership to Organize the Unorganized." In Bronfenbrenner et al., pp. 135–149.

———. 1999. "Cross-Border Alliances in the Era of Globalization." In Tillman and Cummings, eds., pp. 239–254.

———, ed. 1999. *Which Direction for Organized Labor?* Detroit: Wayne State University Press.

O'Kane, Trish. 1994. "New Autonomy, New Struggle: Labor Unions in Nicaragua." In *The New Politics of Survival*, ed. Morton Sinclair, pp. 183–208. New York: Monthly Review Press.

Pattee, John. 1996. "'Gapatistas' Win a Victory." *Labor Research Review* 24: 77–85.

Perez, Martin. 2001. Testimony to *Centro de Apoyo Trabajar.* Reported by USAS, "Kuk Dong Update," May 16.

Pitkin, Daisy (national CLR coordinator). 2001. "Background on Chentex Campaign." *CLR Rapid Action Network Alert.* February 9.

Reed, Thomas, and Karen Brandow. 1996. *The Sky Never Changes: Testimonies from the Guatemalan Labor Movement.* Ithaca, NY: Cornell University Press.

Ross, Andrew, ed. 1997. *No Sweat: Fashion, Free Trade and the Rights of Garment Workers.* New York: Verso.

Safa, Helen. 1995. *The Myth of the Male Breadwinner: Women and Industrialization in the Caribbean.* Boulder, CO: Westview Press.

Sims, Beth. 1992. *Workers of the World Undermined: American Labor's Role in U.S. Foreign Policy.* Boston: South End Press.

SITEKIM. 2001. "Letter from the Independent Union of Workers at the Company Kuk Dong International of Mexico." Reproduced in CLR 2001b.

Spalding, Hobart. 1988a. "U.S. Labor Intervention in Latin America: The Case of the American Institute for Free Labor Development." In *Trade Unions and the New Industrialization of the Third World,* ed. Roger Southhall. Pittsburgh: University of Pittsburgh Press.

———. 1988b. "AIFLD and the Labor Movement." *NAACLA Report on the Americas,* May–June.

———. 1993. "The Two Latin American Foreign Policies of the U.S. Labor Movement." *Science and Society,* Spring.

Stahler-Sholk, Richard. 1995. "The Dog That Didn't Bark: Labor Autonomy and Economic Adjustment in Nicaragua under the Sandinista and UNO Governments." *Comparative Politics* 28 (October).

———. 1996. "Structural Adjustment and Resistance: The Political Economy of Nicaragua under Chamorro." In *The Undermining of the Sandinista Revolution,* eds. Gary Prevost and Harry Vanden, pp. 74–113. London: Macmillan.

Stalker, Peter. 2000. *Workers Without Frontiers.* Boulder, CO: Lynne Rienner.

St. Louis, Melinda. 2000. "Personal Account of Mil Colores Worker Tour." In Campaign for Labor Rights, "Honduras, Nicaragua Update," *Labor Alert,* June 3.

Stillerman, Joel. 2000. "Labor Internationalism and NAFTA: Theoretical, Historical and Practical Dilemmas." Paper presented at the Latin American Studies Association Twenty-Second International Congress, Miami, March 16–18.

Sturmthal, Adolf F. 1973. *The International Labor Movement in Transition.* Urbana: University of Illinois Press.

Tillman, Ray M., and Michael S. Cummings, eds. 1999. *The Transformation of U.S. Unions.* Boulder, CO: Lynne Rienner.

Tong, Mary E. 1993. "Reaching Across the Rio." *Beyond Borders,* Spring. Republished in Kamel and Hoffman, eds., pp. 74–78.

USAS/NLC. 1998. "Behind Closed Doors: The Workers Who Make Our Clothes." New York: National Labor Committee.

———. 1999. "Fired for Crying to the Gringos." New York: National Labor Committee.

Usenmez, Ozgur. 2001. "Editorial." *Monthly Review,* April.

US/LEAP. 1999. "Phillips–Van Heusen: An Industry 'Leader' Unveiled." Chicago: US/LEAP.

———. 2000a. Press release, May 26.

————. 2000b. No. 2 (August).

————. 2000c. "Yoo Yang Wins Legal Recognition!" No. 3 (December).

————. 2001. "Honduran Maquila Union Contracts: One Step Forward, Two Back." No. 1 (May).

USTR. 2000. "Fact Sheet: Caribbean Trade Partnership Act." October 3.

Waterman, Peter. 1998. *Globalization, Social Movements, and the New Internationalisms*. London: Mansell.

Weinrub, Al, and William Bollinger. 1987. *The AFL–CIO in Central America: A Look at the American Institute for Free Labor Development*. Oakland: Labor Network.

Williams, Heather. 1999. "Mobile Capital and Transborder Labor Rights Mobilization." *Politics and Society* 27, 1: 139–166.

Windmuller, John. 1954. *American Labor and the International Labor Movement, 1940–1953*. Ithaca, NY: Cornell University Press.

Witness for Peace. 1998. "Sewing Justice: U.S. Solidarity and the Workers' Struggle in Nicaragua's Maquilas." Washington, DC: Witness for Peace.

4

UNION GLOBAL ALLIANCES AT MULTINATIONAL CORPORATIONS

A CASE STUDY OF THE AMERITECH ALLIANCE

JEFF RECHENBACH AND LARRY COHEN

It has been at least ten years since unions have discovered the need for international work of a different sort in an economy that is increasingly global in both production and consumption. International Trade Secretariats (ITS) have tried to foster cooperation among unions in the same firms across national lines since at least the late 1980s. Led by the food, metal, energy, and textiles industries, this approach soon spread to communications, transportation, and even health care. And unions at specific firms generated world councils of different types at General Electric (GE), Ford, Nestle, and Northern Telecom (now Nortel Networks).

Now the need for much deeper ties among workers in the same firm is evident. For example, GE management uses international competition among nations, unions, and workers to drive costs down at suppliers as well as within GE. GE differentiates between high value-added and low value-added production, shedding all but high margin goods and services and then demanding lower prices from suppliers. GE is now valued at more than $500 billion, or roughly ten times the value of Ford and General Motors (GM). Its approach has universal appeal among global managements.

Given the increasingly transnational nature of employers and their business operations, unions must develop new forms and methods of operation that extend well beyond simple exchanges and meetings of top level leadership. Doing so will require a new vision and new ways of building worker power worldwide. So far, an alternative has not been found. The experiences of unions are too limited as they search for unity around an alternative vision. But reviewing recent experiences of attempts to redefine the international work of individual unions might lead to suggestions for future action.

The Communications Workers of America and Telecommunications

Our union, the Communications Workers of America (CWA), numbers 650,000 members in the United States and Canada. At least two-thirds of those members are technical and professional staff at many of the largest global information sector firms, including Lucent, Southwest Bell Communications (SBC), Verizon, AT&T, Dow Jones, Disney, and GE. Others work in similar technical and professional jobs in the public sector or in information-related jobs at other firms, such as the 10,000 reservations and passenger agents at U.S. Airways. In the past fifteen years, our union has had to deal with an industry that has been changing dramatically.

The growth of the global economy has been led in part by the telecommunications industry, which is comprised of companies that provide a variety of strategic communications services vital to economic development. In 1999, telecommunications firms generated worldwide revenues of $1 trillion. Among the largest companies are Nippon Telephone and Telegraph of Japan, with market capitalization of $190 billion, revenues of approximately $100 billion, and 225,000 employees; AT&T, with capitalization of $150 billion, revenues of approximately $65 billion, and 150,000 employees; and Deutsche Telekom (DT) of Germany, with capitalization of $120 billion, revenues of approximately $45 billion, and 180,000 employees.

The services offered by the telecommunications industry are diversifying rapidly, driven in part by changes in the regulatory environment. The economic liberalization policies (the "neoliberal agenda") adopted by numerous countries in the 1980s spurred competition in the provision of equipment, long distance and wireless services, Internet access, cable television, satellite communications, and submarine cables. By

1997, sixty-eight countries had agreed to allow competition in voice, data, and fax transmissions.

Governments around the world have moved to privatize telecommunications following the 1984 privatization of British Telecom (BT), and many telecommunications companies that once were under public domain and operated in regulated markets are now competing in the private sector. New services seem to be launched on a weekly basis, and traditional definitions of telecommunications employers have become outdated by technological developments. Because deregulation and liberalization of the telecommunications market is occurring in almost every region of the world, there has been a restructuring of telecommunications companies. American companies, in particular, are creating joint ventures abroad. In New Zealand, for example, two U.S. "Baby Bells"—Bell Atlantic and Ameritech—played a key role in the sell-off and reorganization of Telecom New Zealand (TNZ), acquiring a $2.5 billion stake in TNZ when it was privatized.

Deregulation in foreign countries has created many opportunities in service markets that American companies could not enter at home due to remaining regulatory restrictions. For example, two other Baby Bells—U.S. West and NYNEX (now part of Verizon)—entered the United Kingdom (UK) market, offering combined cable television and local telephone services in competition with BT before they could do so in the United States.

In the United States and other industrialized economies, telephone service is nearly universal. Additional growth must rely on the sale of other information services, such as video and electronic publishing and extra lines for fax and Internet services. On the other hand, in most developing countries less than 10 percent of the people currently have access to residential service. Hence, the big profit potential in Third World markets lies in extending basic telephone service to those without service or, in the worst of cases, focusing activities and development primarily in highly profitable products such as cellular telephony.

The governments of developing countries expect the privatization of telecommunications entities to be a quick source of cash for balancing federal budgets and improving currency valuations. At the same time, companies that invest in developing countries expect a high rate of return because the government typically guarantees a continued monopoly over basic telecommunications services for a fixed period. All too often, however, the private investors expect to be able to recoup their initial investments quickly by means of job cuts, price hikes, or market growth (typically manifest in high customer rates)—or all three methods. Under such conditions, SBC—originally known as Southwestern Bell—bought a stake and management role in Telmex, the former national telephone monopoly in Mexico, and a multinational consortium led by GTE (now merged with Bell Atlantic into Verizon) now operates the Venezuelan phone system.

Globalization also reduces the influence that any one nation has over the multinational enterprises operating within its boundaries. In the past, local, state, or national governments could set some operating standards. Today's global telecommunications firms are increasingly well positioned to dictate their own terms of business, especially those that relate to working conditions and labor–management relations.

One result of the globalization of telecommunications has been the lowering of labor standards in an industry where, under private or public ownership, strong unions had previously been able to achieve good wages and benefits. For example, NYNEX and U.S. West—before selling their UK cable TV subsidiaries in 1996—introduced employment practices in Britain that were patterned on the worst practices of predominantly nonunion cable operators in America. These new cable systems farmed out their entire network construction and maintenance to contractors who in turn employed workers as individual subcontractors. The latter were paid for each task they completed. Thus employees of these firms were denied workers' compensation when injured and had no right to collective bargaining since in theory they were self-employed. Since taking over from the two American companies, Cable and Wireless Communications (CWC) has maintained its anti-union stance.

For telecommunications workers and their unions, the bottom line resulting from industry restructuring and ownership changes has invariably been bad. Employment in some of the leading telecommunications companies has declined noticeably. Between 1982 and 1992, 289,931 jobs were eliminated in telecom enterprises in OECD countries alone. Additional job losses have been due to centralization and technological change. For example, in the United States, AT&T's creation of national service centers for customer support resulted in the closing of numerous smaller customer service sites around the country. New technology had its greatest impact on the employment of telephone operators. Complex switching systems for long distance calling, the development of the Operator Service Position Station, and voice recognition technology reduced the number of operators employed by AT&T by 75 percent between 1950 and 1996.

Throughout the world, the telecommunications industry had been one of the most highly unionized industrial sectors prior to the 1980s. With a limited number of companies and employers in any country, this high level of unionization undoubtedly enhanced the ability of unions to defend their members and to influence the direction of the industry. In several cases, this influence was manifest in negotiated reductions in force that minimized their disruptive impact on the lives of workers and communities. However, as telecommunications monopolies have been broken up, traditional unionized companies now constitute a smaller portion of a much broader, more competitive industry with many new players. Workers at most of the newer companies are not unionized. CWA has won card check agreements (agreements to recognize the union after a majority of workers sign union authorization cards) at SBC and Verizon. This is resulting in significant organizing among wireless workers in the United States, but the new lines of business and new entrants are still significantly nonunion. Consequently, the overall level of unionization has been declining, and, concomitantly, the ability of trade unions to affect public policy and corporate decision making is also decreasing.

Union power is at risk even within highly unionized companies. Many of these firms are investing abroad and now generate a significant percentage of their revenues in other countries. In 1993, for example, then AT&T chief executive officer (CEO) Robert Allen stated that one of his strategic goals was to ensure that more than half of the company's revenues were generated overseas. Further, U.S.-based firms attempt, wherever possible, to operate nonunion in their foreign ventures (as NYNEX did with its multibillion dollar cable television venture in Britain) or to operate with the benefit of corrupt, company–union arrangements (as Lucent Technologies—formerly part of AT&T—does at its Mexican maquiladora plants).

Meanwhile, the multinationals headquartered abroad that have expanded into the United States (e.g., the Canadian-based telecom equipment manufacturer Nortel Networks) have largely succeeded in operating free of collective bargaining agreements here. The $3.7 billion capital infusion that CWA's bitter adversary, Sprint, received in the mid-1990s from DT and France Telecom greatly strengthened its market position and ability to spread anti-unionism abroad through Global One, a jointly owned international subsidiary. In sum, trade union leverage in collective bargaining tends to decrease as employers are able to rely on revenues derived from nonunion international operations. This challenge is exacerbated when companies that seem to accept the existence of trade unions in their home countries try to avoid unionization in their foreign operations.

Finally, adoption of increasingly automated technology also has weakened unions. Telecommunications companies can withstand strikes better because fewer people are required to maintain and operate telephone systems. A union post mortem on CWA's lengthy 1989 walkout at NYNEX concluded that it was two months before the strike had much impact because of the company's high degree of automation and ability to maintain service using managers, retirees, and temporary workers.

The CWA is the world's largest union of telecommunications workers. During the last fifteen years—when more than 100,000 jobs have been eliminated in its traditional jurisdiction—the union has undergone considerable diversification and amalgamation. It now includes more than 80,000 health care and public employees, 45,000 newspaper and printing industry workers, and 15,000 workers in cable television and broadcasting. Some of this growth has been the product of mergers with the remaining independent telephone unions or smaller AFL–CIO affiliates, including the Newspaper Guild, International Typographical Union, and National Association of Broadcast Employees and Technicians. But much of the growth—particularly in health care and the public sector—has been the result of aggressive outreach to nonunion workers.

Nationally, CWA now allocates 10 percent of its budget to membership recruitment, while a network of 200 "organizing locals" also contributes a growing share of local union financial resources. The union has emphasized the recruitment and deployment of its own members as organizers, rather than hiring extensively from outside its ranks. Approximately 1,000 rank-and-file activists have received CWA organizer training and participated in actual campaigns. Within companies where it retains significant bargaining clout, the union has been able to facilitate organizing by negotiating agreements that provide for management neutrality, union access to nonunion workplaces, and recognition through card check procedures, rather than Labor Board elections. A five-year struggle with SBC secured such an agreement covering the company's cellular phone subsidiaries; now, more than 6,000 SBC wireless employees belong to CWA.

CWA organized by emphasizing strong workplace committees to re-cruit activists one-on-one and solid, strong majorities. By the late 1980s, it was clear that this type of approach was needed not only in organizing drives, but also in long-established CWA bargaining units, where man-agement was seeking contract concessions and displaying a new will-ingness to take strikes to get them. The union responded by developing a unionwide program called "CWA Mobilization," which applies the lessons of successful external organizing to contract campaigns. Em-ployed in each round of telephone bargaining since 1989, mobilization seeks to strengthen and revitalize the union through systematic internal organizing and greater membership participation in the negotiating pro-cess. Within CWA, mobilization became a key strategy to increase the power of the union.

However, with increasingly global employers, mobilizing members at home was not enough. Telecommunications firms are changing rap-idly in ways that make them less vulnerable to strikes or other forms of workplace and community pressure in their traditional lines of busi-ness. Consequently, the CWA's success in future bargaining and/or or-ganizing involving multinational firms depends, to an increasing degree, on its ability to develop international alliances and joint ventures of its own that enable American workers to act in concert with their brothers and sisters abroad.

When multinationals attempt to boost their power and profits at the expense of workers, unions must mobilize long-term, cross-border cam-paigns based on careful research and analysis, membership education and involvement, organizing, and international labor solidarity.

Partly in reaction to the global nature of our employers, more than ten years ago we began to experiment with various attempts to build union solidarity internationally within a firm. Led by our own president, Morton Bahr, in 1987 we met with unions from around the world to discuss organizing efforts, bargaining, and mutual support at IBM. In 1989, during a strike of 800 Nortel technicians, we realized that without the help of Canadian unions, this Canadian-based firm would wipe us out (see below). At CWC, under the auspices of the Postal, Telecom, Telegraph International (PTTI, the ITS for this sector), we participated as part of a group of unions stretching from the Caribbean to England and Hong Kong as we collaborated on organizing and bargaining strat-egies. We formed an Atlantic Alliance among CWA and two UK unions— the Communications Workers Union (CWU) and the Society of Telecom

Executives (STE). The purpose was to focus on joint organizing in the cable TV sector, and then to build one union at a jointly owned BT-AT&T cable company. In 1998, we formed a similar alliance at Ameritech, then Chicago-based with 35,000 CWA members and now part of the much larger SBC, where we have 90,000 members and which is a dominant player in Mexico, South Africa, Belgium, and Denmark.

Our challenge is to see if we can redefine the basic *activity* of union internationalism as worksite-based rather than as mostly a series of meetings. International union work has long been characterized by meetings of different types where problems of translation and logistics were time consuming and follow-up and real results that members could see were often lacking. Aided by the new technology of the information age—communications tools like e-mail and the Worldwide Web—some CWA activists are now networking with trade unionists overseas just as if they belonged to another local union in the United States. A growing number have had the chance to meet and talk face to face with their counterparts abroad: telephone workers from Mexico, factory workers in Canada, cable TV technicians in England. By joining forces, they clearly have enhanced their ability to maintain or increase union strength, defend wage and benefit standards, and have a greater impact on public policymaking.

However, if major changes are going to occur in the balance of power between labor and capital in the new global economy, far more union resources will have to be devoted to grass-roots organizing and rank-and-file activity. The budgets of various ITSs—like Union Network International (UNI, the ITS for the information and postal sectors)—total millions of dollars a year. More of that money needs to be spent on joint organizing projects like the 1997 CWA–CWU experiment and coordinated solidarity campaigns involving workplace protests and direct action by workers within the same transnational firm. More union members must be encouraged to act locally to be effective internationally because real solidarity—as opposed to symbolic gestures—often requires the exercise of shop floor power at home. If that power has been eroded because a union has no program for internal organization and membership mobilization to meet day-to-day challenges by management, its members will be much less able to help workers elsewhere.

Today, even some of the best organized, most innovative cross-border initiatives by unions are clearly too little, too late. That is because the existing pace of labor's organizational work at the international level does not match the great speed with which transnational corporations are restructuring themselves and redirecting the flow of investment. If unions pursue a business-as-usual approach to building their own international alliances and actions, they will be outmaneuvered and increasingly marginalized.

Worker representatives must themselves feel—and convey to their membership—a far greater sense of urgency about the global anti-union trends that are undermining collective bargaining and workplace protection for millions of people. Unions must be willing to break more rules, take more risks, ignore protocol, and change long-established modes of organizational behavior so that workers can unite and fight more effectively. If we fail, the telecommunications revolution will end up forging what for our members may be a new set of chains.

The Ameritech Alliance

In this chapter, we will examine union solidarity work across national borders by reviewing the experience of the Ameritech Alliance, initiated by the CWA in 1997. We will discuss the international alliances that CWA has been engaged in building with a worker focus for many years, at least since the 1989 strike of CWA technicians at Nortel. The strike was supported by Nortel's two Canadian unions. Other alliances with Mexico and the UK will be described as well. We will show how the Ameritech Alliance included the CWA, the Belgian CGSP-T (General Union of Public Services–Telecom), the Danish TKF (Union of Telecommunications Workers), and Hungary's MATASZ. Ameritech, the regional bell phone company in the Midwest, owned controlling interest in these countries' phone systems. The alliance has organized a series of workplace actions and educational activities around the world. When Ameritech was acquired by SBC, the alliance reached out to include other unions at SBC around the world.

The Ameritech Alliance developed a Statement of International Operating Principles. Its activities have moved Ameritech to operate in ways closer to those principles. While the percentage of members that were involved in worksite activities was small, these efforts were a serious first step in making international solidarity a reality in the workplace. Finally, we will review what can be learned by this modest experience.

One of CWA's first cross-border campaigns involved Nortel and grew out of the crucial international assistance that CWA members received during a five-week strike in 1989. Nortel produces telephone equipment in factories throughout North America, Western Europe, and the Third World. It began as the manufacturing arm of Bell Canada, but in the 1980s it increased its worldwide workforce by 80 percent and its sales by 400 percent. The unionized percentage of its workforce declined by 50 percent during the same period. In Canada, it generally remains heavily organized; about 40 percent of its 22,000 Canadian employees are union-represented. Nortel's U.S. workforce is about the same size, but the unionization rate is less than 5 percent.

By the summer of 1989, the CWA's largest field technician unit consisted of about 500 workers in eight northeastern states. Nortel was clearly preparing to press for concessions that would force a strike. The members readied themselves for this struggle by creating an active mobilization network, issuing regular contract bulletins, and engaging in a variety of on-the-job actions before walking out three weeks after their contract expired. Almost immediately, management deployed replacement workers, who were confronted at key customer locations by teams of mobile pickets and their supporters from other CWA locals. The ensuing strike was militant and well organized, but it almost certainly would have failed if CWA had not lined up international allies as well.

Prior to bargaining, the CWA approached leaders of the company's two main Canadian unions, the Canadian Auto Workers (CAW) and the Communications Workers of Canada (now known as the Communications, Energy, and Paperworkers Union, or CEP). Soon after the U.S. installers struck, both the CAW and CEP intervened in the dispute. Then CAW president Bob White and CEP president Fred Pomeroy sent letters of protest to Nortel's CEO, copies of which were widely distributed among members of all three unions to inform them about the emerging cross-border solidarity campaign. The Canadian unions immediately launched their own grass-roots mobilization in support of the strike. Leaflets distributed in CAW and CEP workplaces throughout Canada recounted Nortel's history of "anti-worker, anti-union activities in the United States" which were linked to the export of jobs from Canada to the United States.

The CWA's ongoing relationship with Mexican telephone workers provides another important example of how international solidarity can and must be a two-way street. The 1990 privatization of Telmex, SBC's management role with the company since then, and the creation of "free trade" links among Canada, the United States, and Mexico have led telephone worker unions from all three nations into a joint venture of their own. This alliance was formalized in an agreement signed by the CWA's Bahr, the CEP's Pomeroy, and Francisco Hernández Júarez, general secretary of Sindicato de Telefonistas de la República Mexicana (STRM). STRM represents 50,000 workers at Telmex and is among the largest independent unions in Mexico. The joint venture commits the participating organizations "to defend union and workers' rights" through "joint mobilization" of members in Mexico and throughout North America.

In September 1995, fifteen CWA organizers and eighteen from STRM spent three days together at a training and strategy session in Laredo, Texas. All of the U.S. participants were bilingual and had experience organizing immigrant workers from Mexico and Central and South America. The STRM activists were eager to learn about the CWA's organizing work, including its efforts to unionize firms that have entered the telecommunications field since deregulation in the United States. As a follow-up to this meeting, two STRM organizers spent a week working on a CWA campaign in Los Angeles among 5,000 Spanish-speaking truckers who transport freight from the city's harbor. By 1999, as part of its own expanded organizing program, STRM had succeeded in winning bargaining rights for 3,000 workers at a customer calling center run by Techmarketing, a Telmex contractor.

The Americanization of telecom industry labor relations in the UK has also fostered increasingly close ties between CWA and its counterparts in Britain. The Thatcher government's sell-off of BT in the 1980s and BT's subsequent downsizing weakened both the 300,000–member CWU and the smaller 27,000–strong STE. Like STRM in Mexico, the CWU and STE were confronted with the task of recruiting new members at the growing number of new cable television and telecom companies—including U.S.-based ones—that are now competing with the former state-owned monopoly. For example, UK cable TV providers now employ more than 30,000 nonunion workers; many of them are hired, American-style, as independent contractors.

CWA's relationship with CWU and STE began modestly with an exchange of information about the problems of organizing new members in a privatized, deregulated market environment. The formal cooperation agreement that was then developed—known as the Atlantic Alliance—states that whenever members of the three unions are bargaining with a common multinational employer, they will establish some form of direct "communication and joint education." In addition, a "contract mobilization timeline" will be developed and the resulting "joint action will be more an expression of basic union strategy in negotiations and less an exceptional example of international solidarity." The agreement declares that "joint organizing strategies" will be developed for key information sector firms operating in both countries.

With their multinational character, a large concentration of Americans in top management positions, and large nonunion workforces, CWC and Telewest became the logical targets for the Atlantic Alliance's highly unusual joint organizing project in 1997. Three CWA organizers— Andrea DeMajewski from Seattle, Hank Desio from Tulsa, and Shannon Kirkland from Detroit—were sent over to spend four months working with CWU branches in Manchester and London.

During their 1997 stay in the UK, DeMajewski lived in Manchester, Desio worked in Brighton, and Kirkland stayed in the London area. All three roomed with union families as part of their cross-training experience. The members providing their housing received a stipend from the CWU. While these living arrangements sometimes created additional adjustment problems, they increased the organizers' credibility among CWU activists and ultimately deepened their connection to the people with whom they were working. The most important outcome of their stay was the development of greater organizing capability in twenty different CWU branches, whose membership is still almost entirely based within BT. As CWU organizing officer Grace Mitchell observed, "We always thought of recruiting as the main job—signing up new members in places where we had recognition already. Now, we focus more on developing small groups of organizers in branches who in turn support committees inside locations where we do not have recognition. This provides a support structure for a recognition campaign."

Through these and other efforts, the idea of international alliances began to be a part of CWA's strategic thinking. In part, this was driven by the success of these efforts. Mostly, it was a result of the changes that were taking place in the industry.

Led by deregulation and technological advances, the telecommunications industry in the United States has been going through dramatic changes during the past twenty years. In 1983, as a result of a consent decree reached between AT&T and the Justice Department, Judge Harold Greene ordered the divestiture of the Bell System. That decree split off

AT&T and saw the creation of seven Regional Bell Operating Companies (RBOCs). These RBOCs provided local telephone service in geographical regions throughout the United States. The five Midwest states of Illinois, Indiana, Michigan, Ohio, and Wisconsin fell within the jurisdiction of Ameritech.

This divestiture was implemented in 1984. The telecommunications industry in the United States went from being a heavily regulated monopoly to a more competitive, somewhat less regulated provider of telecommunications services. Faced with the dramatically changing environment, Ameritech was forced to develop a new business plan to survive in a more competitive arena. Initially, Ameritech followed a business strategy that it referred to as "Fortress Ameritech." This plan was focused almost exclusively on growth and new lines of business within the five-state region. In 1990, that focus shifted slightly as Ameritech ventured into international business for the first time in a major way.

In September 1990, the government of New Zealand sold its interest in TNZ to an American consortium made up of Ameritech and Bell Atlantic. The purchase price for the state-owned telecommunications company was $2.46 billion and gave the two American companies a majority interest. The New Zealand government then changed its position and required Ameritech and Bell Atlantic to reduce their combined ownership position to less than 50 percent by September 1994. In order to comply, the two companies sold a 31 percent stake to the public in TNZ's public offering, reducing their share to 49.9 percent.

This endeavor was a first for Ameritech, which had been standing on the sidelines watching many of the other RBOCs venturing beyond American shores in pursuit of business interests. When Ameritech and Bell Atlantic took over TNZ, they inherited 15,000 represented employees covered under a single collective bargaining agreement. The management and union in New Zealand had a history of worker–management cooperation that was hallmarked by the fact that in the 100–year history of the union, there had never been a full, national strike. The Ameritech–Bell Atlantic alliance quickly changed the management style to one of aggressive cost cutting.

Within four years of Ameritech–Bell Atlantic's taking over the reins, employees had been cut from 15,000 to 9,000, and plans had already been announced to cut another 1,000 within the next twelve months. The 2,000 workers who had previously been covered by a union contract were no longer afforded that benefit. Bitter contract negotiations resulted in a historic, first-ever, seven-day national strike. Benefits and working conditions were under a full-scale assault, including the elimination of a company-subsidized pension plan. By 1997, when Ameritech decided to leave New Zealand and sell its interest of 24.95 percent, the company had just over 8,000 employees; of those, fewer than 2,000 were covered by a collective bargaining agreement.

This de-unionization of TNZ took place in a variety of ways. In addition to the extensive layoffs, TNZ also spun off a number of different work functions to new subsidiaries. Workers were offered opportunities to go to the new subsidiaries; however, existing collective bargaining agreements would not cover them. TNZ would lay off employees one day, pay them a termination allowance, and rehire them the next day in a newly formed subsidiary without a union contract.

Work throughout the company was routinely contracted out to companies where there was no union representation. Contracting out also took place in pieces of the business in places that would have been considered traditional telephone work, such as cable installation and repair work. The Ameritech–Bell Atlantic strategy was apparent. They were bound and determined to cut all expenses out of the business and reap the largest possible profits in a short-term investment.

This strategy was made crystal clear by the payment of dividends. In New Zealand companies, approximately 60 percent of net earnings were paid to shareholders in the form of dividends. From 1992 until 1997, TNZ never paid a dividend lower than 89 percent of net earnings. When one considers that nearly 50 percent of the stock was held by Ameritech and Bell Atlantic, the strategy comes into focus. In fact, there were two years where more than 100 percent of net earnings was paid out as dividends. The average payment during that five-year stretch was 96 percent of net earnings—not a strategy for reinvesting in a company for future growth.

Shortly after the initial purchase of TNZ, Ameritech announced its public strategies for growth: (a) growth of core communications business; (b) creation of new services; and (c) international expansion.

Growth of Core Communications Business

Ameritech sought to increase its revenues from its traditional wireline telephone network. It did this in two ways. First, it promoted new call management (access) services, that is, Caller I.D., Call Waiting, and additional lines of service. Second, it sought to cut costs. Downsizing and consolidation cut network employment by 22 percent over the years 1993–2000. During that same period, the company saw a nearly 16 percent increase in the number of telephone lines sold. Overall cost cutting and job elimination enabled Ameritech to increase network revenue per network employee (a traditional efficiency measurement used in the telecommunications industry) by 51.7 percent—more than three times the rate of increase in the access line of revenue.

New Services

The most successful of the new services Ameritech has launched was Ameritech Cellular. In the upper Midwest, Ameritech currently has over 4 million wireless customers, selling its service through more than 1,000 retail locations.

Beyond cellular, Ameritech has introduced new services in the telecommunications marketplace. These services were almost exclusively nonunion since they were, as the company described, "non-traditional telephone" products. In 1995, Ameritech purchased SecurityLink, a security monitoring company. In subsequent months, it purchased the assets of a number of other small security firms, quickly moving SecurityLink into position as the second largest security company in the United States. Ameritech created a cable television business that has seen rapid expansion over the past five years. It offers cable television service in over 100 municipalities across the five Ameritech states. It was involved in marketing integrated desktop communications services to major customers such as United Airlines, work that included the design, installation, support, and finances for such systems. Ameritech also was active in selling electronic commerce systems networks, which link state and local government document systems. It offered Internet service. Finally, it laid claim to being the world's leading provider of library automation, working in 3,700 libraries in thirty-two countries.

All of these new ventures were entered at least initially without the involvement of Ameritech's union partners, the CWA and the International Brotherhood of Electrical Workers (IBEW). Organizing at SecurityLink was met with stiff resistance. An early agreement was reached to represent workers at Ameritech's cable operation, but at a lower wage rate than that for workers in its traditional telephone business. Attempts to organize other lines of business were generally futile.

International Expansion

Ameritech also began a very aggressive move in the international marketplace. Following the joint investment with Bell Atlantic at TNZ, Ameritech began a rapid international expansion that focused primarily on Europe. During the 1990s, Ameritech made acquisitions or secured controlling interest of the Danish telecommunications company TeleDanmark, the Belgian telephone company Belgacom, the Hungarian telephone company Matav, a cellular operation in Norway, and a business directory company in Germany.

This three-pronged strategy by Ameritech —cost cutting in the traditional telephone business, expansion to new lines of business, and international acquisitions—focused its greatest expansion outside of the core business, which is under union contract. In its wireless, security, financial, and library services, Ameritech refused to offer recognition and ran union avoidance campaigns. At the same time, in other unorganized parts of Ameritech where it had not traditionally run union avoidance campaigns, in the mid-1990s these quickly became the practice.

In nine separate elections during the mid-1990s, CWA signed up over 65 percent of workers in an unorganized Ameritech unit and only twice was able to secure a majority vote in favor of the union. In each instance, the company ran a well-financed, anti-union campaign. It was clear that Ameritech intended to drive the union out of its future business through cost cutting in the represented portions of the corporations and freezing out the union from any new ventures. CWA, which in combination with the IBEW at one point represented nearly 70 percent of the Ameritech workforce, was faced with a shrinking power base and diminished leverage within a rapidly growing company.

CWA had to employ a new strategy to regain its position. This new strategy had to address all three of Ameritech's initiatives. Fortunately, the path was clear as it applied to Ameritech's international expansion. Ameritech's acquisitions had taken place almost exclusively in countries with highly unionized workforces and, more specifically, highly unionized telecommunications workforces.

In the fourth quarter of 1997, Ameritech announced that it had purchased a controlling interest in TeleDanmark. At the time of the earlier acquisitions, Ameritech had portrayed a union-friendly image. CWA had, in fact, responded positively to inquiries from the Belgian CGSP-T about Ameritech. However, by the time of the TeleDanmark acquisition, this reputation had changed due to Ameritech's role in New Zealand and increased conflict over the growth of nonunion subsidiaries in the United States. Thus when the Danish TKF contacted CWA following the TeleDanmark deal, CWA shared these concerns with Danish leaders. This led to an invitation for CWA to come to Denmark and meet with TKF leaders. The TKF and CWA shared a concern about the future of telecom jobs in their respective countries. They believed that union leaders in Belgium and Hungary would likely share the concerns as well.

CWA and TKF worked with the Communications International to call a meeting of all the Ameritech unions. This meeting took place on January 29–30, 1998, in Brussels. The meeting was attended by unions from four countries: CGSP-T from Belgium, TKF from Denmark, MATASZ from Hungary, and CWA from the United States. Representatives of the Communications International were also in attendance. After each union reported on its respective situation, the following was concluded: "It was clear that the unions face many common problems. . . . Almost everywhere [Ameritech] attempts to eliminate or contract-out activities even including what were once considered core activities. In this way it reduces the permanent employees and apparently boosts the productivity figures" (*Ameritech Alliance Newsletter*, February 1998).

Faced with a global employer who was pursuing similar strategies around the world, these four unions decided to create an alliance that became known as the Ameritech Alliance. The alliance had a ten-point statement of principles and programs that "will seek to increase the leverage of our member organizations through greater joint activity. Joint action will need to be more an expression of basic union strategy and less an exceptional example of international solidarity" (*Ameritech Alliance Founding Principles*, January 30, 1998).

Consistent with this action message, the alliance decided that its next meeting would be April 14–15, 1998, in Chicago, Illinois, to coincide with the Ameritech shareholders' meeting. Leaders from Ameritech unions around the world could use the shareholders' meeting as an opportunity to speak out on these key issues. The Chicago alliance meeting would also plan an International Day of Workplace Action to take place later in the year, and it would develop a declaration of "Operating Principles" to present to Ameritech.

CWA began to mobilize its members to attend the shareholders' meeting. CWA had been preparing for its upcoming contract negotiations since September 1997. Even though the contract did not expire until August 1998, CWA recognized that there would be a major fight over key issues. A membership bargaining survey led to a bargaining resolution adopted by leaders of all CWA Ameritech locals in April 1998. The resolution included the following statement:

> Addressing the various aspects of Ameritech's disrespect for its workers and their union will be the primary issue on the bargaining table this year. The results of this round of bargaining will define the future of our relationship with this company as employees and as a union because the Telecommunications Reform Act of 1996 has set our industry on a rapidly expanding course. We have already seen that these changes will vastly increase the number of jobs in our industry. The number of jobs at Ameritech increased by 8,231 in 1997. Yet, the growth is in the nonunion parts of the business such as cellular or Security Link. In 1997, the number of jobs in CWA's jurisdiction declined by 258. As yet, our union has not broken the grip of anti-union hostility, which strangles the path by which our members should be able to access the fastest growing portions of the telecom sector.

CWA knew that the shareholders' meeting would be the opening shot in the struggle to address these key issues in the future. Working together with the IBEW, which represented 10,000 Ameritech employees in Illinois, over 500 union activists attended the shareholders' meeting.

On April 15, 1998, leaders from the four alliance unions and the IBEW led these 500 activists to the shareholders' meeting at Chicago's Art Institute auditorium. The sea of union jackets and caps filled the room and required an overflow room to be set up with TV monitors. In part because of Ameritech's announcement the day before of 5,000 job cuts (ironically all managerial or nonunion), there was significant press attention paid to the meeting. The alliance-led action became international news, with coverage throughout the United States and Europe. The lead in the *Chicago Tribune* story read, "Union leaders from the US and Europe heckled Ameritech Corp.'s Chief Executive at the company's shareholders' meeting Wednesday for entertaining customers at Bulls basketball games, golf outings, and tennis tournaments while laying off thousands of workers." ("Union Chiefs Heckle Ameritech Chairman," April 16, 1998).

Inspired by the actions of members, the alliance leaders announced an International Day of Action for June 24, 1998. Its purpose was to raise awareness and involve members in workplace actions in support of the right to organize and to protect jobs at Ameritech around the world. The call to action stated that "Ameritech has systematically opposed Union organizational activity in the U.S. and Europe. . . . Ameritech's strategy of 'rationalization' and 'downsizing' has had a devastating impact on both employment levels and service quality around the world." Each union was to develop membership-based educational activities that were appropriate to its situation, and the alliance developed a common sticker stating "solidarity" in all of the languages of the member unions. Workers in four different countries would all be wearing these stickers.

Unknown to the leaders of the alliance, Ameritech was in the final planning stages of a merger with telecom giant SBC. Evidently, the display at the shareholders' meeting created concerns that the climate for this merger (which required regulatory and government approval, in both the United States and Europe) would be adversely affected by international labor strife. One week after the shareholders' meeting, Ameritech approached CWA leaders with a proposal for early contract negotiations that included a pledge that there would be no company demands of any kind and that the company would address the union's key concerns.

CWA reached agreement on a new contract in early June 1998, two months before the previous contract expired. In addition to substantial improvements in wages, benefits, pensions, and employment security, the contract contained provisions for card check recognition and neutrality in organizing. This was a major step forward in giving CWA the opportunity to organize the growing nonunion parts of the business.

Notwithstanding an agreement on a new contract, the Day of Action went on as scheduled on June 24, 1998. Activities took place in worksites throughout the world. In Denmark, members wore the stickers. Morning meetings were held at all worksites throughout the country. The union sent a letter to TeleDanmark management. In Belgium, workers wore stickers and were involved in regional activities. An article was placed in the union newspaper, which is sent to the 13,000 CGSP-T members. In Hungary, 350 members attended a mass meeting in Budapest. Other members throughout the country wore stickers. In the United States, CWA members wore stickers and distributed the alliance newsletter among the 30,000 CWA members at Ameritech.

The Day of Action was a positive experience for all of these unions and their members. As one CWA local stated in a flier to its members, "Be proud that you are part of a network of solidarity with your sisters and brothers from overseas, and be sure that wherever Ameritech goes, the Alliance will follow" ("Solidarity Forever International Day of Action," leaflet issued by CWA Local 4309 in Cleveland, Ohio, on June 24, 1998).

While planning for the Day of Action, the alliance had continued to develop a consensus on a set of principles—"The Ameritech Alliance Declaration of World-Wide Operating Principles":

June 11, 1998

"Ameritech Alliance Declaration of World-Wide Operating Principles"

The Communications International and the Ameritech unions, (The Ameritech Alliance), are seeking consultation with Ameritech to discuss operating principles for Ameritech's world-wide operations.

These are the basic principles and rights that the Ameritech Alliance believes should be part of Ameritech's world-wide plans wherever the company may operate.

1. Recognition of the right to organize and the recognition of the rights of trade unions to represent and negotiate for workers.
2. Respect for and compliance with the conventions and recommendations of the International Labour Organisation (ILO) as a minimum.
3. Respect for and compliance with national customs.
4. Maintenance of the highest possible standards regarding the environment.
5. Employment and job security with adequate training and retraining opportunities.
6. No shifting of work from union to non-union jobs.
7. Commitment to deliver and extend a high quality of service that is accessible and universally affordable.
8. Commitment to long term and high levels of investment in local operating companies, to develop and extend the companies' services and jobs.
9. Commitment to convene regular meetings with Communications International and affiliated unions to consult with and share information concerning the companies' global strategies.

However, by the time these principles had been developed, the alliance realized it was dealing with a new and larger global entity—SBC.

On May 10, 1998, Ameritech announced that it had entered into an agreement to be acquired by SBC. SBC was another RBOC providing local and wireless telecommunications to customers in Arkansas, Kansas, Missouri, Oklahoma, and Texas. In addition, SBC was in the process of completing a merger with Pacific Bell and had just announced a merger with Southern New England Telephone Company.

As the merger proceeded through a variety of regulators in the United States, it was also necessary that approval be secured from the European community. CWA has had a very positive relationship with SBC over the past several years. In order to ensure the approval of the merger, we contacted the international secretary at the PTTI and asked PTTI to intercede on behalf of SBC, which it willingly did. The intervention of the PTTI resulted in quick approval by the European community for the merger. Following that approval, CWA vice president Ben Turn contacted SBC chairman Ed Whitacre and requested a meeting of the Ameritech Alliance partners with SBC, a meeting that, despite several overtures, had been rejected by Ameritech management in the past. Within a matter of days, Chairman Whitacre responded positively, and a meeting was set for February 5, 1999, in San Antonio, Texas. Alliance representatives from the United States, Denmark, Hungary, and a representative from the PTTI attended the session. The Belgians were unable to attend due to a scheduling conflict.

At that session, the Ameritech Alliance partners presented the "Declaration of World-Wide Operating Principles," for consideration by SBC in a postmerger environment. Whitacre, while constrained by the Securities and Exchange Commission during the merger approval process, committed to the alliance members that he would sit down with them in a postmerger environment to discuss these matters. Also up for discussion would be the creation of European and global works councils, extending a European-style workplace advocacy to an American-based employer.

The merger has also meant a change in the makeup of the alliance partners. Now that the merger has been completed, we anticipate inviting representatives of unions in countries where SBC has significant holdings. They include France, Mexico, South Africa, Israel, and South Korea. Plans are currently under way to expand the Ameritech Alliance into an SBC alliance. UNI is currently making arrangements to invite all SBC international partners into a global affiliate. However, changes continue in the international activities of SBC. As this chapter was being written, SBC had started to withdraw from Europe, beginning with the Hungarian company and soon followed by Denmark.

Analysis

The transition from Ameritech to SBC has clearly lessened the antagonism between management and labor. SBC has agreed to recognition based on card check and open consultation with its unions on a global basis. In the information sector, this is as good as it gets. CWA has used card check to successfully organize more than 5,000 technical and customer service staff at SBC wireless companies, including Southwestern Bell Mobile, Pacific Bell Wireless, and Cellular One.

We could claim victory, argue for this case as a model, and move on. But we understand that we have so far demonstrated only a limited commitment of our members, shop stewards, and local leaders, as well as those in the other global unions, to a process for coordinated worksite education and action. While the activities in June 1998 on the International Day of Action or in December 1999 in our coordinated action around forced overtime and staffing pressures were serious attempts, only a small percentage of our members participated in these activities. We still need to implement an education program that shows how we are connected internationally at this firm and why we need to be ready to act to support any of the member unions in our alliance.

At least in the information sector an international framework is crucial for the work in any single nation. Management understands this clearly as it moves its investments and restructures work. Management at SBC and the other large information sector firms realizes that coordinated action by labor unions across national lines can either help or hurt its plans. Management has to really stretch to build political clout in more than a single nation—each of these firms is still viewed as based in one nation, and they are often at least somewhat suspect everywhere else.

The failure of the Worldcom–Sprint merger is a good case in point. European Commission (EC) approval of the merger was necessary since both Worldcom and Sprint exceeded the revenue thresholds in Europe that trigger review. Worldcom was already suspect since the EC had placed conditions on its previous merger with MCI regarding divestment of Internet backbone in Europe, and it was widely believed that Worldcom's subsequent sale of Internet properties to CWC had been insufficient.

Through UNI, an educational effort and eventually opposition to the merger was generated among the European affiliates in the EC countries. Greece and Portugal, where the telecom unions are particularly close to the labor-oriented governments, played decisive roles, as did the UK, where CWA has worked closely with union partners Connect and the CWU through a long-term alliance. A delegation from CWA traveled to Brussels and met with members of the European Parliament, explaining the absence of dialogue between the 4,000 CWA-represented members at Sprint and Worldcom management, despite the obvious implications of the pending merger. The delegation also documented Worldcom's failure to contribute in any way to universal service obligations and the dominance it would have globally if the merger were approved. In June 2000, the EC indicated to the U.S. Department of Justice that it would not approve the merger, and subsequently both agencies opposed the merger, effectively terminating the deal. The coalition built around merger opposition demonstrated again that unions could provide local clout on international issues more effectively than management in a single multinational firm.

Information policy issues are also a bridge to greater involvement. On the network side, the main issue is universal access to high-speed, multimedia information. Currently, the digital divide blocks the overwhelming majority of the world's population from any meaningful access to voice communications, let alone multimedia over Internet. Yet the costs to build wireless broadband networks that could at least supply unlimited information to community centers around the world could be funded by a surcharge of 1 percent on global information sector revenues and could provide universal access in a few years. The ability of unions and international organizations such as UNI to effectively build support for proposals such as this could well be decisive in the years ahead.

Diversity of information is a major issue on the content side—what information can flow over these expanding networks and how we promote cultural and intellectual diversity in the process. Information in this case includes news, policy issues, health care data, and even entertainment. These issues are key for economic development and, as such, could unite our members and their communities as an offset to simple market forces controlling not only labor issues, but information issues as well.

A new starting point for all of this may flow from the technology itself. Connecting up shop stewards on a global basis at the same firm through the Internet could begin to move union solidarity work from the conference room to the worksite. At least in high-tech occupations like communications, the majority of the members in North America, Europe, and Japan already are connected to the Internet. We need only to make the investment to connect them to each other. In developing economies we might need to subsidize union Internet connections, but this would be well worth the effort if the result were consistent interchange of information and the capacity to act together. Interestingly enough, Ford management may be spearheading this effort by offering a computer and Internet connection to its employees worldwide.

Coordination at Ameritech/SBC provides some clues toward a redefinition of international unionism. Our efforts to develop a joint strategy around key issues like union recognition and hours of work, coupled with coordinated action and consultation, certainly provide a basis for further action. For CWA this becomes even more urgent in 2001, when contracts expire covering more than 100,000 members in thirteen states. Redefining the union's role and broadening acceptance of the new vision is not going to be easy. Doing it in an international context will be harder, but the potential results could be enormous.

Part II

RESPONDING TO IMMIGRATION

5

NEW WORKERS, NEW LABOR, AND THE NEW LOS ANGELES

RUTH MILKMAN

To the surprise of many observers, Los Angeles emerged in the 1990s as a key site of labor movement experimentation and as a showcase for successful immigrant organizing, an embryo of the broader revitalization effort that the new AFL–CIO leadership and its allies are currently attempting to jump-start. While the long-term prospects for that effort remain ambiguous, L.A. labor has won a series of important union organizing victories in recent years, with over 90,000 new members recruited in 1999 alone (Meyerson 1999). The L.A. County Federation of Labor has also become a formidable political force, launching massive voter registration and get-out-the-vote campaigns among newly enfranchised immigrants that have been pivotal in a wide variety of local, regional and even statewide electoral contests.

Immigrant workers, mostly from Mexico and Central America, comprise the overwhelming bulk of the working class in contemporary southern California, which has more foreign-born residents than any other part of the nation. Although many of the region's Latino immigrant workers are undocumented, and despite the widespread belief that such workers are extremely difficult to organize, they have been at the core of the L.A. labor movement's revival. In a range of low-wage, blue-collar occupational settings, from janitorial work to construction to home health care (to name only the most prominent examples), Latino immigrants have swelled the ranks of unions in L.A. and have demonstrated a capacity for militancy that is second to none.

This chapter traces the metamorphosis of L.A.—once a legendary citadel of the open shop—into what Mike Davis recently called "the major R&D center for 21st-century trade unionism" (2000, 145). It analyzes the relationship between immigration and unionization and exposes the dynamics that have galvanized foreign-born Latino workers into such a vital ingredient of L.A.'s model of labor renewal. And it examines the other crucial ingredients in the mix: the new activist leadership of key unions, at both the local and national levels, and of the L.A. County Federation of Labor, who have cleared a path out of the wreckage of union decline and sclerosis that marked the 1970s and 1980s, developing key prototypes of innovative organizing in the 1990s.

Historical Background

"There is probably no city in America where such unfriendly sentiment obtains against organized labor as in this beautiful city of Los Angeles," a printing union official commented in 1912 (cited in Stimson 1955, 426). Indeed, for most of the twentieth century, L.A. had a reputation as a "company town," where the powers that be were intransigently antiunion. The classic comparison was to San Francisco, once the state's largest metropolis, where unions gained a foothold early on and where public sympathy for labor was widespread. L.A.'s labor history was quite different, as economist Ira Cross pointed out in 1935. There, "almost a century passed [after the city was founded in 1781] before unions appeared, and at no time have they played an important part in the industrial or political life of the community" (268).

Indeed, in the early 1900s, the city was a proud bastion of the open shop whose economic and political elite, led by notorious *Los Angeles Times* proprietor Harrison Gray Otis, was unabashedly hostile to unionism. Antilabor animus was not just Otis's personal idiosyncrasy, but rather was woven into the very fabric of L.A.'s political economy, as Carey McWilliams pointed out long ago:

> Otis and his colleagues were quick to realize that the only chance to establish Los Angeles as an industrial center was to undercut the high wage structure of San Francisco. . . . Having land to burn, the Southland dangled the bait of "cheap homes" before the eyes of the prospective homeseekers. "While wages are low," the argument went, "homes are cheap." . . . From 1890 to 1910, wages were from twenty to thirty and in some categories, even forty percent lower than in San Francisco. It was precisely this mar-

gin that enabled Los Angeles to grow as an industrial center. Thus the maintenance of a cheap labor pool became an indispensable cog in the curious economics of the region. For the system to work, however, the labor market had to remain unorganized; otherwise it would become impossible to exploit the homeseeker element. The system required—it absolutely demanded—a non-union open shop setup. It was this basic requirement, rather than the ferocity of General Otis, that really created the open shop movement in Los Angeles. (1973 [1946], 276–277)

Periodic forays into the city by unionists from northern California, who hoped to organize their southern brethren, accomplished little. "Los Angeles, in spite of its name, is a wicked city and sadly in need of someone who can point out the benefits of trade union organization and the iniquities of rampant capitalism," the San Francisco building trades publication *Organized Labor* lamented in July 1910 (cited in Kazin 1987, 202). The catastrophic bombing of the *Los Angeles Times* building later that year, which killed twenty people, served only to dramatize labor's weakness, particularly after two union men unexpectedly confessed to what Otis called "the crime of the century" (see Stimson 1955, ch. 21) Two decades later, despite periodic efforts to revitalize the local labor movement, the situation was virtually unchanged. As Cross summarized:

There have been continuing and costly attempts to unionize the workers in various occupations [in L.A.], but for the most part with no tangible results. Strikes, usually insignificant in extent, have been called only to be lost because of the overwhelming supply of laborers and the anti-union attitude of employers, the newspapers, and the community. (1935, 287–288)

Only in the late 1930s and 1940s, when industrial unionism swept across the nation, did organized labor finally penetrate the City of Angels' heavily guarded gates. By 1939, L.A. mayor Fletcher Bowron could state, "Even the most conservative manufacturers have come to realize that workers must organize, that bargaining cannot be with individuals, and that the effort to maintain the open shop is a lost cause" (cited in Perry and Perry 1963, 521). Among the first sectors where unionism gained a lasting foothold in L.A. was garment manufacturing, starting in 1933 with a dramatic strike that brought many Mexican American women into the International Ladies' Garment Workers' Union (ILGWU). Soon afterward, the ILGWU left the American Federation of Labor (AFL) for the newly established Congress of Industrial Organizations (CIO), which appeared on the scene in 1935 carrying the banner of union revitalization.

But the new industrial unionism was less central to the labor movement in L.A. than elsewhere in the country. The ILGWU did play a pioneering role in the 1930s, as did the International Longshoremen's Association (ILA), which launched the massive 1934 strike that established collective bargaining for waterfront workers in all the ports on the Pacific Coast. The ILA's West Coast locals soon left the AFL to form the CIO-affiliated International Longshoremen's and Warehousemen's Union. But these were small islands of progressive unionism in a vast sea where the open shop still dominated. The real breakthrough for the L.A. labor movement did not come until 1937, and it came not from the CIO but rather from old-fashioned business unionists in the International Brotherhood of Teamsters (IBT). The IBT deployed a bold secondary boycott strategy that leveraged union strength in northern California and Seattle to extract a collective bargaining agreement from L.A.-area trucking employers. This was an extremely successful effort, but it bore little resemblance to the massive worker mobilizations that were emerging elsewhere in the United States during the 1930s. Rather the Teamsters engaged primarily in top-down union organizing directed at employers, with minimal rank-and-file worker participation (Garnel 1972).

The Teamsters' 1937 victory paved the way to labor breakthroughs in other sectors, most notably construction, where unionism took a similar form and where in 1941 a Master Labor Agreement was signed covering the bulk of southern California's building industry. During World War II, with the rapid expansion of aircraft and other defense industries, unionization spread far more widely through the L.A. workforce, although the CIO continued to lag behind the AFL. Moreover, much of this wartime growth also took a top-down form, through "maintenance of membership" and other union security arrangements, rather than through bottom-up organizing. Labor's strength continued to grow in this fashion during the late 1940s and 1950s, as unions in the city consolidated their wartime gains.

Attempts to build unionism from the bottom up in L.A. were not entirely absent in the 1930s and 1940s, but rank-and-file labor organizing of this type produced meager results relative to those of top-down business unionism. For example, the ILGWU's organizing efforts during the depression years brought only about 3,000 new members into the L.A. labor movement by 1937, whereas the Teamster campaign that year yielded over 20,000—equal to the combined 1937 membership of some two dozen CIO unions then active in the city, according to one estimate (U.S. Senate 1940, 23613–23614). On the whole, organized labor in L.A. in this period was dominated by conservative forms of union organization, unlike many Eastern and Midwestern cities, where the new industrial unionism took center stage. As late as 1955, when the AFL and CIO merged, the historic pattern of AFL predominance in the local labor movement remained intact. At that time 77 percent of all union members in L.A. were in AFL-affiliated unions, with only 16 percent in the CIO (the balance were in independent unions). In the United States as a whole, the CIO's share of union membership was 29 percent, almost double the level in L.A., while the AFL accounted for 61 percent (California Department of Industrial Relations 1952–1989, 9).

The ethnic and racial composition of L.A.'s population in this period also contrasted sharply with that of such union strongholds as New York and Chicago. In those cities, the working class was dominated by first- and second-generation immigrants from southern and eastern Europe who formed the core constituency of the industrial union organizing drives of the 1930s. L.A.'s white (or "Anglo," as it is still colloquially known) working class was much more heavily native born, although the city already had a sizable population of Mexican Americans, African Americans, and Asian Americans (see Fogelson 1967). Insofar as these non-"Anglo" groups were employed in the industries that were newly unionized in the 1930s and 1940s, they entered the ranks of L.A. union members. As early as the 1930s, at least half of the city's unionized garment workers were Mexican American (Wuesthoff 1938, 109), and by 1950, half of all its unionized janitors were African American (Greer 1959, 172–175). But the vast majority of members in L.A.'s largest unions in this period, such as those in trucking and construction, were native-born whites.

After the war, L.A.'s unionization rate gradually approached that in the state as a whole. In 1951, 34 percent of nonagricultural wage and salary workers in L.A. were union members, compared to 41 percent statewide, and at the 1955 peak, the figure was 37 percent in L.A., just below the state level of 39 percent. While organized labor was still far stronger in San Francisco (51 percent unionized at the 1955 peak), the north–south gap was much smaller than in previous decades (California Department of Industrial Relations 1952–1989).

L.A.'s historic reputation as an anti-union town persisted well into the late twentieth century. But in fact, from the mid-1950s on, its unionization rate was similar to that in California as a whole, as Figure 5.1 shows, and close to the national average. As was the case throughout the United States, union density in L.A. gradually fell over the following decades, and by the time the state stopped collecting unionization data in 1987, it had dropped to only 19.6 percent, half the 1955 peak. This was actually slightly above the state figure of 19.1 percent for 1987, however, and the decline reflected national as much as local and regional developments. The collapse of basic industries like auto, steel, and later aerospace, along with the national employer anti-union offensive that began in the late 1970s, fueled the deunionization process in L.A., as elsewhere.

Unionization Patterns in Contemporary L.A.

In the 1990s, despite the revitalization of the local labor movement described here, the overall level of union density in L.A. continued to decline, as ongoing membership losses and rapid economic growth in the nonunion sector more than offset the gains from new organizing. As Figure 5.2 shows, in 1998 only 15.2 percent of L.A. workers were union members (in between the national average of 13.9 percent and the state average of 16.1 percent).[1] L.A. lagged slightly behind both the state and the nation in the private sector, where only 9.0 percent of workers were union members in 1998 (compared to 9.5 percent nationally and 9.8 percent in California), and more sharply in manufacturing, where only 7.7 percent of workers were union members, half the national figure. However, public sector workers were more highly unionized in L.A. than in the state or the United States, with well over half (54.8 percent) counted as union members in 1998 (Hirsch and Macpherson 1999). With nine out of every ten private sector workers entirely outside the ambit of organized labor, L.A. was once again a citadel of the open shop—although there was nothing distinctive about this by the end of the century.

The few unionized enclaves that remained were mostly relics of an earlier era. Figures 5.3, 5.4, and 5.5 highlight some of the basic characteristics of L.A.'s union members in the 1990s, using merged data from the U.S. Current Population Survey (CPS) for 1994–1997.[2] As Figure 5.3 shows, unionization is distributed extremely *unevenly* through the city's economy. For example, only 10 percent of L.A.'s workers are

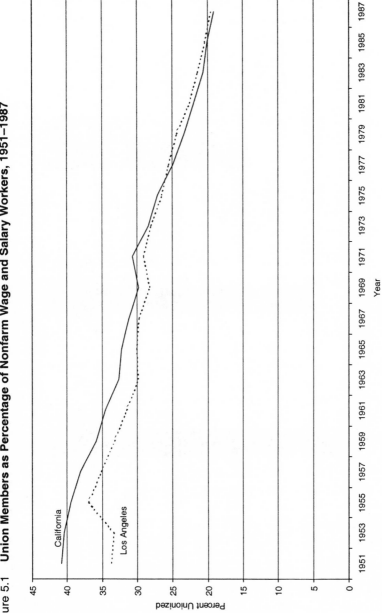

Figure 5.1 Union Members as Percentage of Nonfarm Wage and Salary Workers, 1951–1987

Source: California Department of Industrial Relations (1952–1989).

Figure 5.2 **Union Density by Sector, L.A., California, and the United States, 1998**

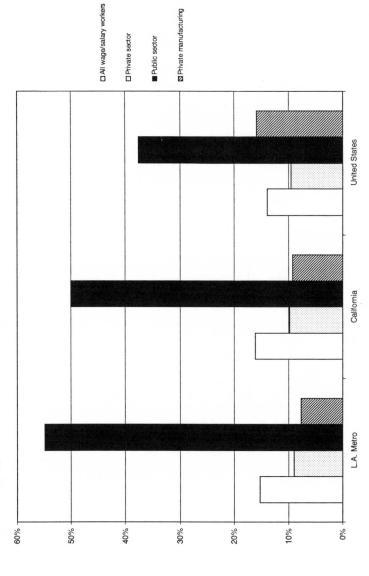

Source: Hirsch and Macpherson (1999).

111

Figure 5.3 **Employed Workers and Union Members in Greater L.A., 1994–1997, by Industry**

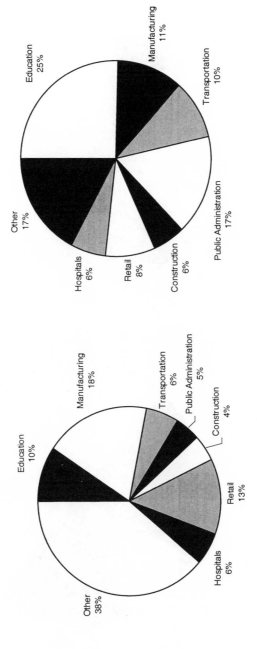

Employed Workers

Union Members

Figure 5.4   Employed Workers and Union Members in Greater L.A., 1994–1997, by Nativity and Ethnicity

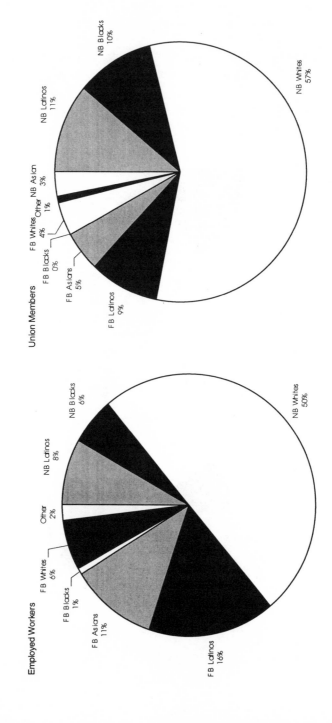

NB = Native born; FB = Foreign born.

Figure 5.5　Employed Workers and Union Members in Greater L.A., 1994–1997, by Sector, Nativity, and Ethnicity

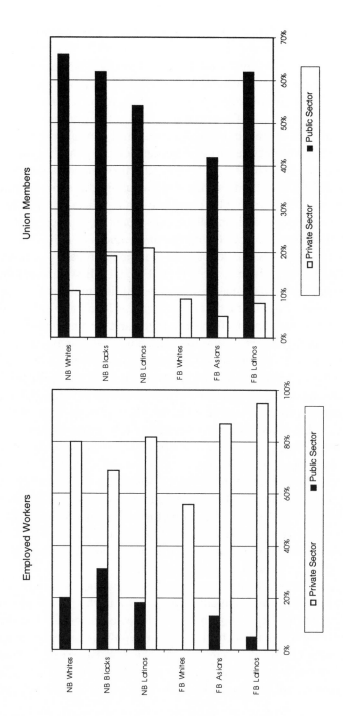

NB = Native born; FB = Foreign born.

employed in education, but 25 percent of all union members work in that sector. By contrast, 18 percent of all workers, but only 11 percent of union members, are employed in manufacturing. This unevenness is an artifact of the highly peculiar U.S. industrial relations system, which since 1935 has been based not on individual decisions about union affiliation, but instead on the requirement that entire workplaces be unionized through the arduous and increasingly employer-dominated winner-take-all electoral process administered by the National Labor Relations Board (NLRB). Thus the pattern of unionization shown in Figure 5.3 reflects the fact that some industries, at some point in the past, have been successfully organized while others never have (or if they have, they were deunionized subsequently). And crucially, these data tell us nothing about the current preferences of individuals, much less the preferences of categories of workers, in regard to union membership. In short, given the structure of the NLRB system and the erosion resulting from the past few decades of de-unionization, the main determinant of whether a given individual is a union member today is where he or she happens to be employed and whether that workplace became (and remained) unionized at some previous point in time—regardless of his or her pro- or anti-union sympathies.

The data on unionization levels among immigrants and native-born workers and among various ethnic groups, shown in Figure 5.4, must be interpreted with these caveats in mind. There is no question that immigrants are less likely than the native born to be union members in contemporary L.A.: although native-born whites comprise only about half of all employees in the area, they account for 57 percent of its union members. In contrast, foreign-born Latinos are 16 percent of all employees in L.A. but only 9 percent of union members; similarly, foreign-born Asians are 11 percent of all employees but only 5 percent of union members. (On the other hand, L.A.'s African Americans are overrpresented in union ranks: 10 percent are union members, although they are only 6 percent of L.A employees.)

Figure 5.5, which shows unionization rates and employment distribution by nativity and ethnicity separately for the highly unionized public sector and the largely nonunion private sector, suggests the underlying dynamics. The public sector is far more highly unionized than the private sector not because public sector workers have a more favorable attitude toward unions (though they may), but because there is far less resistance to unionization when the employer is the federal, state, or local government than when it is a private sector corporation. Indeed, as Figure 5.5 reveals, *regardless of race, ethnicity, or immigration status*, public sector workers are far more extensively unionized than their private sector counterparts. Indeed, the unionization rate for foreign-born Latinos employed in the public sector in L.A. is 62 percent—the same as for native-born blacks and only slightly below the 66 percent rate for native-born whites! However, only 5 percent of the area's foreign-born Latinos work in the public sector (compared to 31 percent of native-born blacks and 20 percent of native-born whites), which all by itself goes a long way toward explaining the relatively low immigrant unionization rate.

That rate is also affected by the fact that recently arrived immigrants are less likely to be union members than those who have been in the United States longer. Among L.A.'s foreign-born Latinos, only 7 percent of those who arrived in the country after 1980 were unionized in 1994–1997, compared to 16 percent of those who arrived before 1980. The latter figure is only slightly below the overall unionization rate of 19 percent for this sample.[3] This reflects the distinctive employment patterns of newcomers, who are far less likely to obtain jobs in unionized workplaces than their more settled compatriots. Newcomers are virtually excluded from public sector employment and generally relegated to the bottom of the labor market, where unions are, almost by definition, unlikely to exist.

The Myth of Immigrant Unorganizability

If, for historical reasons, immigrant workers are less likely to be unionized in contemporary L.A. than their native-born counterparts, what are the prospects for organizing them today and in the future? The conventional wisdom, widely accepted until very recently, is that immigrants are vulnerable, docile persons who are intensely fearful of any confrontation with authority, who accept substandard wages and poor working conditions because their standard of comparison is drawn from their home countries, and who therefore are extremely unlikely to actively seek unionization. For the undocumented, the assumption that immigrants lack real potential as union recruits is especially widespread. As Hector Delgado reported in his case study of a successful union organizing drive among undocumented Latino immigrants that took place at an L.A. factory in the 1980s, "The unorganizability of undocumented workers because of their legal status has become a 'pseudofact'" (1993, 10, citing Merton).

Because of their vulnerability to deportation, one might indeed expect undocumented workers to be fearful about the risks involved in union organizing, particularly when confrontations with state authority are likely. Yet Delgado found that this was far less of a problem than is generally presumed. In the case he studied,

> Undocumented workers' fear of the "migra" did not make them more difficult to organize than native workers or immigrant workers with papers employed in the same industries. Workers reported giving little thought to their citizenship status and the possibility of an INS raid of the plant. . . . A forklift driver at Camagua [pseudonym for the company] claimed that he had never been afraid of the INS, adding, "I've never seen them here. Only in Tijuana." . . . [Another worker] said that he had a better chance of "getting hit by a car"—and he didn't worry about either. . . . In response to the prospect of deportation, Camagua's workers responded that if deported they would have simply returned (in some cases, "after a short vacation"). Julia Real [pseudonym], a sewer, commented, "They're not going to kill you! The worse [sic] thing they [the INS] can do is send me home, and I'll come back." (1993, 61, 63)

Recent efforts to tighten restrictions on immigration and renewed initiatives to deport the undocumented may have altered the climate in the years since Delgado did his fieldwork. Yet the findings of his pioneering study are confirmed by developments in the 1990s, when Latino immigrants, many of them undocumented, emerged as the central protagonists of the new unionism in L.A. and elsewhere. Indeed, among the dozens of union organizers Kent Wong and I interviewed in the course of our fieldwork over the past several years, not one endorsed the once conventional wisdom that immigrants were more difficult to recruit than natives (see the examples in Milkman and Wong 2000b).

On the contrary, despite the large numbers of undocumented immigrants among foreign-born workers, there is survey evidence, albeit fragmentary, suggesting that foreign-born workers'—especially Latinos'—attitudes are actually more favorable toward unions than are those of native-born workers (DeFreitas 1993). "It's not true that immigrants are hard to organize," a northern California hotel union organizer told a researcher. "They are more supportive of unions than native workers" (cited in Wells 2000, 120). One reason for this may be that many recent immigrants—especially those from Central America—have some positive experiences of unionism in their home countries. Although there is no systematic evidence on this point, it is striking that many of the new rank-and-file immigrant union leaders have a history of union activism and/or left-wing political ties in their native lands (Acuña 1996, ch. 8, cites several examples). And although many immigrant workers are from rural backgrounds, a substantial number arrive in the United States far better acquainted with the idioms of unionism and class politics than their native-born counterparts. Among the workers involved in the L.A. Justice for Janitors (JfJ) campaign in 1990, for example, organizers reported "a high level of class consciousness," as well as a willingness to take the risks involved in organizing, that was shaped by experiences back home. "There, if you were for a union, they killed you," one organizer noted in discussing the role of Salvadorans in this effort. "Here, you lose a job for $4.25 an hour" (cited in Milkman and Wong 2000b, 24).

The fact that immigrant workers rely so heavily on ethnic social networks for such basic survival needs as housing, jobs, and various other forms of social and financial assistance may also make them easier to recruit into the labor movement than native-born workers. Southern California is famous for its highly atomized social arrangements and weak sense of community, but that reputation is based entirely on the "Anglo" experience. In contrast, L.A.'s working-class immigrants have vibrant ethnic networks and communities rooted in extended kinship ties, as well as the shared experience of migration from particular communities in their countries of origin. The intricate web of social connections among immigrants can be a key resource in building labor solidarity, particularly if unions can identify and recruit key actors in kin and community networks.

Yet another factor that may enhance the appeal of unionism is the shared ordeal of immigration itself and the persistently high level of stigmatization foreign-born workers are forced to endure in their adopted home. The sense of being under siege in a hostile environment, rather than generating passivity and fear as the conventional wisdom assumes, may actually foster solidarity. In this context, if labor unions extend a helping hand to immigrant workers, offering economic and political resources that can be utilized to ameliorate the conditions of daily life, they may be received far more enthusiastically than by native-born workers, who do not feel so entirely excluded from access to other opportunities for improving their economic situation.

For all these reasons, immigrant workers have proven ready recruits
to labor unionism in recent years, and the once ubiquitous assumption
that they are unorganizable seems to be dying. Indeed, the *New York
Times*, the nation's newspaper of record, attributed the success of a 1999
strike at a Washington state meatpacking plant, where 90 percent of the
workers were foreign born, to "the receptivity that many immigrants
feel toward union activity and their growing confidence that . . . the
potential benefits of pressing for better wages and working conditions
outweigh any risks" (Verhovek 1999, A8). Similarly, the *Times'* account
of the historic 1999 union victory at the Fieldcrest Cannon textile plant
in Kannapolis, North Carolina—where over the past quarter century several previous efforts to unionize that plant had failed—presented the
success as due in part to "growing numbers of immigrants in the work
force who tend to be more likely to support unionization" (Firestone
1999, A1). And many unionists today endorse the view that workplaces
with large concentrations of immigrants—especially Latinos—are among
the most promising organizing targets. An L.A. janitors' union activist
put it forcefully: "We Latino workers are a bomb waiting to explode!"
(cited in Waldinger et al. 1998, 117).

Immigrant Organizing and the New Labor Movement in L.A.

Latino immigrants are the economic lifeblood of the sprawling metropolis that is contemporary L.A. Fully a third of the labor force is
foreign born (compared to about 10 percent nationally), and the proportion is far higher in blue-collar industrial and service jobs. (see
Lopez and Feliciano 2000). The new arrivals who poured into southern California over the past few decades, mostly from Mexico and
Central America, have been rapidly incorporated into the increasingly
deregulated and de-unionized regional economy. Latino immigrants
are the core of contemporary L.A.'s burgeoning low-wage, nonunion
workforce, much like the native-born migrant "homeseekers" that
Carey McWilliams (1973 [1946]) described for an earlier era. Employers, although often skeptical initially, quickly became enamored
of the new immigrants' apparent willingness to work hard, at long
hours, for minimal (sometimes subminimal) pay. In contrast, L.A.'s
organized labor movement, which suffered steep membership declines
in the 1970s and 1980s, initially was hostile toward the newcomers,

who were arriving in vast numbers during precisely those years, fearing that they would undercut hard-won wages and labor standards.

As the numbers of immigrants grew, however, and as they became the bulk of the workforce in industry after industry, union leaders slowly began to change their views. Necessity being the mother of invention, over the years L.A. became a national laboratory for a series of experiments in immigrant unionization. The ILGWU was the first to explore this terrain, beginning in the late 1970s, and although its efforts yielded few lasting results in terms of union membership, the union served as a crucial training ground for the new generation of local Latino labor leaders, who would go on to lead a rich variety of immigrant organizing efforts in later years (Milkman and Wong 2000b, 3).

The real breakthrough in organizing L.A.'s foreign-born workers on a significant scale, however, came more than a decade later, with the 1990 strike victory of the JfJ campaign. This was a successful effort by the Service Employees International Union (SEIU) to recapture its old base in building services, in this case janitors cleaning large office buildings. During the late 1970s the SEIU had about 5,000 of L.A.'s private sector janitors among its members, but by the mid-1980s the figure had fallen to only 1,800, even as the number of janitors in the city had grown. As wages and conditions deteriorated with de-unionization, native-born workers left janitorial work in droves and were quickly replaced by recently arrived Latino immigrants. These were the workers the SEIU successfully recruited in the late 1980s, culminating in the 1990 strike. As a result of JfJ's triumph, by 1990 the SEIU had more than recouped its janitorial membership in the city, which now stood at 8,000.

This was the largest private sector immigrant-organizing victory since the United Farm Workers' successes in the 1970s. It has since become the gold standard for immigrant organizing, not only in L.A. but nationally. (It is even the focus of a feature film by British director Ken Loach, *Bread and Roses*, which premiered in L.A. to an audience of janitors on the tenth anniversary of the 1990 strike victory.) It dramatically demonstrated not only the potential for galvanizing immigrant workers into a militant, solidaristic force for labor movement revitalization, but also the critical role of union leadership in that process. The JfJ campaign combined grass-roots rank-and-file mobilization, on the one hand, with careful strategic planning on the part of experienced union leaders with access to extensive financial resources as well as expertise, on the other. It would not have succeeded without both elements (Milkman and Wong 2001).

The L.A. campaign was part of a national JfJ organizing drive spear-headed by then SEIU president John Sweeney (who became president of the AFL–CIO as part of the "New Voice" leadership slate in 1995), but L.A.'s effort proved to be the most successful anywhere in the United States. The organizers deliberately avoided the traditional NLRB elec-toral system in favor of an innovative approach that combined careful research into the power structure of the industry, strategic planning, and militant, media-savvy rank-and-file mobilization tactics (see Waldinger et al. 1998 and Savage 1998 for details).

The JfJ effort showed not only that immigrants could organize suc-cessfully on a large scale, but also, and equally important, that their initial organizing successes could be sustained. Indeed, despite difficult internal conflicts in the local union in the aftermath of the initial break-through, the L.A. janitors went on over the course of the 1990s to con-solidate their success, holding the line against the ever-restless building owners and office cleaning companies, winning a series of contract im-provements, and keeping union members active, informed, and involved in the internal life of the union (Fisk et al. 2000).

In April 2000 the L.A. janitors launched another spectacularly suc-cessful strike to improve their wages and to narrow geographical pay differentials. As it had done ten years earlier, the SEIU not only mobi-lized rank-and-file janitors on a huge, highly visible scale, but also used the occasion to skillfully expose and critique the social inequality and ethnic polarization that are so deeply embedded in contemporary L.A. In the context of a period of unprecedented prosperity for the city as a whole, the union's demands for improved pay and conditions for low-wage Latino immigrant workers whose daily labor involved cleaning up after mostly native-born "Anglo" lawyers and other professionals in the city's glitzy office towers immediately captured the moral high ground, and the strike won unprecedented public support (see Meyerson 2000).

Later the same year there was a wave of strikes in L.A., involving bus drivers, SEIU-represented public sector workers, and actors (see Cleeland 2000). Although they succeeded to varying degrees, none of them en-joyed the kind of public support that the janitors were able to galvanize. There were a number of reasons for this. The unions involved did not engage in the detailed strategic planning for a strike that the janitors had undertaken for nearly a year prior to their strike. Nor were the workers involved, especially the actors and bus drivers, in the same desperately low-wage category as the janitors. And whereas the services the janitors provided benefited mostly the privileged classes, the opposite was true of bus drivers and public workers, on whom the poor depended for basic survival-level services in hospitals, welfare offices, and similar public settings (see Riccardi 2000). Thus the unions did not have the moral high ground nor the imagination that had served the janitors so well, ingredients that can be extremely important in labor struggles, as Steven Lopez (2000) has pointed out in another context.

The janitors' success remains unmatched in its scale and visibility, but it is part of a larger set of pathbreaking unionization efforts that emerged in the 1990s among L.A.'s vast immigrant workforce. Two years after the janitors' 1990 breakthrough, a five-month strike by thousands of Mexican immigrant drywall hangers (workers who install the sheetrock panels that make up the interior walls of modern buildings) halted residential construction throughout southern California (see Milkman and Wong 2000a). This yielded a union contract that doubled drywallers' wages in the region and brought 2,400 previously nonunion Mexican immigrant workers into the carpenters' union. One important element in the campaign was the legal assistance coordinated by the California Immigrant Workers' Association (CIWA), an AFL–CIO sponsored organization founded in 1989 (but abandoned not long after this strike) that was staffed by a group of talented labor and immigration activists and attorneys. Although the aftermath of the drywallers' campaign was far more problematic than in the case of the janitors, with the carpenters' union failing to sustain the market share it had won at the time of the strike settlement and also leaving the internal structure of the union untransformed, this example too shows the potential for organizing success among Latino immigrants when rank-and-file militancy and experienced union leadership are coordinated (Milkman and Wong 2001).

And there are others. The L.A. local of the Hotel Employees and Restaurant Employees (HERE) union, although it has yet to achieve an organizing victory comparable in size to those of the janitors and drywallers, has been highly effective in smaller-scale recruitment among immigrants. It is now headed by Maria Elena Durazo, who rose to power in 1989 after a challenge to an old-line union bureaucracy that, among other things, had refused to translate the union contract or union meetings into Spanish. Under Durazo's leadership, L.A.'s HERE local has become a leader in "internal organizing"—that is, activating its existing membership to both strengthen the union where it is already entrenched and to organize new workplaces (see Milkman and Wong 2000b, 11–22).

Even in manufacturing, often seen as a hopeless sector in which to organize given its vulnerability to capital mobility, there have been some successful unionization efforts among L.A.'s immigrant workers. The largest involved 1,200 Latino wheel workers who launched a wildcat strike at the L.A. American Racing Equipment factory in July 1990, leading to a union victory in a representation election held later that year and in 1991 to a union contract. This was a rank-and-file-initiated campaign, and the resulting local union, the International Association of Machinists Local 1910 (named for the year the Mexican Revolution began), remains vibrant and highly independent and has won significant contract improvements over the years since the strike (see Zabin 2000).

All these initiatives notwithstanding, the story here is still one of *potential* rather than actual transformation. Even the 90,000 new union members (most of them low-wage immigrants) recruited in 1999 are a drop in the bucket, hardly likely to turn the tide of union decline.[4] After all, L.A. is the nation's second largest metropolis, with a labor force of over 6 million, a third of them foreign born, and in the private sector over 90 percent of workers remain outside the union fold, as we saw above. And while a few unions, most important the SEIU and HERE, have developed tremendous dynamism, the rest remain staid fortresses of labor bureaucracy and do hardly any organizing at all. Still, the recent experiments that have occurred in L.A. have assumed importance beyond that suggested by the numbers of workers and unions involved, for at least two reasons.

The first reason involves timing. The janitors, drywallers, and American Racing Equipment successes all antedate—but by only a few years— the 1995 coup in the AFL–CIO that brought former SEIU president John Sweeney, who had overseen the JfJ campaign, to the helm of the federation. Sweeney and his "New Voice" leadership slate came to power with a commitment to making organizing central to the labor movement once again, as the SEIU itself had done under his leadership in the years immediately preceding. The displays of militancy in L.A. during the period just before Sweeney's ascent and his intimate familiarity with the case of the JfJ campaign there in particular therefore have generated considerable attention at the highest levels of the U.S labor movement (Cleeland 1999). Even the Los Angeles Manufacturing Action Project, an effort to develop industrywide organizing strategies for L.A.'s vast manufacturing sector, although it was never fully funded and was abandoned entirely in 1997 (only three years after its official establishment), continues to be an important reference point in discussions among the hopeful architects of new labor (Delgado 2000). While historically L.A., with its notorious reputation as a company town, was barely on the radar screen for the national labor movement, in recent years it has captured the imagination of the many progressive unionists who ally themselves with labor's revitalization efforts in the Sweeney era.

The second reason the immigrant unionization breakthroughs of the 1990s are of greater significance than their modest scale would otherwise warrant is that they have so radically transformed L.A.'s political scene, in which labor is now a formidable presence. The L.A. County Federation of Labor (or County Fed)—headed since 1996 by Miguel Contreras, a former farmworkers' organizer widely respected in the Latino community—has become a key power broker thanks to its repeated mobilization of newly enfranchised Latino immigrant voters. The County Fed has been extraordinarily successful in translating its affiliates' past organizing successes into political power, and in a virtuous circle, so that political leverage in turn has become a resource helping to foster further organizing.

Ironically, California's passage in 1994 of Proposition 187, which involved a variety of restrictions on immigrant rights, led to a surge in naturalization among the eligible foreign-born population, producing thousands and thousands of new citizens with the right to vote. The Latino proportion of all California voters doubled over the four years that followed Proposition 187, reaching 12 percent in 1998 (Pyle et al. 1998). And because the proposition had been sponsored by Republican governor Pete Wilson, the new voters tended to gravitate toward the Democrats. These developments, combined with the long-standing political apathy on the part of L.A.'s native-born citizenry, created an opportunity for Latinos to become a significant electoral force, and the County Fed has nearly singlehandedly turned that opportunity into a palpable reality. As veteran L.A. political journalist Harold Meyerson recently noted,

> Since Contreras assumed its leadership in 1996, the federation has intervened in 17 district races—all hotly contested, at all levels of government—and has prevailed in 16 of them. . . . [There is] a new order in the

political firmament of Latino California. The janitors, in tandem with the hotel workers, have supplanted the United Farm Workers as the political powerhouse and moral beacon of local Latino politics. (2000, 26)

In 1996, five of the six County Fed–backed Democratic candidates for the state legislature won their races, helped by $160,000 in union campaign contributions (Rodriguez 1998). The following year the County Fed orchestrated a whole series of political victories: in a head-on confrontation with Republican mayor Richard Riordan, labor candidates won a majority of seats on the elected city charter reform commission; the City Council passed a union-backed "living wage" law; and former SEIU official Gil Cedillo was elected to a state assembly seat. The most impressive Latino labor electoral showing of all came in June 1998, when labor—again led by the L.A. County Fed—mobilized successfully to defeat Proposition 226, a ballot measure designed to curtail the use of union dues for political purposes. The measure was defeated by a narrow 53–47 margin and might well have passed if not for the fact that 75 percent of Latinos voted against it, according to exit polls (Pyle et al. 1998).

L.A. labor has parlayed its political clout, in turn, into leverage in ongoing worker organizing efforts. The April 2000 janitors' strike once again provides the shining example. The SEIU launched the strike with official endorsements from forty-eight local elected officials and by the end had won support from politicians across the board—including members of both houses of the state legislature, the entire City Council (some members of which were arrested for civil disobedience in support of the strike), and even Mayor Riordan. The strike became a litmus test of loyalty to the formidable County Fed for L.A.'s politicians, and above all for aspiring Latino politicians, for whom "to have been missing in action, or deemed insufficiently pro-janitors, would have amounted to political suicide" (Meyerson 2000, 29).

Labor's accumulating political influence has also been translated into organizing breakthroughs in other arenas in the past few years. For example, in a political quid pro quo, Riordan recently appointed Contreras to the Airport Commission, a useful point of leverage in the ongoing "Respect at LAX" campaign that has made considerable headway in its efforts to win union recognition for baggage handlers and other airport service workers. Another example is the City Council's worker-retention ordinance, which protects workers' jobs when a new contractor takes over work directly under contract to the city and which was extended in 1999 to cover recipients of economic development grants as well (Meyerson 1999). Thus by the late 1990s organized labor had not only become "the 800–pound gorilla in local politics," as the *Los Angeles Times* reported (Schuster 1998, A1, A22), but also had managed to create effective links between its newfound political power and the continuing uphill struggle to build its organizing capacity—the most critical task in labor revitalization.

Conclusion

As the L.A. examples illustrate, immigrant workers, undocumented or not, are highly receptive to organizing efforts. The major impediment is not a lack of interest in unions on their part, but rather the still relatively limited efforts to tap that interest on the part of the labor movement— itself reinforced by the intensely antilabor environment that makes organizing workers of any type extremely difficult in the contemporary United States. But since 1995, the new AFL–CIO leadership has signaled a strong commitment to recruiting new members and has poured unprecedented resources into the effort. Such leadership support from the top is an absolutely critical ingredient in the innovative unionism that emerged in the 1990s (Voss and Sherman 2000). And the AFL– CIO's historic announcement in February 2000 of a new immigrant worker policy initiative, calling for blanket amnesty for undocumented immigrants and an end to sanctions against employers who hire them, is a bold step that should help foster new organizing among immigrants in particular (Greenhouse 2000).

Yet what has been achieved so far remains fragile, and the obstacles to further progress are formidable. The AFL–CIO's affiliated unions vary widely in the extent to which they are willing to embrace the national leadership's new initiatives, and while it can reward compliance, the Sweeney administration cannot force it on the many affiliates that remain captives of the old guard. For all the sterling examples of new immigrant organizing strategies offered by unions like the SEIU and HERE, there are at least as many cases of campaigns that failed due to union ineptitude, a lack of strategic leadership, or unrelenting employer opposition (see Milkman and Wong 2001). Moreover, many unions still are not seriously undertaking new organizing at all. Even those that are successfully recruiting immigrant workers often fail to move on to the next step—namely, transforming their internal organizational and leadership structure in such a way as to fully incorporate immigrant workers and their specific concerns. This is a critical task if immigrant unionism is to have any lasting significance—and is often as difficult as new organizing itself.

If the labor movement is to survive into the new century, however, it has little choice but to take on these tasks. To be sure, the odds are very heavily stacked against unions in confrontations with employers in this historical period. If JfJ and some of the other examples mentioned here show that winning is possible—even in such an unlikely venue as L.A., once a redoubt of vicious anti-unionism—no one can argue that it is easy. Ironically, however, the surge of low-wage Latino immigration that was generally presumed to be a threat to organized labor until quite recently may be one of the few trump cards that could help New Labor beat the odds.

Notes

1. Note that the 1998 figures in this paragraph are taken from a different data series (part of the U.S. Current Population Survey [CPS]) and are not strictly comparable to the 1951–1987 data cited above. (In 1988, 16.4 percent of L.A. workers were union members in the CPS data series, whereas the California state data found a 19.6 percent unionization rate for 1987.) Like the 1951–1987 data, however, the figures cited here include only union members and not workers covered by union contracts who are nonmembers. Obviously these 1998 data do not include the 90,000 new union members recruited by L.A. area unions in 1999. For details about the 1998 data, see Hirsch and Macpherson (1999).

2. Thanks to Roger Waldinger for providing access to this special merged data set. Because the local sample sizes for each year in the CPS are very small, the merged four-year set is especially valuable. Even here, however, the numbers of observations are quite small, so these data should be interpreted with caution. In the merged data set, N = 1,194 for the five-county L.A. workforce (including L.A., Orange, San Bernardino, Riverside, and Ventura Counties), and for union members in the five counties, N = 232. For further discussion and analysis of these data set see Waldinger and Der-Martirosian (2000).

3. This figure is higher than those cited earlier because the sample includes not only union members, but also workers who are covered by union contracts under agency shop and other such arrangements, even though they are not union members. The data cited above from Hirsch and Macpherson (1999) are for union members only, as mentioned in note 1 above.

4. Moreover, 74,000 of the 90,000 new members recruited in 1999 were public sector home health care workers who became SEIU members after an eleven-year campaign that mainly involved lobbying and other political efforts to make unionization legally feasible (see Greenhouse 1999; Cobb 1999).

References

Acuña, Rodolfo F. 1996. *Anything but Mexican: Chicanos in Contemporary Los Angeles*. New York: Verso.

California Department of Industrial Relations, Division of Labor Statistics and Research. 1952–1989. *Union Labor in California*. San Francisco.

Cleeland, Nancy. 1999. "L.A. Area Now a Model for Labor Revival." *Los Angeles Times*, September 6, pp. A1, A20, A21.

———. 2000. "In L.A., Striking Similarities on Picket Lines." *Los Angeles Times*, October 29, pp. A1, A20.

Cobb, Rachael. 1999. "Background Memo: Unionizing the Home Care Workers of Los Angeles County." Unpublished mimeo, Massachusetts Institute of Technology.

Cross, Ira. 1935. *A History of the Labor Movement in California*. Berkeley: University of California Press.

Davis, Mike. 2000. *Magical Urbanism: Latinos Reinvent the U.S. Big City*. New York: Verso.

DeFreitas, Gregory. 1993. "Unionization Among Racial and Ethnic Minorities." *Industrial and Labor Relations Review* 46: 284–301.

Delgado, Hector. 1993. *New Immigrants, Old Unions: Organizing Undocumented Workers in Los Angeles*. Philadelphia: Temple University Press.

———. 2000. "The Los Angeles Manufacturing Action Project: An Opportunity Squandered?" In Milkman, ed., pp. 225–238.

Firestone, David. 1999. "Victory for Union at Plant in South Is Labor Milestone." *New York Times* (national edition), June 25.

Fisk, Catherine L., Daniel J.B. Mitchell, and Christopher L. Erickson. 2000. "Union Representation of Immigrant Janitors in Southern California: Economic and Legal Challenges." In Milkman, ed., pp. 199–224.

Fogelson, Robert M. 1967. *The Fragmented Metropolis: Los Angeles, 1850–1930*. Cambridge, MA: Harvard University Press.

Garnel, Donald. 1972. *The Rise of Teamster Power in the West*. Berkeley: University of California Press.

Greenhouse, Steven. 1999. "In Biggest Drive since 1937, Union Gains a Victory." *New York Times* (national edition) February 26, p. A1.

———. 2000. "Labor, in Switch, Urges Amnesty for All Illegal Immigrants." *New York Times* (national edition), February 17, p. A23.

Greer, Scott. 1959. *Last Man In: Racial Access to Union Power*. Glencoe, IL: Free Press.

Hirsch, Barry T., and David A. Macpherson. 1999. *Union Membership and Earnings Data Book: Compilations form the Current Population Survey*. Washington, DC: Bureau of National Affairs.

Kazin, Michael. 1987. *Barons of Labor: The San Francisco Building Trades and Union Power in the Progressive Era*. Urbana: University of Illinois Press.

Lopez, David, and Cynthia Feliciano. 2000. "Who Does What? California's Emerging Plural Labor Force." In Milkman, ed., pp. 25–48. Ithaca: Cornell University Press.

Lopez, Steven H. 2000. "Contesting the Global City: Pittsburgh's Public Service Unions Confront a Neoliberal Agenda." In *Global Ethnography: Forces, Connections, and Imaginations in a Postmodern World*, ed. Michael Burawoy, Joseph

A. Blum, Sheba George, Zsuzsa Gille, Teresa Gowan, Lynne Haney, Maren Klawiter, Steven H. Lopez, Sean O'Riain, and Millie Thayer, pp. 268–298. Berkeley: University of California Press.

McWilliams, Carey. 1973 (1946). *Southern California: An Island on the Land*. Salt Lake City, Utah: Gibbs M. Smith.

Merton, Robert. K. 1959. "Notes on Problem-Finding in Sociology." In *Sociology Today: Problems and Prospects*, ed. Robert K. Merton, Leonard Broom, and Leonard S. Cottrell, Jr., pp. ix–xxxiv. New York: Basic Books.

Meyerson, Harold. 1999. "The New Unionism Finds a Home." *L.A. Weekly*, (October 8–14).

———. 2000. "A Clean Sweep." *American Prospect* 11, 15 (June 19–July 3).

Milkman, Ruth, and Kent Wong. 2000a. "Organizing the Wicked City: The 1992 Southern California Drywall Strike." In Milkman, ed., pp. 169–198.

———. 2000b. *Voices from the Front Lines: Organizing Immigrant Workers in Los Angeles*. Los Angeles: UCLA Center for Labor Research and Education.

———. 2001. "Organizing Immigrant Workers: Case Studies from Southern California." In *Strategies for Renewal: Transforming the Labor Movement in the 1990s and Beyond*, ed. Lowell Turner, Harry C. Katz, and Richard Hurd. Ithaca, NY: Cornell University Press.

Milkman, Ruth, ed. 2000. *Organizing Immigrants: The Challenge for Unions in Contemporary California*. Ithaca, NY: Cornell University Press.

Perry, Louis B., and Richard S. Perry. 1963. *A History of the Los Angeles Labor Movement, 1911–1941*. Berkeley: University of California Press.

Pyle, Amy, Patrick J. McDonnell, and Hector Tobar. 1998. "Latino Voter Participation Doubled Since '94 Primary." *Los Angeles Times*, June 4, pp. A1, A28.

Riccardi, Nicholas. 2000. "When Strike Can't Hurt Decision Makers." *Los Angeles Times*, October 13, p. B2.

Rodriguez, Gregory. 1998. "Labor Pains: After Decades of Bowing to Big Business, L.A.'s Unions Are Grabbing Votes—and Power." *Los Angeles Times*, November, p. 34.

Savage, Lydia. 1998. "Geographies of Organizing: Justice for Janitors in Los Angeles." In *Organizing the Landscape: Geographical Perspectives on Labor Unionism*, ed. Andrew Herod, pp. 225–252. Minneapolis: University of Minnesota Press.

Schuster, Beth. 1998. "Latinos May Give Labor Key to City Hall Control." *Los Angeles Times*, December 29.

Stimson, Grace Heilman. 1955. *Rise of the Labor Movement in Los Angeles*. Berkeley: University of California Press.

U.S. Senate. Hearings before a subcommittee of the Committee on Education and Labor. 1940. *Violations of Free Speech and Rights of Labor*. 76th Congress, Third Session, Part 64, "Supplementary Exhibits."

Verhovek, Sam Howe. 1999. "The New Language of American Labor." *New York Times* (national edition), June 26.

Voss, Kim, and Rachel Sherman. 2000. "Breaking the Iron Law of Oligarchy: Union Revitalization in the American Labor Movement." *American Journal of Sociology* 106 (September): 303–349.

Waldinger, Roger, and Claudia Der-Martirosian. 2000. "Immigrant Workers and American Labor: Challenge . . . Or Disaster?" In Milkman, ed., pp. 49–80.

Waldinger, Roger, Chris Erickson, Ruth Milkman, Daniel J.B. Mitchell, Abel

Valenzuela, Kent Wong, and Maurice Zeitlin. 1998. "Helots No More: A Case Study of the Justice for Janitors Campaign in Los Angeles." In *Organizing to Win: New Research on Union Strategies*, ed. Kate Bronfenbrenner, Sheldon Friedman, Richard W. Hurd, Rudolph A. Oswald, and Ronald L. Seeber, pp. 102–119. Ithaca, NY: Cornell University Press.

Wells, Miriam J. 2000. "Immigration and Unionization in the San Francisco Hotel Industry." In Milkman, ed., pp. 109–129.

Wuesthoff, Marie Louise. 1938. An Inquiry into the Activities of the International Ladies' Garment Workers' Union in Los Angeles. Unpublished M.A. thesis, Department of Economics, University of Southern California.

Zabin, Carol. 2000. "Organizing Latino Workers in the Los Angeles Manufacturing Sector: The Case of American Racing Equipment." In Milkman, ed., pp. 150–168.

6

UNIONS AND IMMIGRANTS IN SOUTH FLORIDA

A COMPARISON

BRUCE NISSEN AND GUILLERMO GRENIER

As the U.S. economy has increasingly become "globalized," both the U.S. labor movement and labor-oriented academics have paid greater attention to trade policy, international labor rights, and even cross-border solidarity issues (Brecher and Costello 1994; Frundt 1998; Nissen 1999). The main stimuli for the new attitudes have been growing import penetration in highly unionized industries (garment, auto, steel, etc.) and the export of jobs abroad as companies closed U.S. plants and reopened in foreign countries, often at much lower wages (Browne and Sims 1993).

Immigration has not received similar attention, but it too is a part of the same process. In complex ways, the new immigration is intimately tied to the worldwide opening of trade and investment borders in recent decades. Globalization of capital is leading to a smaller but still significant globalization of the workforce in the form of immigrants to the United States, largely from Asia and Latin America (Stalker 2000). While there is no simple one-to-one relationship between mobility of capital and mobility of workers, the globalization of capital through direct foreign investment has set up a complex constellation of relationships that turn immigration into a labor-supply mechanism in advanced industrial (or postindustrial) nations like the United States.

By uprooting local economies and driving people in less developed countries out of agriculture and/or formerly protected industries and by creating opportunities for people to emigrate through the establishment of ties through military and political policies aimed at promoting international capital mobility, the new globalized form of capitalism has created a "push" for such emigration to the United States (Sassen 1988). On the receiving end, the growth of "global cities," with low-wage employment needs easily filled by immigrants from less developed countries, creates a significant "pull" (Sassen 1994, 1998, 2000). Reduced costs and greater ease of transportation and communication globally also facilitate the process. Explanations based simply on intercountry income differentials or poverty and slow growth in countries of origin do not explain modern emigration/immigration, but more complex explanations based on the evolving world' political economy show that immigration is intimately related to current globalization trends.

Some scholarly attention has been paid to contemporary union attitudes toward, and relationships with, immigrant workers (Delgado 1993; Ness 1998; Milkman, ed. 2000). But more typical are historical works focused on either supporting or debunking the myth of the "unorganizable immigrants" as an explanation of the AFL's failure to incorporate newcomers at the end of the nineteenth and beginning of the twentieth century (Brody 1965; Dubofsky 1968, Bodnar 1982, 1985; Poyo 1986; Lane 1987; Mink 1990). These analysts and others suggest that immigrant participation in unions had more to do with conditions the newcomers encountered upon arrival than on their particular characteristics as immigrants. Labor market structures and conditions, the extent and nature of contacts with the broader society, and the level of ethnic solidarity are determining factors in the immigrants' enthusiasm for or rejection of union activities. In each case, labor had to contend with a "foreign" labor force clustered in unskilled occupations, and living in tightly knit, relatively stable, long-lasting community enclaves providing considerable interclass interaction and separating them from mainstream American life (Greene 1968; Fenton 1975; Asher 1982).

Some analysts have looked at internal union practices. Craft union conservatism, the belief that minorities would jeopardize the unions' stability by "taking over," market pressures that encouraged monopolistic union control, the AFL–CIO's nativist sentiments—all have been invoked to explain why some labor organizations failed to incorporate immigrants and minorities (Gutman 1976; Olson 1970). Race- and ethnicity-based exclusionary practices of craft unions were the focus of intense national political and legal action in the late 1960s and 1970s (Gould 1977; Hall 1969; Marshall and Briggs 1967; Marshall et al. 1976).

Even from its earliest origins, the U.S. labor movement has vacillated between impulses toward international solidarity and nativism or exclusionism. Aside from the Native American population, which was killed in large numbers while survivors were mostly relegated to reservations, the country was composed entirely of immigrants. Earlier European immigrants—mostly German, Irish, and English—frequently brought with them traditions of socialist and labor union activism that inclined them toward a natural fraternity and solidarity with their brethren abroad. Mid- to late-nineteenth-century labor organizations and ethnic workingmen's associations tended to favor unlimited immigration from Europe, both because of recent ties to the old country and for ideological reasons tied to the "producerist" thinking prevalent among skilled artisans in the country at the time. Particularly, immigrants from northern and western Europe were welcomed due to their cultural and national similarities to the skilled workers comprising most labor organizations (Lane 1987, 9–32).

But a countertendency was illustrated by attitudes toward Chinese immigrants, particularly in California. The labor movement in that state led a vicious and racist attack upon Chinese immigrants, including murderous riots and successful pressure to stop all further Chinese immigration for twenty years in 1882 (Saxton 1971). Chinese, and later Japanese, were considered the "other" and hence were attacked rather than welcomed. Samuel Gompers, leader of the American Federation of Labor (AFL) and its predecessor (the Federation of Organized Trades and Labor Unions—FOTLU) led the lobbying for exclusion, despite his denials that he had any prejudice against "Asians."

In fact, Gompers and many other labor leaders considered the Chinese an inferior race of people who were not capable of assimilation into the American nation. Hence, they would degrade labor standards and lower the conditions of working people. Here the immigration question merged with the race question: who got defined as a legitimate part of the nation (who was "us" rather than "them") shifted uneasily along lines of racial and nationality classifications. While socialist, anarchist, and other left-wing class-conscious ideologies existed within the U.S. workforce and labor movement, they were not dominant. Hence, the belief that workers of the world should unite was heavily modified in the United States in the second half of the nineteenth century by national and racial solidarities that could quickly undercut class-based solidarity.

Nevertheless, there was within the U.S. labor movement a considerable identification with all workers (and all "producers") in the late nineteenth century. Historian A.T. Lane has shown how prolonged and reluctant was the shift from international solidarity and republican egalitarianism to exclusionism and nativism in the labor movement from 1880 to 1900. Only when technological and economic change had weakened the position of skilled craftsmen did anxieties about immigrants become pronounced. A shift in European immigration patterns from northern and western countries to those in the south and east further weakened a sense of working-class solidarity since the newest immigrants were culturally considered "other" and inferior (Lane 1987, 37–52). But the change in attitude from positive to negative occurred only because the skilled craftsmen became convinced that the very survival of their unions depended on exclusion, requiring a sacrifice of the lingering principles of worker solidarity.

By 1900 the "official" labor movement was anti-immigration. (The "unofficial" Industrial Workers of the World [IWW] carried on the internationalist tradition in the 1900–1920 period.) The shift toward exclusion accompanied a trend toward business unionism within the AFL craft unions. Solidarities of all types narrowed; the broad interests of workers as a class were sacrificed in order to win increased wages and benefits for the fortunate few inside the ranks of the unions. The AFL strongly supported the 1917 imposition of a literacy test on immigrants and was a main force for the draconian 1921 and 1924 laws freezing future immigration to small numbers based on formulas favoring northern and western Europeans (Parmet 1981; Lane 1987).

This chapter utilizes case studies from a heavily immigrant city to update our understanding of alternative recent union responses to mass immigration. It examines four Miami area union responses to mass immigration. Two are building trades unions with a craft structure and a long "exclusionary" history: the United Brotherhood of Carpenters and Joiners of America (UBC) and the Ironworkers Union. Two are industrial unions, one operating in the service sector (Hotel Employees and Restaurant Employees [HERE] and one in apparel production (the Union of Needletrades, Industrial, and Textile Employees [UNITE]). Explanations for differing responses are sought in the structure of the union, the external environment within which the union operates, the leadership's vision and ideology, and the union's internal "cultural" practices. Finally, we note which practices best help unions to be successful in integrating and promoting immigrants.

Methodology

The authors utilized U.S. census data to determine percentages of immigrants in Miami–Dade County, Florida, and in the various industries with workers represented by the four unions. Public documents such as newspaper and journal articles were gathered and studied, as well as internal union files and documents when we were allowed access. Finally, structured interviews were conducted with leaders, ex-leaders, employees, ex-employees, retirees, and activists from the unions in 1988 and 2000. From these data sources, information on the historical reaction of union leadership and the policies of the unions toward the growing immigrant population was obtained. We describe, categorize, and evaluate varying approaches taken toward the immigrants.

Changing Workforce in South Florida

The population and the workforce of South Florida changed greatly in the second half of the twentieth century. The percentage of foreign born in the Miami area grew from under 10 percent in 1940 to almost 60 percent of the total population in 1998. Table 6.1 shows the changes. Changes in the adult civilian labor force generally paralleled those for the population as a whole; by 1998 an even larger 65.5 percent of the adult labor force in Miami–Dade County was foreign born. For particular industries, we have data only from 1980. They too show increasing percentages of immigrants. Table 6.2 shows the percentage of immigrant labor in various industries. The immigrants in Miami–Dade County primarily came from Cuba, followed by other South and Central American and Caribbean nations. Table 6.3 shows countries of origin.

Patterns of Union Relations with Immigrants

As the previous section shows, the four Miami-area unions were operating in an increasingly immigrant workforce, mostly from South and Central American and Caribbean nations. How and why they reacted to this changed workforce is the subject of this study. The following four subsections will relate the reaction of each union.

Table 6.1

Percentage of Foreign-Born Residents in the Miami Standard Metropolitan Statistical Area (SMSA), Selected Years

Year	1940	1950	1960	1970	1980	1990	1998
Percent foreign born	9.7	12.1	16.9	41.8	53.7	59.7	53.6

Source: For 1940–1990: Website http://www.census.gov/population/www./documentation/twps0029/tab22.html; for 1998: *Current Population Survey*, March 1999.

Table 6.2

Percent Immigrant Labor in Various Industries, Miami–Dade County, 1980, 1990, and 1998

	Immigrant labor in industry (in percent)		
Industry	1980	1990	1998
Construction	39.4	60.2	74.6
Eating and drinking	29.9	51.3	67.3
Hotel/motel	39.8	65.7	67.4
Apparel	82.6	85.7	85–95*
Nursing home	19.5	54.0	75–85*

Sources: For 1980: U.S. Census Bureau 1981, table 227, pp. 941, 942; for 1990: 1990 Census, analysis of Public Use Microdata Sample (PUMS) data; for 1998: *Current Population Survey*, March 1999, except for apparel and nursing home industries, which are authors' estimates.

*Sample size too small to be usable; number range shown is an estimate.

Table 6.3

Country of Origin of Immigrant Workers in Miami–Dade County, 1998

Country of origin	Cuba	South America (Colombia)	Central America (Nicaragua)	Haiti	Dominican Republic	Jamaica
Percentage of all immigrants	54	14 (7)	12 (6)	6.4	4.3	2.2

Source: Current Population Survey, March 1999.

Ironworkers Local 272

Ironworkers Local 272 was a typical U.S. building trades craft union in the post–World War II period. It represented craft workers doing steel and iron work in building and construction projects by referring workers to construction projects done by unionized contractors. Workers stayed with a job until completion, then returned to the union hiring hall for referral to another construction job. A skilled workforce was maintained through a three-year union apprenticeship program, which the nonunion segment of the industry has been unable to duplicate. When the local was unable to supply enough union workers, it would refer nonunion workers to job sites, but only so long as all union workers were employed.

Consistent with post–World War II building trades tradition, the local had only two basic categories of worker: apprentices (whose wages would steadily rise toward full pay as they progressed through the program) and full-fledged journeymen. The pay levels of both were specified in the union contract. Also consistent with traditional U.S. building trades union practice, entry into the apprenticeship program was greatly restricted, often to relatives of those already in the local. In the words of Dewey Tyler, the local's current business manager:

> Ironworkers Local 272 was a closed local in the 1960s. . . . You couldn't get into the apprenticeship school—you had to be a relative. . . . So when the Cubans came over and tried to get work with us, our union kept them out. They didn't let anyone in. So they had to work wherever they could. And we said, well, they can't do our work. We thought we were infallible. (Tyler interview)

The exclusion was so complete that at one time the local had 200 members but 3,000 people working out of the union hall. In 1971 the national union forced the local to take in 500 new members, but only a token number were minorities or immigrants (Tyler interview). Throughout the 1970s and 1980s the numbers of immigrants and African Americans in the local crept up slightly, but the local was still overwhelmingly native born and white. The one leader who attempted to bring in Hispanics to the local was voted out of office after one term, at least partly due to a backlash against the more open policy (Phillips interview).

The union's immigrant membership lagged behind the industry as a whole prior to the 1990s. Table 6.4 shows the percentages for the last four decades of the century. During this period the attitude of the local's leadership and the rank-and-file membership toward immigrants was not positive, according to the current local president, Dave Gornewicz:

> [They were] typically prejudiced attitudes. Stereotyping people: "*Some of them are alright. They don't have the same skills as we do. You can't*

Table 6.4

Immigrants in Construction Industry, Iron Work, and Union Membership, Selected Years

Position	Percentage of immigrants in position			
	1960s	1970s	1980s	1999
In construction industry	unavailable	unavailable	39–60	75
Doing iron work (est.)	10	15–30	40–50	60+
In union (est.)	1–2	10–15	20	Over 50

Sources: For construction industry: U.S. census figures; for iron work: estimates from Dewey Tyler and Dave Gornewicz, business manager and president, Ironworkers Local 272; for union: estimates from Dewey Tyler.

trust them all." Every backward thing you can imagine . . . completely racial—not anything to do with the skills. (Gornewicz interview)

The union's exclusionary practices, coupled with the changing labor force, slowly caused it to decline as more and more of the work went to nonunion contractors employing heavily immigrant labor. At the time of the 1992 union election, there were only seventy-three union members working in the five-county jurisdiction of this local, which was on the verge of collapse. Union workers represented less than 1 percent of the local ironworker labor force (Tyler interview). Dewey Tyler was elected business manager on a platform calling for change, although members were unclear about what the change would be.

As Tyler began bringing more immigrants into the union, he immediately faced intense opposition from members and the local's president at that time. So he instituted an extensive education program on the need to organize the relevant labor force for the union to survive. Beginning with the leadership and eventually extending to much of the membership (by early 2000 almost 40 percent of the local's members had received formal training), he eventually won over the majority to the need to end the "country club unionism" and to organize all workers, including immigrants.

By the mid-1990s the majority of the union's executive board and membership favored a shift to aggressive organizing of *all* workers with the necessary skills, irrespective of racial or immigrant status. In 1996 the local began a formal organizing program, including special Hispanic and Haitian organizing committees. Membership has grown rapidly ever since. Table 6.5 shows the figures.

Table 6.5

Membership of Ironworkers Local 272, Selected Years

1996	1997	1998	1999	March 2000	December 2000 goal
538	549	653	810	844	920–950

Sources: Data through 1999 from "Local 272 Moves into a New Millennium: The Real Deal-Organizing"; slide show prepared by the union, January 29, 2000; March and December 2000 data from interviews with Dewey Tyler and David Gornewicz.

The number of contractors signing the union contract grew from three in 1992 to ninety as of March 2000. Tyler estimates that the local's "market share" (percentage of the work that is done union) grew from under 1 percent in 1992 to 20 percent by early 2000.

The new leadership has appointed a more representative staff. Gregorio Cisneros, a Peruvian immigrant, is the primary organizer of Hispanic workers. His skill and impressive track record have catapulted him in a few short years into the third highest rank in the local's informal chain of command, after Tyler and Gornewicz. Antonio Parker, a black immigrant from Jamaica, was elected local recording secretary in 1998 (the first elected immigrant leader), and he was subsequently appointed apprentice director (Parker interview). Monthly membership meeting attendance (averaging 50–85 persons) has been about 40 percent immigrant (Gornewicz interview; Tyler interview).

Internal opposition to the change was eventually isolated and defeated: the opposing presidential candidate received only fifteen votes in the 1998 election against Dave Gornewicz, a strong reform supporter. Gornewicz attributes success in overcoming backward attitudes to two factors: (1) an extensive education program, lasting years, and (2) a growing "interfacing" with immigrants within the union and on the job, leading to a recognition that they are capable of doing the job.

Despite lingering fears from long-term non-Hispanic white members, the new leadership is fully reconciled to the complete transformation of the union local, including at leadership levels, as indicated by the following statement by Dewey Tyler:

> I've had people concerned, saying, "What's going to happen? Is this local going to be where the business manager and the business agents are black and Hispanic?" And I say, "Well, I would certainly hope so! Be-

cause I would hope that the membership gets to vote on who's going to be there." That's democracy. Greg Cisneros, at some point in time, will be the president or the business manager of this local. (Tyler interview)

Changes in the composition of the ranks of the apprenticeship program show that the changeover to a new membership base will be permanent. Of the 124 apprentices in the Florida East Coast program, 50–60 are Hispanic, 40–50 are black (both African American and African Caribbean), and only 17 are non-Hispanic whites. Similarly, new job categories accommodate nonunion immigrant workers who are too skilled to be apprentices but not skilled enough to be full journeymen. The union now issues a "structural steel" book to some new members and a "rodman" book to others, and it even has a "utility program" with three classifications for those with very low skill levels. Through classroom training and/or on-the-job experience, those in lower categories can attain full journeyman status.

Nevertheless, the local has not fully changed to an immigrant-friendly union. Neither of the two secretaries at the union hall speaks Spanish or Creole, and only one of the two apprenticeship school secretaries speaks Spanish (but not Creole). The local's website is in English only, although some literature used for recruitment and education is written in English and Spanish. More important, the local's five-person executive board has only one Hispanic (and no black) member. Reportedly, the constitution and bylaws requirements imposed by the national union regarding meeting attendance and past dues payments make it difficult to diversify the executive board more.

South Florida Regional Council of the UBC

Like the Ironworkers Union, the UBC was traditionally a virtually all-white, male craft union operating through a hiring hall. The UBC's South Florida Regional Council was large and powerful in the 1960s, with membership of almost 12,000. The UBC admitted immigrants in the 1960s in larger numbers than any other building trades union. It was the "only trade to open its doors" to Cuban immigrants, according to Ernie Taylor, council president when interviewed in 1988 (Taylor interview).

But the union failed to match the growing percentage of immigrants in the craft in later years. Relatively few Haitians have become carpenters in the United States, so we use Hispanic percentages as a rough

Table 6.6

UBC Membership and Hispanic–Non-Hispanic Breakdown, Selected Years

Year	Total members[a]	Non-Hispanic	Hispanic
1973	7,505 (100%)	6,165 (82%)	1,340 (18%)
1980	3,303 (100%)	2,520 (76%)	7,830 (24%)
1988	3,834 (100%)	2,740 (71%)	1,094 (29%)
2000	3,841 (100%)	2,567 (67%)	1,274 (33%)

[a]Figures for 1973, 1980, and 1988 were derived from Hispanic surname count of membership lists. The figure for 2000 is from the official records of the South Florida Regional Council on March 15, 2000.

proxy for immigrant penetration of the union. From 1980 to 1999 the construction industry moved from 39 percent to 75 percent immigrant. In the same years, the union moved from 24 percent to only 33 percent immigrant membership. Table 6.6 shows the union's lagging membership trends for the relevant years.

While the union's early acceptance of some immigrants was probably the best of any building trades unions in the area, attitudes were never very friendly. Kennie Peckel, a union local president, stated in 1988 that the members confronted the "Cuban problem" with prejudice, with some exceptions (Peckel interview). Generally, immigrants were viewed by both members and leaders as threats to union jobs. Organizing them was a radical idea.

The union's passive acceptance of immigrants, coupled with indifference and neglect, changed in the 1970s, when an unusually forceful and talented Cuban immigrant leader emerged within its ranks. Jose "Pepe" Collado became a member of the South Florida Local 405 in 1969. His initial reception was far from promising, as he relates:

> What they gave me was a desk and a test, and they told me that the test would cost me $20 or $25. I . . . paid the $20 or $25, did not pass the test because, number one, I did not read English. I had problems with the language. And number two, the type of test they can give you . . . are [*sic*] so that one will not pass it. Three weeks after . . . there were ads in the newspapers . . . looking for people. I returned. They gave me a little better attention this time, did not give me the test, but they did not let me in, either. I got in on the third time because my [Anglo] father-in-law was a member of the local and had become a friend of the local representa-

tive. I came in recommended by him and the business agent helped me to pass the test, and I started working. (Collado interview 1988)

In 1976, Collado was elected trustee of Local 405, and in 1979 he became the first Hispanic business representative in the council. He achieved this position by mobilizing his local's Hispanic workforce and forcefully making its needs known to the other council leaders. Collado used the growth of Hispanic contractors as leverage to increase the presence of Hispanics in the appointed ranks of leadership. With him came the first wave of Hispanic organizers and executive board members with surnames like Fajardo, Figueroa, Leon, and Jiménez.

As the organizational attitude toward immigrants changed, the union also partially reversed a decline in membership from the early 1970s. By the mid-1980s, most of the "hard work" in the local was being done by immigrants, including not simply Cubans, but also other Hispanic workers, particularly Nicaraguans and Dominicans (Jiménez interview; Bittle interview).

Collado's influence made the UBC the most progressive of all South Florida construction unions in its practices in the 1980s and helped the union partially reverse a decline in membership. When Collado resigned his business representative position in 1985, he was immediately offered a staff job by the union's national president.

Soon after, the council was placed under supervision by the international, and a top-down strategy for creating institutional diversity was adopted. Shortly, two of six business agents were Hispanics, as was the state organizing director. Apprenticeship classes were made more immigrant-friendly, contracts were translated into Spanish, and a new training level, journeyman training, was instituted to upgrade skills of workers, particularly Hispanic workers, who would not come in as apprentices because they were already working or had experience.

Collado moved up in the national union; today he is a national executive board member in charge of the entire southeastern portion of the United States and is the union's highest ranking Hispanic. Yet most of the local changes he compelled or initiated were reversed in the decade after he left. None of the Hispanic leaders who walked through the doors he opened are any longer there. By the mid-1990s, a new leadership was dealing with the very issues that Collado had tackled a decade earlier. Simple procedures, such as translating contracts and tests into Spanish, had to be reinitiated. Collado states, "They just buried our work when I left. Didn't keep it up" (Collado interview, 2000). Walter Seidel, the union's executive secretary in 1999, confirmed the regression to previous backward practices:

> When we started doing the tests and contracts (in Spanish), I called Pepe and he said that all that had been done back when he was around. Nobody could remember . . . . Nobody knew where the stuff was. (Seidel interview)

In 1995, the national union reorganized the district council. Once again, the purpose was to force more diversity and accountability in the council. The executive secretary of the regional council reports to Collado and is the only officer elected by the members. The business agents, rather than having their own base, now are appointed by the executive secretary.

The changes have diversified the union staff. Of the seven local unions, two have Hispanic business agents, one Cuban, and one Puerto Rican. This is called the regional council side of the organization. The other is the organizing side, directly funded by the national union, and five of the six organizers are Hispanics (two Cubans, one Colombian, one Salvadorean, and one Puerto Rican). The organizing director at the time of our interviews was a first-generation Cuban American raised in Boston; later he was replaced by another Cuban American when he moved up to the executive secretary position. The organizing division is seen as a way of implementing the vision of top union leadership of a diverse and representative leadership structure within the council. Collado states, "Top leadership in our union has always wanted more immigrants in the ranks and in positions of power. Middle leadership has been the stumbling block" (Collado interview, 2000).

The national union's attempt to bypass local leadership antipathy or indifference has brought mixed results. The regional council office has only one Spanish-speaking secretary, in the safety and health program, and its newsletter is published in English only. Some locals hold "unofficial" meetings in Spanish to supplement regular union meetings. The council has run an organized educational program directed at changing long-standing attitudes in the year 2000. It also is implementing plans to recruit immigrant leaders from the rank and file and appears to be having some initial success.

Ambivalence toward organizing immigrants has been hard to overcome. The council's organizing director in 2000 described the ambivalence clearly:

> Immigrants are positive and negative for our unions. . . . The massive cheap labor they provide helps the nonunion shops, no question. . . . It's a double-edged sword. "They are out there, doing our job, we should organize them." But also, "we should exclude them, deport them . . . because our trade is being diluted." But if we keep them out, like the union has been doing, they become a double negative. . . . If we go after them, it can revitalize us . . . give us purpose. . . . We have 5 percent market share. . . . The attitude [of exclusion] has changed. (García interview)

Angel Domínguez, a talented organizer who later became the union's organizing director, was very critical of the union at the local level in a year 2000 interview:

> They [union regional council leadership at the time] are lost. They don't know what they are doing. They don't understand the people we need to organize and want to keep doing the same thing that hasn't worked for years. (Domínguez interview)

Domínguez launched a series of community-based activities among Mexican workers in Homestead, a town just southwest of Miami. Mexican immigrants now are a dominant force in the Homestead area "and to organize them, we have to go where they are and do what they do." So he established nontraditional organizing strategies, such as setting up a booth at a crowded flea market or running a radio program serving the Mexican community in Homestead.

The regional council leader at the time could not understand why Domínguez was doing this, which Domínguez saw as a symptom of the lack of vision of the current leadership. He felt business agents and leaders, uneducated about immigrants, did not recognize their significance other than as a threat and therefore did not use the union to defend immigrant worker rights. This restricted the union's ability to recruit and develop leadership from immigrant members (Domínguez interview).

Despite resistance, the union's hierarchy made tremendous progress in the second half of the year 2000 and 2001. As noted, Domínguez was promoted from chief critic of the union's organizing strategy to its organizing director. The tempo of organizing has picked up rapidly, and Domínguez has been leading a campaign for amnesty for undocumented workers in the Homestead area. Previously unsympathetic union leaders and staff are backing him fully, despite some remaining puzzlement about why they are being pulled into something so far removed from their traditional idea of union affairs.

The deterioration of the union's treatment of immigrant workers from the late 1980s until the late 1990s shows that dependence on one leader to advance the interests of immigrants is risky. When that leader moves up or on, reforms may disappear if changes have not been institutionalized and if the cultural practices of the union local are not systematically altered.

The contrast with the Ironworkers is striking: Ironworkers leadership systematically set up a plan, conducted education, and solidified majority leadership support for a major change in orientation toward immigrants. Only then did the union implement its new organizing strategy. No such systematic process has taken place in the UBC, where change imposed from above has been more difficult to deepen than was the case with the internal local insurgency in the Ironworkers. It remains to be seen if the UBC now has the necessary unified leadership, clarity of vision, strategic plan, and transformed internal cultural practices to make for a lasting change.

HERE Local 355

HERE Local 355 (known as Local 255 prior to a 1973 merger with two other locals) is an industrial union local with a jurisdiction over service workers employed in lodging and eating establishments. It organizes all workers irrespective of skill or craft. Its main employers are a couple of larger hotels in Miami Beach and airline food preparation workers at the Miami Airport, although it also represents workers at assorted other employers and runs a "roll call" hiring hall for catering jobs.

The local has always represented relatively low-paid service workers in a sector where immigrants often first seek employment. We lack data on the percentage of union membership that was immigrant in the decades following 1960, but minutes of executive board meetings show that seven of the twenty-one executive board members in the latter half of 1962 were Hispanic (executive board minutes, August 6–December 3, 1962). However, only one of the union's seven office staff in August 1963 had an Hispanic surname: the woman who answered the telephone (executive board minutes, August 6, 1963).

Paid officers and field staff also became somewhat integrated in the 1960s, although two white Anglos were president and business manager. As of 1965, four of the local's nine business agents had Hispanic surnames (executive board minutes, August 1965). By 1967, the general organizer for the local was an Hispanic, Armando Vázquez (executive board minutes, December 4, 1967).

The local's willingness to accommodate recent immigrants was tested in 1972, when executive board member Ricardo Torres requested that local meetings be conducted in both English and Spanish. Torres stated that a big percentage of the membership did not understand meeting proceedings due to language problems. According to the minutes:

> Brother Schiffman [local president] explained that the By-Laws of our International Constitution clearly spell out that any meeting can be conducted only in English language. Therefore the constitution will supercede anything. A motion cannot be introduced in this respect. (executive board minutes, March 6, 1972)

Despite Schiffman's lack of accommodation of immigrant language needs, current leaders claim that Schiffman was well liked by the workers, including the Hispanics in the local. Partly this may have been due to "good times" for the local, whose membership reached 7,400 in 1965.

In December 1976 "Pinky" Schiffman was convicted for accepting gratuities from hotel owners (Vaira and Roller 1978), and in 1978 the local was put into trusteeship by the national union for nonpayment of dues and financial irregularities. Trustee Alvaro González was elected secretary-treasurer when the local left trusteeship in April 1979. Another Hispanic, Antonio Fernández, became president and business manager. Twelve of the fifteen officers and business agents of the local at the time had Hispanic surnames (executive board minutes, April 23, 1979).

In 1980 the issue of bilingual meetings was again raised at the executive board, bringing about "lengthy discussion." Arguments that this would unduly prolong the meetings carried the group, but they stipulated that the president should ask (in Spanish) at the beginning of the meeting if anyone could not follow the discussion in English. If any could not, the room would be divided for simultaneous translation. Although the original motion failed, considerably more accommodation was provided than had been the case eight years earlier (executive board minutes, September 23, 1980).

In the late 1970s and early 1980s, large numbers of Haitian immigrants began to enter the hotel industry. In 1981 the local hired its first Haitian organizer for a one-month trial period (executive board minutes, October 27, 1981). However, subsequent records from the 1980s do not indicate continued hiring of Haitians to organize and service this growing segment of the workforce.

The 1980s through the mid-1990s were years of stagnation and decline for the local. Membership dropped and many unionized establishments went nonunion. Alvaro González ran the local in an autocratic manner, continuing the Schiffman legacy. In the early 1980s a power struggle between González and local president Fernández led to accusations of inept organizing and squandered resources, financially shady relations with insurance companies, breakaway union attempts, and sensational accusations on local Cuban talk radio shows.

The internal culture of the local was focused on these matters rather than on immigrant issues. Immigration came up only as part of internal feuding when González tried to remove an executive board opponent, Wilfredo Fariñas, for lack of U.S. citizenship (executive board minutes, September 25, 1984). The national union's constitution required U.S. citizenship of board members. In late 1984 Fariñas was ejected from the meeting despite his pleas that he had applied for citizenship and would be hearing back soon (executive board minutes, December 4, 1984). This behavior is consistent with current business manager Andy Balash's assessment of González: AAl did not care about immigrants. Al did not care about anything but Al, as far as I heard" (Balash interview).

In 1990 Al González moved to a higher position in the national union, replaced by his son Robert González. In 1994 the local was put into trusteeship for financial irregularities (it owed the national union half a million dollars) (Balash interview). When trusteeship ended in 1996, assistant to the trustee Andy Balash became the new secretary-treasurer and business manager. Balash developed a union leadership slate that includes the union's major immigrant groups: a non-Hispanic white (Balash), a Cuban American president (Jorge Santiesteban), and a Haitian American vice president (Maria Angie Badio).

The local's executive board is appointed to mirror the local's national and ethnic membership. It has six Hispanics, three Haitians, one African American, and one Caribbean American (West Indies). The proportional breakdown of the membership of the local is shown in Table 6.7.

Table 6.7

HERE Local 355 Membership by Nationality, March 2000 (in percent)

Cuban	Haitian	Non-Cuban Hispanic	Other
40	30–35	20	5–10

Source: Estimates by HERE Local 355 business manager Andy Balash and president Jorge Santiesteban.

Today the local runs membership meetings in one, two, or three languages (English, Spanish, Creole) on an "as needed" basis. Average attendance is 30–50 people, and 75–90 percent are estimated to be immigrants (Balash interview; Santiesteban interview). Of the eight office staff (including business agents and organizers), all speak English, six speak Spanish, and one speaks Creole. The local's quarterly newsletter is printed in English only because the local cannot afford to print in all three languages, and rather than offend the group left out if two languages were used, the "universal language" of English is used (Santiesteban interview; Balash interview).

The local's leadership attaches little significance to its immigrant membership base, beyond requirements of representative leadership and staff. The local is not involved in Cuban, Haitian, or other immigrant community issues. And it does not consciously utilize national cultures or events to build the union. This statement by business manager Balash regarding immigrants is representative:

> They're our members. They're reflective of our workforce. We have to represent them. . . . I, myself, running this union: I'm running it on behalf of *workers*. I really do not see Cuban, Haitian, or Nicaraguan. I see these are dues paying members who happen to be immigrants. And we service them and try to take care of their needs as best we can. (Balash interview)

Thus HERE Local 355 is a union whose members happen to be mostly immigrant. It neither uses this fact to its advantage nor to damage itself by exclusionary practices.

UNITE

UNITE was formed in 1995 from the merger of the Amalgamated Clothing and Textile Workers Union (ACTWU) and the International Ladies'

Garment Workers' Union (ILGWU). Both ACTWU and ILGWU operated in South Florida prior to this merger, and here as elsewhere they
were "immigrant unions." As with HERE, the garment unions operated
in a workforce environment that had long been heavily immigrant. By
1980 the industry's workforce was 83 percent immigrant; by 1990 the
figure was 86 percent.

When union staffer Anita Cofino (daughter of the leader of Cuba's
largest prerevolutionary labor federation) transferred to the ILGWU office in Miami from New York in 1971, she found an "immigrant union
with an immigrant staff":

> By the time I came down from New York with the ILG, the workforce
> was practically all Cuban. Not Hispanic. Cuban. Some blacks were in it
> but not many other immigrants. We had nearly 8,000 members in twenty
> some factories. . . . It was our peak. (Cofino interview)

At that time, the entire garment industry in the Miami area employed
approximately 20,000, so the union had a healthy 40 percent of the
workforce under contract.

The union's two Anglo regional managers during the decade had
"no love" for Cubans, according to Cofino. Only when she was appointed education and political director of the region in 1973 was she
able to become more independent of what she calls "the manager's
anti-immigrant opinions." She organized citizenship classes for members and developed a newsletter in Spanish.

The ILGWU lost the majority of its organized plants to plant closings in the 1970s, and it failed to organize existing and newly opened
nonunion shops, so its membership dropped precipitously. By 1981 it
had only 806 members, and by 1987 the union was down to 231 workers, an insignificant 1.2 percent of the 19,000 still working in apparel
manufacturing.

At the same time, the workforce increased in diversity. Hispanic immigrants still dominated, but they came from Nicaragua, Colombia, the
Dominican Republic, and other Central and South American countries.
Haitians as well began to work their way into the mix, the women in
sewing and the men in the pressing departments.

Cofino was laid off in the mid-1980s and went to work for ACTWU,
which had followed large unionized companies like Hart, Schaffner, and
Marx and Kuppenheimer's when they moved production to Miami. The

virtually all-Cuban female workforce approached 100 percent membership, demonstrating more union/class consciousness than stereotypes about Cuban immigrants would depict (Grenier 1990).

Since the production of suits and formal wear requires a more skilled workforce, the ACTWU plants survived the first wave of plant shutdowns. The Alabama-based ACTWU regional managers in the 1980s had a much more positive attitude than their ILGWU counterparts, according to Cofino (Cofino interview). With their support, she started citizenship classes and a bilingual newspaper. By the early 1990s, the newspaper was trilingual, for the growing numbers of Haitians in the shops.

Shifting demographics motivated a structural adjustment in the union. Traditionally ACTWU amalgamates workplaces into one large local—the Miami structure until the early 1990s. Local 694 represented six worksites and nearly 2,800 workers with a twelve-person executive board. Nine of the twelve executive board members were Cubans, along with two Anglos and one Haitian man.

This structure had worked in the past, but by the 1990s the executive board was not representing the younger Central American and Haitian immigrant members. The board met once a month, and membership meetings were not held at all. So the union de-amalgamated, creating worksite locals united under a South Florida Council (Russo interview; Russo 1993, 39).

ACTWU was hit hard by a second wave of plant closings in the mid-1990s that weakened the nonamalgamated model. By the time ILGWU Local 415–475 merged with the ACTWU South Florida Council to create UNITE Local 2000 in 1995, the need for another restructuring process was evident, according to UNITE's Florida district manager, Monica Russo:

> Our initial reason for de-amalgamating was to involve the members, but with plant closings, board members losing their jobs and their base, [and] constant elections, the model became problematic. Our base was going and we needed to find a new direction in organizing. (Russo interview)

Many unemployed members from the closed garment plants were retrained to become Certified Nursing Assistants (CNAs) and went to work in the nursing home industry. UNITE at that point chose to follow these immigrant members and established an organizing focus on nursing homes.

Local 1115, a non–AFL-CIO union, had also been organizing nursing homes. It merged with the Service Employees International Union (SEIU) at exactly the time when UNITE and SEIU were drawing up plans to establish a joint organizing project named Unite for Dignity (with Russo as executive director). Thus UNITE became an important force in a new immigrant industry, with approximately twenty-five nursing homes under SEIU contract and a handful already organized by UNITE. (Later, in the year 2000, the national UNITE union decided to cede the Unite for Dignity formation entirely to the national SEIU union and to return to a more traditional jurisdiction in Florida centered on laundry workers.)

Unite for Dignity during its years with two parent unions was not officially a labor organization, so the workers joined either UNITE Local 2000 or SEIU Local 1115. The Unite for Dignity council combined members of both unions to devise strategies and plan activities. The attendance at these meetings was overwhelmingly immigrant. English was seldom spoken, and the meetings were run in Creole and Spanish.

UNITE's local structure prior to its departure from Unite for Dignity changed considerably as the union tried to maintain its commitment to immigrant workers. The industrial division, with a few remaining garment-cutting and distribution centers and a growing focus on industrial laundry shops as well as a few miscellaneous businesses, had a mix of Haitian, Cuban, non-Cuban Hispanic, and African American organizers. Unite for Dignity, both as a joint project and later as an SEIU union, has been staffed primarily by Haitians, including the organizing director. These staffing patterns reflect the predominant nationalities in the workforces being organized. In the year 2000, months prior to UNITE's withdrawal from Unite for Dignity, Russo estimated that its membership was 40 percent Haitian, 30 percent Hispanic, 20 percent African American, and 10 percent other (mostly immigrant) workers.

UNITE and its eventual breakaway offspring, Unite for Dignity, have had an active presence in immigrant communities unmatched by any other union in South Florida. They have played a leading role in many social movements involving immigrant and African American communities in Miami. The union hall is open to progressive community groups throughout the county. They are well known for active intervention in immigrant community concerns and are thought of as "community unions." This is in striking contrast with HERE or other local unions with a predominantly immigrant membership that take a much more passive stance toward immigrant community affairs.

Analysis and Discussion

What can explain such different patterns of union response to immigration? Four factors appear to have a direct impact on the relationship established between unions and immigrants: union structure; changing labor force and employer characteristics; union leadership, vision, and ideology; and internal organizational practices.

Union Structure

Union structure can greatly influence a union's likely response to immigrants. The two building trades unions in this study are structured as craft unions representing relatively skilled workers performing iron work and wood work in constructing buildings. Both operate a union hiring hall that refers first union then nonunion workers to construction projects done by unionized contractors. A skilled workforce is created through a union apprenticeship program. This structure allowed the building trades craft unions to operate as "country clubs" for many decades following World War II. They jealously guarded entry to the trade by restricting apprentice openings.

These exclusionary practices overlapped with racial and nationality boundaries. The traditional membership of these unions was virtually all white and all native born. Thus the exclusionary practices and the structure that made them possible and natural also had discriminatory racial and nationality impacts. African Americans and immigrants were excluded.

For these structural reasons, the two building trades unions in this study were much tardier than their industrial union counterparts to admit representative numbers of immigrants to their ranks. By the 1960s both HERE and UNITE's predecessor unions, admitting anyone working in the hotel and apparel industries, had admitted large numbers of (usually Cuban) immigrants, and both had immigrants in leadership and staff. This was especially true for the apparel unions, which had a long history of being "immigrant" unions in New York and elsewhere from the turn of the twentieth century.

The building trades' traditional dichotomy of workers into journeyman or apprentice had also excluded many immigrants working in the trade who were more highly skilled (and more highly paid) than apprentices but less highly skilled (and less well paid) than full-fledged journeymen. Ironworkers Local 272 surmounted this problem in the late 1990s by creating four or five other categories for workers with intermediate skill levels. The UBC recognizes the same problem and in a less clear fashion is attempting a similar type of solution involving structural flexibility.

At least at the local level, UNITE had two other types of flexibility helpful for the integration of immigrant workers. First, it continuously amalgamated and de-amalgamated itself, depending on external circumstances and challenges, to keep its internal structure fully representative of all cultures and nationalities. Second, at least in the short run, it maintained extreme jurisdictional flexibility by following immigrant workers to the nursing home industry, far from its traditional apparel base. (The national union's abandonment of the Unite for Dignity project shows that the national union was less flexible in this regard and less committed to following its previous workforce to new jobs than were local leaders such as Monica Russo.)

The HERE local has displayed neither extraordinary flexibility nor a lack of it. With only one category of membership and a clearcut employer base, it has neither a restricting rigidity nor an acutely sensitive responsiveness and flexibility.

Finally, national and regional union structures can influence a union local's relationship with immigrants, although the relationship is not one of simple causality. National union influence on this issue ranges from mere indifference (Ironworkers, HERE until very recently) or perhaps mild support for immigrant-friendly initiatives (UNITE). The UBC's attempt to force top-down change onto local structures illustrates some limitations. The international has funded organizing, with five of the six organizers and the organizing director being Hispanics. But at the local level the necessary leadership vision and internal cultural practices needed to make immigrant workers feel welcome have been developing only very slowly.

Changing Labor Force and Employer Characteristics

As noted above, the population and workforce of South Florida changed greatly in the second half of the twentieth century. The workforce changed even more than the proportion of immigrants in the area; by 1998 almost two-thirds of workers in the county were immigrants. The industrial labor forces within the jurisdiction of the four unions in this study had similar and sometimes even stronger trends this time. Thus the four unions were operating in local industries that were increasingly composed of immigrants, most from South and Central American and Caribbean nations.

Even though all unions faced a growing immigrant labor force within their jurisdictions, they were not all equally prepared for the changes they confronted. The building trades unions had a traditional union membership that had long been virtually immigrant-free, making racist and prejudiced responses to immigrant workers much more likely than in the hotel and garment unions, which had long histories working with immigrant laborers. Consequently the two construction unions were the slowest to deal with immigrants systematically.

The growth of nonunion employers and market segments employing large numbers of immigrants usually undermines union survival. For example, unions such as those in the building trades with little attachment to immigrants are hurt when the economy shifts from traditional unionized employers or market segments because immigrants work for the newer, nonunion competitors and segments. However, unions so attached to immigrant members that they follow them, such as UNITE did locally (and temporarily) by following ex-members into nursing homes, can use their immigrant ties to advantage. Immigrants then provide new organizing opportunities and a loyal membership base.

Finally, decline almost to the point of irrelevance or extinction can force a previously hostile or indifferent union leadership and membership to reevaluate and change their attitudes toward immigrants and the need to organize them. Ironworkers Local 272 illustrates this most fully. But the UBC's decline from a purported 95 percent of market share in the 1960s to 5 percent today is also an example of an external push to change old ways of thinking and doing.

Union Leadership, Vision and Ideology

While union structural characteristics and labor force and employer characteristics put limits and pressures on union leaders, the vision and ideological outlook of that leadership play a large role in explaining the varying paths taken by the unions examined in this chapter. In fact, leadership vision can be absolutely crucial; the complete turnaround in the Ironworkers local is the clearest example. Until the 1992 election, Ironworkers Local 272 leadership was traditional for a U.S. building trades union. The vision was narrow; economic gain for existing members was the only motive. The self-interest of the local's members was seen in terms of excluding others from the monopolistic country club known as the union, which could bring high incomes to the fortunate few inside the club. Ideology was conservative; larger interests of workers as a class were downplayed or ignored.

The leader who turned the local around had a vision with a strong moral component: the "uplift" of the membership, of the trade, and of working people as a whole. His vision was inclusive rather than exclusive and heavily influenced by a strongly held Christian faith. From his "born again" faith, Dewey Tyler concluded that racism and exclusionary thinking must be rejected. Tyler's coleader of the local, Dave Gornewicz, tends to see the world in more traditionally left-wing, class-conscious terms. Yet he and Tyler are united on the direction for the local: inclusion; organizing all workers, including immigrants; equality of treatment of all workers irrespective of race or nativity; a union hall that feels like home to all nationalities.

In contrast, the South Florida leadership of the UBC has been less clear and more conflicted, both in vision and ideological commitment to immigrant organizing, although this changed considerably in late 2000 and early 2001. UBC leaders of the past understood that they needed to organize immigrants to survive in South Florida, but collectively they exhibited ambivalence and lack of clarity about how to do it. The national union's pressure has been slowly turning the union around, but the final outcome is still not certain.

The UBC also shows the limits of individual visionary leadership alone, without a corresponding change in union internal institutional and cultural practices. When union leader Pepe Collado moved to higher leadership levels, his reforms faded at the local level. Systematic education of the leadership and then the membership was not conducted, as it was in the Ironworkers union at a later date. The leadership never consolidated a unified understanding of the importance of organizing and welcoming immigrant workers and lacked a conscious plan for integrating cultures within the union.

HERE Local 355 leadership traditionally lacked the vision or the ideology to understand the immigrant influx as an opportunity rather than an unimportant fact of life in the hotel industry. Until 1995 the local was plagued by fiscal irresponsibility, accusations of corruption and incompetence among leaders and aspiring leaders, and autocratic leadership styles. Very little vision is apparent in thirty years of leadership from 1965 through 1995.

The union's current leaders appear to be more competent and fiscally responsible than their predecessors. However, they attach relatively minor significance to the fact that their membership base is largely immigrant, and they do not involve the local in issues of immigrant communities, in striking contrast with Unite for Dignity. The local's leadership is neither strategic nor innovative in its approach to immigrant workers, but neither is it backward or reactionary.

Unite for Dignity's top leader in Miami—Monica Russo, now an SEIU staff member rather than UNITE staff member—combines a strong class-conscious worldview with an intense commitment to organizing immigrant workers. She exhibits a more ideologically driven commitment to immigrant workers than any other union leader in the Miami area. Partially as a result, Unite for Dignity has become the most successful "immigrant" union in the region. Russo has not had to contend with backward views on the immigrant issue within her own membership or the rest of her leadership team. So a progressive immigrant policy is easier to implement here than it would be in a union with a more xenophobic or racist history.

Internal Organizational Practices

Vision and leadership are not enough to create a successful union program to welcome immigrants into a union. The union must also be a comfortable place for immigrant workers to be. It must work out ways for members of different cultural and national backgrounds to intermingle and coexist in the day-to-day workings of the union.

The unions examined in this study have had varying degrees of success in transforming their internal cultures to encompass practices that meld their members with disparate backgrounds. The most successful has been Unite for Dignity, which has constant immigrant cultural, community, religious, and similar activities going on within its building. The union hall has become one of the best known community centers for various meetings, especially for the Haitian community, the union's fastest growing segment.

This cross-cultural interaction within the confines of the union hall is consciously planned by the union's leadership, whose thinking is casptured by this excerpt from an article by Russo:

> In transforming one's attitudes—in transforming our unions—we don't do it by sitting around and talking about it. We have to get out there and roll up our sleeves. We have to live with each other, be with each other, and our human potential and our rich experiences start coming out. That's how we're building a multicultural organizing union in this world called Miami. (Russo 1993, 49)

The UNITE union hall has a multicultural and immigrant "feel" to it unmatched by any other union in the area. Culturally, it is definitely a comfortable place for Hispanic and Haitian immigrants to be.

The Ironworkers local has not gone to the same lengths as has UNITE, but it has probably changed its internal cultural practices as much as any building trades union in the Miami area could. The local's leadership has made the union hall a comfortable place for all nationalities. The local president sums up how this local differs from most building trades union locals:

> Most people don't want to change. It doesn't change because they don't want it to. They might give lip service to it: "We need to do this." But do they hire people to do it? Do they put programs into effect that will do it? Do they carry through on what they promise? Then they tell people that this is a democratic organization, we want you to be part of it. Do they mean it? Do they make them a part of it? When we see people come in here on fire, because they believe this is *their* union, they don't see that we're just letting them come in and get a job. They feel that this is *their* union. That's the only time the change isn't superficial, is when . . . "Esto es *mío*" [This is *mine*]. (Gornewicz interview)

The UBC is struggling to develop the same vision and internal cultural practices and is slowly attempting to diffuse them widely throughout the organization.

The HERE local automatically has an immigrant membership base. Its internal organizational practices are neither particularly praiseworthy nor worthy of condemnation in relationship to this fact. While not in the "vanguard" like Unite for Dignity in its creative relationship to its immigrant membership base, neither is it backward in its general internal practices.

Which Unions Will Successfully Integrate Immigrants?

U.S. unions will all face immigration in the coming years, but their circumstances and internal conditions will vary enormously. Most will not face the same degree of immigration as has occurred in South Florida, and the specific mix of immigrants will be different: no other place in the country will likely have the vast majority of its immigrant population coming from Cuba. Nevertheless, immigration—much of it from Spanish-speaking countries in Central and South America and the Caribbean—will greatly affect virtually all areas of the United States in the years 2000–2030. So the South Florida experience should be useful in showing which unions are most likely to integrate the changing workforce.

Based on the Miami experience, we predict that unions will be most successful if they undertake a number of actions to prepare for in-migration from other countries. First, they will do better if they *think strategically* about this issue and put programs in place immediately, rather than reacting defensively after the immigration issue is forced upon them. Reactive programs are less likely to be well considered or effective than those planned well in advance. Locals that carefully assess their own memberships and surrounding environments will do better.

Second, unions will fare better if they conduct *internal education* to demonstrate the importance of immigrants and their communities to the future of the labor movement. The most successful education would be carried out over a period of time and would attempt to reach a large percentage of the local's membership, for most U.S. union members are sorely lacking in an internationalist outlook necessary for a progressive outlook (Nissen 1999).

Third, more successful unions will seek out and promote staff and *leaders who are ideologically committed* to cultural diversity, antiracism, and pro-immigrant policies. While unions cannot create progressive attitudes or "vision" among their staff and leadership, people with such attitudes can be recruited and developed as staff and leaders. Doing so creates a norm within the union that makes backward attitudes less easy to promote through the union organization.

Fourth, once unions have immigrants within their ranks, the more successful will consciously *develop leadership* from their ranks. This is frequently difficult to do because it challenges established lines of leadership progression, but it is crucial because representation at leadership levels is one of the only ways to ensure that change goes beyond superficial appearances.

Fifth, effective unions will strive to be *structurally flexible*, adapting existing structures to accommodate nontraditional types of workers, including immigrants. This is particularly important in unions with historically rigid structures, such as building trades craft unions. Extreme flexibility may even mean following immigrants into new economic sectors, as UNITE did in South Florida, at least for a time.

Sixth, unions with lasting results will *institutionalize changes* so that the daily practices of the union reflect immigrant input and participation. Simply relying on a leader with vision, as the UBC did in the 1980s, is very risky. The more immigrant-friendly practices can be made to permeate the union organization, the more likely they are to survive over the long run.

Seventh, successful unions will *develop both top-down and bottom-up strategies* for incorporating immigrants into both membership and leadership roles, particularly emphasizing the bottom-up component. The UBC attempts to impose top-down change illustrate the difficulties of relying on that approach alone.

Eighth, the most effective unions will develop practical ways for *intercultural interaction* in a nonthreatening union environment, creating organic working relationships and understandings. UNITE's experience in South Florida shows that this is possible, if difficult, and that it truly does create successful integration of different nationalities when practiced religiously. Finally, the most forward-looking union locals may be able to *involve themselves in immigrant community struggles* and larger battles for immigrant rights. Making this politically feasible is critical to making the U.S. labor movement a broader force for progressive social change and is part of a larger battle to get U.S. unions involved in community social movements.

The Miami experience suggests that unions implementing the above nine suggestions will more successfully organize and integrate immigrant workers. And that will be of crucial importance to the future of the U.S. labor movement and the future of workers throughout the world.

References

Asher, Robert. 1982. "Union Nativism and the Immigrant Response." *Labor History* (Summer): 325–348.
Bodnar, John. 1982. *Workers' World: Kinship, Community, and Protest in an Industrial Society, 1900–1940*. Baltimore: Johns Hopkins University Press.
———. 1985. "Workers, Unions, and Radicals." In *The Transplanted: A History of Immigrants in Urban America*, ch. 3. Bloomington: Indiana University Press.
Brecher, Jeremy, and Tim Costello. 1994. *Global Village or Global Pillage: Economic Reconstruction from the Bottom Up*. Boston: South End Press.

Browne, Harry, and Beth Sims. 1993. *Runaway America: U.S. Jobs and Factories on the Move*. Albuquerque, NM: Resource Center Press.

Brody, David. 1965. *Labor in Crisis*. Philadelphia: J.B. Lippincott.

Delgado, Hector L. 1993. *New Immigrants, Old Unions: Organizing Undocumented Workers in Los Angeles*. Philadelphia: Temple University Press.

Dubofsky, Melvyn. 1968. *When Workers Organize: New York City in the Progressive Era*. Amherst: University of Massachusetts Press.

Fenton, Edwin. 1975. *Immigrants and Unions, a Case Study: Italians and American Labor, 1870–1920*. New York: Arno Press.

Frundt, Henry. 1998. *Trade Conditions and Labor Rights: U.S. Initiatives, Dominican and Central American Responses*. Gainesville: University Press of Florida.

Gould, William B. 1977. *Black Workers in White Unions: Job Discrimination in the United States*. Ithaca, NY: Cornell University Press.

Greene, Victor. 1968. *The Slavic Community on Strike*. Notre Dame, IN: Notre Dame University Press.

Grenier, Guillermo. 1990. "Ethnic Solidarity and the Cuban–American Labor Movement in Dade County." *Cuban Studies* 20: 29–48.

Gutman, Herbert G. 1976. *Work, Culture and Society in Industrializing America*. New York: Random House.

Hall, Richard. 1969. *Occupations and the Social Structure*. Englewood Cliffs, NJ: Prentice-Hall.

Lane, A.T. 1987. *Solidarity or Survival?* Westport, CT: Greenwood Publishing Group.

Marshall, Ray, and Vernon Briggs. 1967. *The Negro and Apprenticeship*. Baltimore: Johns Hopkins University Press.

Marshall, F. Ray, Allan M. Cartter, and Allan G. King. 1976. *Labor Economics: Wages, Employment, and Trade Unionism*. Homewood, IL: R.D. Irwin.

Milkman, Ruth, ed. 2000. *Organizing Immigrants: The Challenge for Unions in Contemporary California*. Ithaca, NY: Cornell University Press.

Mink, Gwendolyn. 1990. *Old Labor and New Immigrants in American Political Development: Union, Party, and State 1875–1920*. Ithaca, NY: Cornell University Press.

Ness, Immanuel. 1998. "Organizing Immigrant Communities: UNITE's Workers' Center Strategy." In *Organizing to Win: New Research on Union Strategies*, ed. Kate Bronfenbrenner et al., pp. 87–101. Ithaca, NY: Cornell University Press.

Nissen, Bruce. 1999. "Alliances Across the Border: U.S. Labor in the Era of Globalization." *Working USA* 3, 1 (May–June): 43–55.

Olson, James S. 1970. "Race, Class, and Progress: Black Leadership and Industrial Unionism, 1936–1945." In *Black Labor in America*, ed. Milton Cantor. Westport, CT: Greenwood Publishing Group.

Parmet, Robert. 1981. *Labor and Immigration in Industrial America*. New York: G.K. Hall.

Poyo, Gerald. 1986. "The Impact of Cuban and Spanish Workers on Labor Organizing in Florida, 1870–1900." *Journal of American and Ethnic History*, Spring: 46–63.

Pozzetta, George. 1991. *Unions and Immigrants: Organization and Struggle*. New York: Garland Publishing.

PUMS. 1990 Census Public Use Microdata Sample—PUMS 5 percent Sample. CD available from the U.S. Census Bureau

Russo, Monica. 1993. "This World Called Miami." *Labor Research Review* 20 (Spring–Summer): 37–49.

Sassen, Saskia. 1988. *The Mobility of Labor and Capital.* Cambridge, UK: Cambridge University Press.

———. 1994. *Cities in a World Economy.* Thousand Oaks, CA: Pine Forge Press.

———. 1998. *Globalization and Its Discontents.* New York: New Press.

———. 2000. *Guests and Aliens.* New York: New Press.

Saxton, Alexander. 1971. *The Indispensable Enemy: Labor and the Anti-Chinese Movement in California.* Berkeley: University of California Press.

Stalker, Peter. 2000. *Workers Without Frontiers: The Impact of Globalization on International Migration.* Washington, DC: International Labour Organisation.

U.S. Census Bureau. 1981. *1980 U.S. Census, State of Florida.* Washington, DC: U.S. Census Bureau.

———. *Current Population Survey.* 1999. Washington, DC: U.S. Census Bureau. March.

Vaira, Peter F., and Douglas P. Roller. 1998. "Organized Crime and the Labor Unions." Memo prepared for the White House by the Chicago Strike Force. Html file: <URL: http://www.laborers.org/VAIRA_MEMO.html>, last accessed October 2001.

Primary Sources

Executive Board meeting minutes, HERE Locals 255 and 355, 1962–1988.

Internal membership documents for Dade County: Amalgamated Clothing and Textile Workers Union, 1980–1995.

Internal membership documents for South Florida: International Ladies' Garment Workers' Union, 1980–1995.

Internal memos and slide show: Ironworkers Local 272, 1996–2000.

Internal membership documents: South Florida UNITE, 1995–1999.

Membership lists of the South Florida Regional Carpenters Union: 1973, 1980, 1988. Ethnicity of union members was established by identifying Hispanic surnames from the original membership lists. The accuracy of this method for identifying ethnic representation within a population is supported by research on the Mexican American population by Karen Gottlieb, "Genetic Demography of Denver, Colorado: Spanish Surname as a Marker of Mexican Ancestry." *Human Biology* 55, 2 (1983): 227–234.

Personal interviews with: Andy Balash, David Bittle, Anita Cofino, Jose "Pepe" Collado, Angel Domínguez, Jorge García, Dave Gornewicz, Paco Jiménez, Gloria Lewis, Antonio Parker, Kenny Peckel, George "Buddy" Phillips, Monica Russo, Jorge Santiesteban, Walter Seidel, Ernie Taylor, Dewey Tyler. The Bittle, Jiménez, Peckel, and Taylor interviews occurred in 1988; with Collado, in 1988 and March 2000. All other interviews were in February or March 2000.

Part III

INTERNAL TRANSFORMATION

MOVING TOWARD SOCIAL MOVEMENT UNIONISM?

7

THE STRATEGIC CHALLENGE OF ORGANIZING MANUFACTURING WORKERS IN GLOBAL/FLEXIBLE CAPITALISM

FERNANDO GAPASIN AND EDNA BONACICH

This chapter focuses on the problem of organizing manufacturing workers in Los Angeles. We make no attempt to cover manufacturing throughout the United States, and some of our statements may not apply beyond southern California, though we suspect that they do. Los Angeles has several key characteristics as a center of manufacturing. First, it has the largest number of manufacturing workers—600,000–700,000—of any city in the country. Second, L.A.'s manufacturing workers are heavily immigrants, primarily from Mexico and Central America. Third, much heavy industry has left southern California, leaving behind mainly light, often nondurable manufacturing, which is spread out over thousands of small factories. The apparel industry is the largest manufacturing employer in the city and is, to some extent, emblematic of the character of L.A.'s manufacturing industries. Fourth, many of L.A.'s manufacturing workers are low paid; they constitute an important segment of the working poor. This appears to be a product of both the character of the industries that employ them and the ability of employers to take advantage of an immigrant, often undocumented, workforce.

According to the Los Angeles Alliance for a New Economy:

> Some 245,000 of the working poor [in Los Angeles], almost one-quarter of the total in the county, work in manufacturing industries. . . . Manufac-

turing workers in Los Angeles are much more likely to be working poor than in the United States as a whole. . . .While nationally only about 16 percent of manufacturing workers live below 200 percent of the poverty level, in Los Angeles about a third are working poor. (2000, 28)

This study also reports that Latinos constitute 26 percent of the total L.A. workforce but 42 percent of manufacturing employees. Moreover, they make up 75 percent of the working poor employed in manufacturing (p. 31).

Much has been written about the recent organizing successes of the Los Angeles union movement, including its progress in organizing immigrant workers (e.g., Milkman, ed. 2000). Los Angeles is often touted as the most dynamic center of union organizing in the country today. Yet if we look at the manufacturing sector, we find that hardly any organizing is going on. Indeed, union density in manufacturing has undergone a steep decline as sectors that were once organized have either left the state or the country, or have managed to reduce the level of unionization in their firms, while few or no organizing campaigns have been initiated to take up the slack. The great successes of the Los Angeles union movement have been either in the area of services or in the public sector. Both of these sectors have an advantage that manufacturing lacks—namely, they are unable or unlikely to move offshore to countries where labor costs are much lower. In addition, organizing in the public sector becomes easier than organizing in the private sector once the legality of such organizing is established. The public sector employer must assume a level of social responsibility and responsiveness to multiple constituencies that the private sector can completely ignore. While the Service Employees International Union (SEIU), in particular, has been able to achieve some amazing victories using brilliant strategies, it has not been faced with the harsher realities confronting the manufacturing industries. Not only are these industries solidly in the private sector, but they also face the threat or actuality of the movement of production offshore in the face of any efforts to raise standards for local workers, let alone union organizing. Moreover, the movement offshore is usually accompanied by the importation of low-cost goods that compete with local production and put a downward pressure on local labor standards.

A good deal of literature has recently appeared on the problems facing the U.S. union movement and its need to reform itself (e.g., Bronfenbrenner et al., eds. 1998; Mantsios, ed. 1998; Nissen, ed. 1999).

Unions have been losing ground over the last several decades, to the point where they represent only a small proportion of U.S. workers and an even smaller proportion of private sector workers. The movement has lost power along with membership and appeared to be caught in a downward spiral toward oblivion. The election of John Sweeney and the New Voice leadership of the AFL–CIO seems to afford the union movement a window of opportunity to reform itself. Much of the new literature focuses on the culture of AFL–CIO unions and the need for its reform. The criticisms include a lack of democracy, a lack of involvement on the part of the membership, and a legacy of exclusiveness particularly toward people of color, women, and immigrants. Suggestions have been made for developing a much greater emphasis on organizing, for involving the membership in an organizing program, for developing strong coalitions with the community, and, in general, for transforming the union movement into more of a real social movement.

These kinds of recommendations and the experiments with internal reorganization that they have fostered are all to be commended. However, they fail to address the way in which the economy is changing and the implications that these changes have for the possibilities of pursuing traditional union organizing drives. It seems to us that the union movement needs to engage not only in organizational self-criticism, for which there is abundant need, but also to develop a careful and thorough analysis of the ways that global/flexible capitalism is changing the nature of work. We believe that the changing nature of work poses a different kind of challenge to the union movement, in which taken-for-granted strategies of organizing may no longer apply. In other words, the crisis of the union movement is not only internal, but also external. While it is widely recognized that the legal and political environment for union organizing has become increasingly hostile (e.g., Friedman et al., eds. 1994), we believe that insufficient attention has been given to the changing work environment. It may be time to rethink the whole enterprise of union organizing, given the changing nature of work, at least in some key industries.

The Importance of Organizing in Manufacturing

Why should there be any special concern about organizing manufacturing workers? Surely the United States is becoming more and more of a service economy, with manufacturing a shrinking area of employment.

The growing power of SEIU attests to this shift. Why even bother with trying to organize U.S. manufacturing workers when it is so patently difficult and when the industries may shut down and move offshore if any headway is made by unions?[1] Putting limited organizing dollars into manufacturing seems like a bad investment with little likely payoff. This is the reasoning that is leading even the major manufacturing unions to shift to organizing in services and the public sector. If they want to survive as organizations, it seems to make little sense to beat this dead horse.

Here are the reasons why manufacturing is important. Following Marxism, the surplus value of capitalism is generated from the exploitation of workers in *production*. Production includes agriculture, manufacturing, and transportation. Service sector workers are also exploited in the sense that they are not paid the value that they produce, but they are part of the distribution system and are paid out of the surplus value that is generated in production (Harvey 1982).

Today, U.S. corporations exploit production workers around the world. They have shifted much of production offshore and import both the products and the surplus value that are generated. The dependence on global production can be seen as the ships laden with containers role into the Los Angeles/Long Beach harbors by the ton. Much of L.A.'s service economy is linked to global production—financiers, lawyers, advertisers, accountants, retailers, communications specialists—and many more occupations are busy coordinating the global economy and taking gigantic profits from it.[2] Many low-wage service workers, employed in hotels, restaurants, child care, house cleaning, and the like, provide personal services for these managers and professionals of the global economy. In other words, Los Angeles as a city sits on top of a system of global exploitation, and its wealth depends on the extraction of wealth from poorer nations. When public and service sector unions pressure capital to pay their workers more, they are, in part, asking for a bigger share of this stolen wealth. Let us repeat: these workers are also exploited, and it is perfectly legitimate for them to demand a bigger piece of the pie. That they should be paid a living wage is consistent with basic human rights and decency. Nevertheless, from an economic point of view, raises in their wages do not threaten the regime of capital accumulation in the same way as do raises in agriculture or manufacturing.

Manufacturing workers in the United States, or at least in Los Angeles, are in a peculiar position. They are generally the leftovers of a system of production that has partially moved abroad. They pick up the sectors of production that either cannot be moved or have not been moved yet. It is no accident that these sectors have a higher proportion of immigrant workers than any other sector and that these are typically among the lowest-paid workers. The very presence of immigrant workers reflects, in part, pressures to migrate that are generated by global capitalism. Moreover, immigrants are favored by the remaining domestic production industries because the industries are able to take advantage of the political disabilities, including the denial of full citizenship rights, of these workers.

It is important that unions pay attention to organizing manufacturing workers in Los Angeles for a number of reasons: they are crucial to capital accumulation and therefore represent an important front in the class struggle that cannot be neglected; they are among the most oppressed and exploited of workers and need the protection of unions to defend themselves; and they are linked to exploited and impoverished production workers in their industries around the world. Let us dwell for a moment on this last point. Many people on the left recognize the need for international solidarity in the class struggle (e.g., Moody 1997). Workers of the world need to unite, and the possibility of such coordination grows as capitalism becomes more and more of a global system. The ideal way to build international linkages is for each country to develop its own union movement, which then joins with others in confederation. Too often the AFL–CIO looks at unions in *other* countries, especially of the global South, with a patronizing disdain, as weak, nonexistent, or corrupt. The U.S. union movement needs to take a hard look at itself in terms of holding up *its* part of the tent. If manufacturing workers in the United States are unorganized, it becomes very difficult for growing unions in the global south to hook up with workers who are employed in the belly of the beast and who are a critical component to any sustained fight against global capital.

The Los Angeles Manufacturing Action Project (LAMAP) may not have said all of these things so explicitly, but we suspect that the leaders chose to focus on organizing in manufacturing for these kinds of reasons. It is a tragedy that LAMAP did not receive the kind of support necessary for it to have a chance at succeeding. And it is even more of a tragedy that nothing has arisen to take its place. We discuss this project in more detail below.

Global/Flexible Capitalism and the Union Movement

U.S. manufacturing unions became major power centers during a particular period of capitalist evolution. This was a period when Fordism was the dominant production regime, when factories were large, and when workers were employed on the assembly line. The height of Fordism coincided with the so-called social accord among capital, labor, and the state. From the 1940s to about 1970, a truce was worked out whereby the U.S. government supported the rights of workers to be represented by unions and to engage in collective bargaining with their employers. In turn, business accepted labor unions as part of the institutional framework in which they operated, on the assumption that unions brought labor peace and prevented the kind of revolutionary fervor that threatened capitalism during the 1930s. In 1949 the unions purged their communist members, ensuring that the union movement would see its interests as lying with an expanding U.S. capitalism, as opposed to operating on the principle that labor and capital were inevitably engaged in a class struggle over the fundamentally exploitative character of capitalism (Mantsios 1998).

The accord has fallen apart for a variety of complex reasons. U.S. corporations no longer feel that they need to work with unions and will use any means necessary to get rid of them. Rather than seeing unions as partners in economic growth that can be shared with all, they see unions as an anachronism whose usefulness has passed. To the corporations, a union is now viewed as a kind of protection racket, where an outside organization comes in and plans to make trouble unless the corporation coughs up some money. They deny that the labor movement has any grounding among the workers and use the capitalist-owned media to propagate an ideology that workers do not need or want unions; that unions are merely corrupt bureaucracies, and that the free market, unimpeded by organizations like unions, is the best means for workers to improve their lives. Any sense that unions are necessary partners in prosperity has completely disappeared.

The Democratic Party (and other previously social democratic parties in Europe) demonstrates the shift away from the social contract. While the party still depends on organized labor for money and support, it has joined the free marketeers on every important policy issue. The AFL–CIO continues to hope that the party will turn around and reestablish the social contract, but such a possibility is long past. The accumulation of capital is now seen to depend on globalization and flexible production, and no kicks and threats by the union movement are going to change this thrust. The golden age of labor relations (which, of course, was not so golden for people of color and women and for countries that faced U.S. imperialism and rabid anticommunism) is dead and cannot be revived.

Global/Flexible Capitalism and the Changing Nature of Work in Manufacturing

One of the major changes associated with the end of the old Fordist regime and the accompanying social contract is that the nature of work has been changing. Globalization and flexible production have brought some major shifts, such that the old model of a large factory with stable employment, where a simple strike can lead to the signing of a collective bargaining agreement, is too often irrelevant. This is certainly evident in the sprawling manufacturing sector of Los Angeles. Here are some of the changes that have occurred and their consequences for traditional union organizing:

Contracting Out

More and more firms are contracting out segments of their work. They keep the most profitable sectors and spin off the less profitable ones, engaging in arm's length transactions with their contractors. By contracting out, companies avoid having to maintain a stable workforce through periods of unemployment. Instead, they use contractors and employ workers on an as-needed basis, substantially cutting their costs and increasing their flexibility. Contracting out has created a large number of firms, many of them small, that work on a contingent basis. The employees who work in these factories are thus made into contingent workers because of the character of their employer.

Contracting out can be devastating to unions. First, the contractors are not profit centers, so that a union contract cannot win much for the workers. Second, the competitive nature of contracting means that big companies will favor nonunion over union contractors and will shift production away from any contractor where labor militancy is brewing. Third, workers in contracting shops have little job stability, and their low wages do not allow them to pay full union dues. These factors tend to create a large and growing nonunion sector among workers who are employed in contracting establishments. Many U.S. companies have learned that they can break unions by contracting out the work.

Offshore Production

U.S. companies have been shifting production offshore to sites where labor is considerably cheaper. This has taken two primary forms: direct investment and contracting. In the latter case, externalizing parts of the work has taken an extreme form as the new levels of fragmentation have become worldwide. The manufacturing sector has been especially hard hit.

The challenge of organizing a particular company's production empire is multiplied enormously when it is spread around the globe. Offshore contracting enables transnational corporations not only to shift production to whatever country offers them the best deal, lowest wages, and most politically controlled workforce, but also to avoid labor trouble in any particular location by shifting to another one. If workers try to organize, they are faced with the threat that their factory will shut down and leave. While this may sometimes be a bluff, it has happened too many times not to carry weight. Thus workers in a particular locale may win a hard-fought union battle only to find that their jobs have disappeared.

Another feature of offshore production, and of contracting out in general, is secrecy. In the apparel industry, for instance, transnational corporations (TNCs) typically hide their production sites, claiming that their contractors and subcontractors are a protected business secret. This means that workers and unions have no idea where their fellow workers are employed and must engage in significant expenditure of resources just to locate connected factories. Moreover, with flexible production, sites keep changing, so that the information problem is chronic.

Apart from secrecy, the shifting around of production meanings that the relationship with particular TNCs is unstable. A maquiladora may do work for more than one transnational corporation (TNC) and may have continuously changing relationships with those who send it work. This can make it impossible to organize all the workers for one particular TNC since the workforce keeps shifting depending on where the TNC sends work.

Obviously, not all manufacturing firms are equally mobile. Some industries and industrial sectors are more regionally tied. These less mobile sectors may afford easier organizing opportunities. Nevertheless, the challenge remains: how do we organize in those industries that *can* flee? Globally mobile industries and sectors are a growing component of the economy. They cannot be set aside as unorganizable.

Flexibility Taken to Extremes

All kinds of new devices keep getting invented so as to fragment the firm still further and externalize the employment relationship. Examples include treating workers, including industrial homeworkers, as independent contractors; employing temporary and part-time workers who are treated as the employees of the temp agency; and increasing the proportion of temporary and part-time workers who have lower wages than regular employees, no benefits, and no claims on the firm. Part-time and contingent workers now account for one-quarter of the U.S. workforce. They typically suffer from low wages and few benefits, reduced employment security, barriers to advancement, and low productivity. They are much less unionized than the rest of the labor force (Carre et al. 1994).

Employment of People of Color, Immigrants, and Women

The changing employment forms have been accompanied by a rise in the number and proportion of workers who are people of color, immigrants (including undocumented immigrants), and women. Marginalized, low-paying jobs tend to be filled by the segment of the population that is most denied any rights.

This creates all kinds of potential conflicts. First, old, unionized, often white male workers, find their good jobs evaporating, to be replaced by the more flexible (i.e., contingent) jobs both here and abroad, and there is a tendency to blame the less advantaged workers for their woes. In other words, racism and sexism are promoted under these conditions of shift. Second, the already unionized workers feel little inclination to reach out to the less advantaged workers because they are different in terms of race or gender or do not speak the same language. Moreover, the economic gulf among the sectors of the working class makes the prospect of organizing the new entrants appear daunting. Third, union officials tend to be entrenched and to come from the ranks of the old, mainly white male membership. They often do not understand the cultures and communities of the newer entrants and have difficulty repre-

senting their interests. Meanwhile, the disadvantaged workers sometimes do not trust the union leaders and feel that they do not have their
interests at heart.

Industrial Employment Instability

Many workers in the low-wage sector cannot count on any form of employment stability. Not only do they shift from job to job within a particular industry, but some also shift from one industry to another.[3] Women
move among garment work, domestic service, janitorial services in offices and restaurants, and street vending. Men shift from restaurants to
serving as day laborers in construction and other fields to gardening and
micro-entrepreneurial enterprises. These workers have truly been transformed into the ideal capitalist proletariat: unskilled hands that can be
moved to whatever job currently needs to be filled. We call them the
hyper-proletariat. They may be trained briefly to fill the specific needs
of the job, but no serious training is given to enhance their skills. However, the industries that employ them maintain their own coherence,
even though the workers themselves have little reason to maintain a
commitment to a particular industry.

Thus at the level of capital, industries such as apparel, shoes, and
toys each have their own competitive structure and their own community of key actors who know each other and form organizations to pursue their collective interests. The floating character of the low-wage
segment of these industries, in contrast, is disorganized as far as work is
concerned. Of course, these workers have various forms of community
organizations and affiliations, including church memberships, soccer
clubs, and clubs of origin and racial/ethnic identification. But the fluidity
of their work lives makes organizing around the job a temporary activity
at best. As a result, the social structures of community become more important to them than the social structures connected with the job.

The Challenge of Organizing in a New World Order

We need to develop means for pursuing the struggle for improving conditions for workers that look seriously at capitalism as it actually is, not
as we would like it to be. This means accepting the fact that the large
plant with a stable workforce is mainly a thing of the past, at least in
many sectors of manufacturing in Los Angeles. Most private sector

workers do not work in such facilities any more. They have a much more tenuous hold on their positions in the workforce. Many workers make such low pay that they live in constant poverty, on the edge of economic disaster. They lack the wherewithal to sustain a long and costly fight against their employer, and they have many other unmet needs. They are the working poor.[4]

The labor movement (including the traditional unions and other efforts by workers and community groups to organize) needs to develop new strategies for organizing and fighting in this changed environment. We believe that new models of organizing are called for under these changed conditions. We believe that the old systems of organizing, based on the ability to win a contract in a particular plant, may be obsolete for many hundreds of thousands of workers. If they are tried, the workers will almost certainly lose the struggle and their jobs as well. For this reason, we are calling for a complete and open rethinking of the old methods of the labor movement.

What Is the Goal?

Traditional unionism has typically focused on a limited goal—namely, redistributing some of the social surplus away from corporate profits and into the hands of workers. Even the New Voice rallying cry, "America needs a raise," speaks to this limited goal. However, from a Marxist point of view, two major questions can be raised. First, one can question whether this goal is systematically attainable in the long run, especially if increasing the workers' share interferes with capital accumulation (Harvey 1982). At best, certain sectors of the working class can carve out a favorable return for themselves, at the expense of other workers, by maintaining exclusiveness. That way they can take a bigger cut of the wage allocation, while other workers, here and abroad, take a lower cut.

Second is the question as to whether greater social equality can ever by achieved under capitalism or whether the working class (and the union and labor movements) should be planning methods for challenging capitalist institutions, including the fundamentally exploitative character of the wage relationship. It is our experience that while some union leaders consider themselves socialists, they also believe that raising socialist issues is wildly idealistic and impractical. They put off these questions to the indefinite future, believing that they need to win more power before they can be raised. Since they are losing power by the ton, the struggle for sheer organizational survival takes precedence. But maybe keeping the higher goals in mind is a prerequisite for being able to win some power. As long as unions play the game of operating solidly within capitalism, accepting its basic rules, unions as we have known them could be doomed. The crisis we face should lead us not to narrow our vision of what needs to be fought for, but to broaden it.

Strategic Possibilities

If the factory is no longer a workable unit of union organizing, then we need to consider changing the unit. This means either moving down or moving up from the factory. Let us consider both of these options.

Moving Down: The Worker as the Unit of Organizing

The basic idea here is to attempt to organize workers, regardless of where they are employed. This approach allows the union to serve workers who do not have stable employment in one factory and who move from one job to the next. It also means that the union cannot be destroyed if a particular factory shuts down. Just as capitalism has become more flexible, so unions must also adopt a more flexible approach to membership.

One way to develop this alternative approach is to build workers' centers that workers can join regardless of where they are employed. A center can be industry-specific or locationally based so that no matter in what industry workers are employed, they can join. Experiments with workers' centers are popping up all over the world, especially among low-wage, vulnerable workers, including immigrants. They can serve a number of functions: provide workers with an opportunity to form a community and share their grievances, present basic education in worker rights, develop political consciousness through low-risk actions, and work toward building a movement of workers that can win significant gains.

Worker-centered organizing overlaps with community-based organizing. Organizing is rooted in the community and is not limited to the worksite. Workers' nonwork concerns become relevent, including housing, transportation, education, health care, police harrassment, and immigration issues. Workers' centers can be concerned about the whole life experience of their members and not simply their work experience, central though this is. In other words, the goal is to build a *working-class* organization that attends to the multiple needs and demands for justice and change of the class as a class in conflict with capital on multiple fronts.

Unfortunately, experiments of this sort too frequently come into conflict with traditional unions. They involve the long-term development of workers, but unions often want quick results. U.S. unions mirror U.S. businesses in terms of their short-range vision. If a local has not won an election or signed a collective bargaining agreement recently, it is seen as a failure. This kind of mentality leads to what is known as hot shop organizing, and to shifting from traditional jurisdictions into easier fields, like services and the public sector. Similarly, the idea of noncontract struggles is too often foreign to traditional unions, even though they may reflect the workers' most pressing needs.

Workers' centers and similar nonstandard formations *could* show unions quick results in terms of growth in membership if the unions are open to treating such workers as union members. In practice, some unions will not allow membership unless the worker has a contract. Others have associate membership programs, under which the associates are treated as second-class citizens. Why will not unions open up their membership to workers who are not employed under traditional, stable conditions? We suspect that one important factor is that union leaders are reluctant to bring in large numbers of new workers who may be militant and who might vote them out of office. They are also afraid that the new members would demand the benefits won under the old regime (like health care and retirement programs), which would be expensive to the union. Moreover, the new members are likely to be both poor and people of color, that is, people who are different, in some sense, from the old leadership and who may insist on changes in the union's culture. In other words, unions have a sad tendency to become exclusive organizations that, despite the rhetoric of need for growth or they will die, do not really want to see their organizations change. Vested interests block their ability to open themselves up, even though doing so might greatly increase their membership and their political clout.

Moving Up: Multi-Union, Transnational, and Human Rights Coalitions

Moving up means expanding beyond the individual factories. Certainly many trade unionists and their supporters have long recognized this need. Organizing an entire sector at once can assuage the fierce antagonism of any single employer who otherwise fears he will be driven out of business because his wage bill will rise above that of his competitors. Similarly, some creative thinking has occurred among certain unions in terms of going after higher levels in subcontracting chains. SEIU's Justice for Janitors and the Farm Labor Organizing Committee (FLOC) are noteworthy in this respect. Still, in both these cases, the work is unlikely to be shifted offshore, opening up the possibility of actually winning multilayered organizing drives through pressure tactics.

Manufacturing unions, faced with subcontracting chains, need to expand their visions beyond U.S. borders. They need to think about organizing drives that bring together the entire global production system of a major brand name producer. The automobile unions have had some success in this kind of cross-border organizing, but they have not had to deal with the incredibly complex production chains and huge discrepancies in wages of such light consumer products makers as Nike, Mattel, or The Gap. Most unions probably cannot afford to take on such campaigns on their own, but the AFL–CIO, through its American Center for International Labor Solidarity (ACILS, also known as the Solidarity Center), may be able to coordinate such efforts.[5]

Forces that can be of significant aid in such cross-border campaigns are the newly emerged antisweatshop movement and the related, fast-growing, antiglobalization coalition of religious, environmental, student, and human rights activists. These groups can help to put intense pressure on companies that are faced with transnational union organizing efforts by demonstrating at their retail outlets and by threatening the high-priced reputation of the brands. While unions worked well with these forces in Seattle at the anti–World Trade Organization (WTO) demonstrations in 1999, the coalition showed strains at the demonstrations surrounding the 2000 Democratic convention in Los Angeles. By pushing for loyalty to Al Gore and the Democratic Party, the unions for the most part abandoned those groups that were demonstrating for all the social justice issues that the unions need to support if they are to be a force in this community.

Given the great variety of small manufacturing shops in Los Angeles and the fact that workers do not have stability of employment, the idea of multi-union organizing seems especially appropriate. Of course, this is not a new idea, and it was one that was tried with LAMAP. Still, the potential for strategic gains could be huge, if only unions could give up their jurisdictional squabbles and consider the greater good that could be gained from working together. Following the model of LAMAP, the Alameda Corridor (discussed below) appears to provide for rich possibilities for strategic collaboration. Not only is the Alameda Corridor an area where large numbers of manufacturing plants are located, but it also contains a number of residential communities with the workers who are employed in those plants. This allows for the coupling of industrial and community organizing. Furthermore, the ports of Los Angeles and Long Beach lie at the end of the corridor, and the unloaded goods are shipped up the corridor to feed the local industries and retail establishments, as well as to be prepared for shipment to the rest of the country. Both the International Longshoremen's and Warehousemen's Union (ILWU) and the Teamsters (IBT) could play a critical role in disrupting these flows if the manufacturing unions of Los Angeles decided to engage in a serious, broad-scale, multi-union organizing drive. Unfortunately, as LAMAP learned, petty power games and concerns over dividing the spoils made it impossible to bring various unions together to work closely enough to pull off such an ambitious project.

The Los Angeles County Federation of Labor (County Fed) seems like a likely place to start thinking outside of the standard limitations of the union movement. Despite great praise for this organization's accomplishments, it seems trapped in certain old-style limitations. The leadership is unwilling to provide a vision for its member unions, but instead is determined only to follow and support what those member unions are willing to do. If no manufacturing unions are willing to take on the difficult task of organizing L.A.'s manufacturing workers, then the County Fed is not going to do anything about it. This leads to a tragic stalemate in which it appears that there is no force willing to move.

How Do We Get from Here to There?

The social forces that impact the nature of work may also be forcing the need for another dramatic restructuring of the union movement, perhaps as dramatic as when the union movement shifted from a local to a national focus at the 1891 AFL convention, or when industrial unionism was created with the founding of what became the Congress of Industrial Organizations (CIO) in 1935. As suggested above, if such a restructuring is to occur, three sometimes conflicting strands must be tied together and be the foundation of the rebuilding: lifting the standard of living for all workers in the United States, linking different sectors of the labor movement (AFL–CIO unions/independent labor organizations/ community forces) around common economic and political demands, and building institutions that can create coordinated worker solidarity movements internationally. These strands must be tied together in four primary arenas: schools, legislatures, working-class communities, and workplaces. Here we address some of the internal constraints that exist in the American union movement and make such a dramatic change difficult.

Ideological Strains in the Union Movement

The challenges of restructuring the union movement are immense. The ideological perspectives that exist within the labor movement present a wide range, from collusion with the purveyors of neoliberalism and global capitalism to calls for the destruction of the capitalist system and imperialism (e.g., Larson and Nissen, eds. 1987). By no means are we suggesting that such a movement could or should become ideologically monolithic. But the internal conflicts present challenges for change in the union movement. For instance, multiple ideological points of view pushed the U.S. union movement from its narrow trade-centered perspective to industrial unionism in the 1930s. Obviously, plain old pragmatism was one point of view, and another advocated some variety of socialism. One addressed the practical needs of a union movement where the nature of work was shaped by Fordism and thus required a more practical way of organizing large groups of workers in order to build and maintain the union movement. The other viewed it as potentially a more effective way to organize workers, providing them the opportunity to improve their day-to-day lives while at the same time offering education around the need for class struggle and the overthrow of the capitalist system itself. Opponents within the union movement to industrial unionism (whole plant or sector organizing), in this case, were those union bureaucrats who believed that the maintenance of the trades orientation (organizing by trade skill) was the best way to preserve their own way of life and the well-being of what they perceived the trade union movement to be, that is, a constituency of white, relatively well-paid workers.

It could very well be argued that other theories about the labor movement influenced these changes (e.g., Larson and Nissen, eds. 1987), but three ideological perspectives seem most relevant. We call them pragmatic, leftist, and traditional, recognizing that each of these positions contains a range of views. Each of these perspectives has its own way of answering three key questions: (1) Who is the constituency of the labor movement? (2) Who are the friends, allies, and enemies of the labor movement? (3) What is the geographic scope of our concern for the working class? The answers that labor activists give to these questions help to define where they fit in relation to the three categories identified.

Labor Movement Constituency

For the pragmatists and the traditional unionists, the answer to the question of labor movement constituency would be union members. Leftists would define it more broadly to include all members of the working class. A recent example of how pragmatic unionists can broaden their constituency is when the AFL–CIO reversed its position on undocumented immigrant workers. Previously, the AFL–CIO had supported the employer sanctions provision of the Immigration Reform and Control Act. Leftists in the union movement undoubtedly played a role in influencing the dramatic shift of the AFL–CIO to a call for repealing employer sanctions and for full amnesty. But the shift occurred mostly because of the increasing numbers of immigrant workers in sectors of the economy that the union movement wished to organize. Thus, for pragmatic reasons, some trade union leaders changed their stance on organizing immigrant, and especially undocumented immigrant, workers.

Allies, Friends, and Enemies

Traditional unionists would probably define "good capitalists," some politicians, the Democratic Party, and community groups like the United Way as friends and allies. Leftists, communists, and socialists would be seen as the enemy. Leftists would probably view friends and allies from the standpoint of where various forces stood on various working-class reforms that would enhance the ability of working-class people to be more powerful. In a strategic sense, allies would be those social movements that objectively weakened imperialism. Pragmatic unionists would usually be viewed as potential allies. Enemies of leftists would be TNCs, the International Monetary Fund, the World Bank, and those parts of the state that supported neoliberal policies. More often than not, traditional unionists would also be seen as enemies of leftists. Pragmatists generally view friends and allies in a similar manner as traditional unionists, but they view leftists, communists, and socialists not so much as enemies as potential allies if the need arises for dedicated and disciplined ground troops, for example, when organizing is a priority of the union movement. Enemies of pragmatists are those forces that threaten the survival of union institutions.

During the social accord of the 1940s and post–World War II, when unions were viewed as part of the American way of life by corporate America, pragmatists did not view capitalism as their enemy. Even now, when it is obvious that the social accord has been abandoned by the capitalist class, union pragmatists are still hoping to reform the system to recreate the social accord. Traditional unionists, on the other hand, always view capitalism as a partner to their interpretation of unionism.

Geographic Scope

Leftists are concerned about workers around the world and seek to unite with their struggles against oppression. Pragmatists are more concerned about workers around the world from the standpoint of how cooperation can help to preserve the domestic union movement. In contrast, since they see their interests as tied directly to the success of U.S. corporations, traditional unionists will tend to support the international policies of the corporations as long as such policies do not directly affect domestic union interests.

These three ideological perspectives or categories persist today. The changes in the union and labor movement can often be measured by which perspective is dominant. Leftists have never been the dominant force in the U.S. union movement. Sometimes they have had more influence—for example, during the era when the Industrial Workers of the World (IWW or Wobblies) were a significant force, and within the CIO up to the purge of the eleven so-called red unions in 1949. One could argue that they had an effect on the 1995 change of leadership in the AFL–CIO, but certainly not as obvious an impact as in the previous two examples. Since the creation of the CIO, leftists have had most impact on the union movement when they were able to influence the direction of the pragmatic trade unionists like John L. Lewis. One reason they were able to influence pragmatist leaders was that they paid per capita dues or had citizenship in the union movement because of their leadership and influence in particular unions within the CIO. Their power in the CIO, and ultimately in the AFL–CIO, was greatly diminished when the eleven red unions were purged.

The post–World War II, McCarthy era saw pragmatists move much more deliberately toward the traditional union forces. This could be seen quite clearly in the isolation of leftists around their opposition to the Marshall Plan. Under the leadership of George Meany, the AFL–CIO institutionalized anticommunism within the union movement. Bylaws were written to exclude communists and other leftists from the union movement. The local central labor bodies of the AFL–CIO specifically excluded non–AFL-CIO bodies from affiliating with them. Internationally, the AFL–CIO became known as the labor arm for the enforcement of U.S. foreign policy. Domestically, during the Vietnam era, local central labor councils were threatened with losing their charters if they officially opposed U.S. policy in Vietnam.

For nearly two decades after the social accord was broken by U.S. corporations in the early 1970s, pragmatic and traditional unionists tried to breathe life into the already dead accord. Only when union density radically dropped, when unions were forced to engage in wide-scale concession bargaining, and when U.S. industry engaged in dramatic and rapid restructuring did pragmatists begin to look for a change in leadership within the union movement. In a less obvious, but not insignificant way, leftists also influenced the change in the union movement from business-as-usual service unionism to an emphasis on organizing to increase union density. The leftists included some people who had remained in the union movement even after the 1949 purges, but they were now joined by many younger, college-educated leftists who entered the union movement during the 1960s and 1970s. Many of these new union leaders were influenced by the antiwar and civil rights movements, solidarity movements in Latin America, and more generally, Marxism.

Union Transformation

These three different ideological categories may help to explain what is required for the union movement to make the necessary changes to ensure its own future. From a leftist perspective, the future of the union movement lies in the ability of local unions to transform themselves. Not only are 70 percent of the union movement's resources tied up in local unions, but it is at the local union level that everyday workers and communities interact with the union movement. We believe like others (e.g., Eisenscher 1999; Fletcher and Hurd 2000) that the shift from business unionism to social movement unionism requires a dramatic cultural, ideological, and structural shift in the U.S. union movement.

In order to understand the notion of culture change, unions must first identify their own culture and its roots. The dominant culture of the U.S. union movement today was largely framed during the McCarthy era. As mentioned above, the fear of leftists infiltrating the AFL–CIO was a major concern of AFL–CIO president George Meany. Anticommunism and the prohibitions against non–AFL-CIO organizations belonging to local central labor councils (the umbrella organizations for multiple local unions), discriminatory policies of unions, and the AFL–CIO's pro–Vietnam War stance all increased the distance between the union movement and other social movements that should have been close allies, for example, the civil rights movement and the antiwar movement. The distance between unions and community groups is an obstacle to the community unionism that is being advocated by the national AFL–CIO in its Union Cities program. Today, this gap has an adverse effect on the ability of the union movement to organize minority and immigrant workers and to move beyond its own white chauvinism.

One of the weaknesses of the AFL–CIO's current concept of strategic organizing is its focus on industries that cannot run away to avoid unionization, such as public sector or service industries. The flexibility of some manufacturing enterprises, like garment factories, to export jobs to nonunion or offshore locations scares the hell out of unions. Into this gap have stepped a number of independent and union-supported projects, such as LAMAP.

LAMAP was founded in 1992 by Peter Olney and other veteran organizers, in conjunction with, but independent of, unions. They envisioned the project as a community development strategy that could bridge multiethnic communities, incorporate the expertise and prestige of universities, and harness the organizing power of unions. LAMAP chose the Alameda Corridor as its organizing target. This is a 120–square-mile corridor that stretches from downtown Los Angeles to the Port of Los Angeles and contains almost two-thirds of the manufacturing jobs in the city. The Alameda Corridor is also a primary U.S. access point for the Pacific Rim. LAMAP pioneered large-scale, multiunion labor organizing drives that targeted whole industries rather than individual shops. It also designed a large-scale community component that included English as a Second Language (ESL) and citizenship (empowerment program) classes and mobilized college students to volunteer in the campaign.

However, LAMAP, like other creative programs such as the California Immigrant Workers Association (CIWA), died for lack of union support. Despite high praise from several international unions and acknowledgment from John Sweeney that LAMAP was a "model" for organizing, the unions would not support an "outside" entity like LAMAP, and it was forced to shut down in January 1998.

One of the consistent messages about the demise of LAMAP was that despite the ties that the founders of LAMAP had with unions, LAMAP was considered an outside organization. The common refrain from some unions was, "Why ask them to do what we should do ourselves?" This statement makes no sense within the self-contained post–World War II context of the U.S. union movement. To do what LAMAP wanted to do, a local union would have to decide that it was going to organize workers industrywide, across industries, and in their communities. Local unions would have to be able to draw upon resources that were large enough to field sufficient numbers of staff and rank-and-file organizers. They would have to have the desire, knowledge, resources, and structure to incorporate community issues and strategies into their own organizations and aid in the accomplishment of community as well as union goals. The local union would also have to be able to clear jurisdiction with unions that represented workers in other sectors. Clearly, very few unions by themselves could do what LAMAP was designed to do.[6] LAMAP attempted to be the vehicle by which unions could participate and learn how to organize in a flexible manufacturing environment, but it was also a way for unions to combine resources to accomplish the organizing of whole geographic areas rather than the traditional organizing of hot shops.

For some leftist trade unionists in the Los Angeles area and around the country LAMAP represented creativity and provided an indicator for what was needed for organizing now and in the future. Many of the staff of LAMAP found work in other unions and the Los Angeles County Federation of Labor (LACFL). The LACFL has attempted to encourage large-scale organizing, union partnerships in organizing, and the building of community ties. Some researchers (e.g., Gapasin and Wial 1998) have suggested that organizing on a broader scale could be facilitated only by central labor councils under the present union structure. But since most local unions are autonomous bodies and the central labor councils cannot force any local union to do anything, a central labor council has only the power of persuasion. In Los Angeles, manufacturing unions, with the exception of the International Association of Machinists (IAM), have not been answering the call to organize. And none of the manufacturing unions has the capacity to organize on the kind of scale that is needed. While overall union density in Los Angeles has climbed from 18.6 percent to 21 percent, density in manufacturing has dropped from 14 percent to 7 percent, with a steady downward trend. Obviously, this precipitous decline is due, in part, to corporate restructuring and the loss of heavy durable goods manufacturing, but the overall number of manufacturing workers in the city is growing, not declining.

The challenges are not new ones, nor have they been ignored before. For instance, the leaders of LAMAP had studied the Campaign for Justice in Santa Clara County, California. There unionists (one of whom is now one of the leaders in the LACFL) attempted to create a multi-union, community campaign to organize in the heart of nonunion, high-tech Silicon Valley. In brief, they could not muster enough local union participation and support to make the campaign viable. LAMAP attempted to build union commitment at the local and national levels. It employed research teams made up of academics and multi-union organizers, encouraged the collective participation of communities and unions, engaged in multiracial organizing, and activated a broad array of supporters to help implement its campaigns. But it could not leverage long-term union support.

As pointed out above, the AFL–CIO's central labor councils appear to be the logical institutions for the creation of such a broad restructuring of the union movement. Central labor councils seem like the place to coordinate resources so that "regional unionism" can occur. Regional unionism in one form or another has been suggested by others, such as author and University of Wisconsin professor Joel Rogers. In our interpretation, it could be focused on cross-sector, whole industry, or geographic organizing. It could develop worker centers, community issue-based organizing, or more orthodox collective bargaining strategies.[7] The key would be the ability to employ regional organizing strategies that effectively combated the regional strategies of the TNCs. At the risk of advocating one big union, it is not far-fetched to suggest that regional unionism could be extended to all of southern California and even to Mexico. There is only one problem. As Samuel Gompers stated, the AFL–CIO is a federation held together with a rope made out of sand. Since national and international unions are autonomous, the AFL–CIO can only attempt to persuade unions to coordinate their efforts. It cannot compel them.

The LACFL has done as good a job as possible, under the present structure, to coordinate and effect broad-scale organizing. This has been primarily the product of an aggressive SEIU region and an active HERE. It is also due to the ability of the LACFL to deliver in electoral politics to the benefit of the Democratic Party (Gapasin 2000). The ability to deliver politically has enhanced the prestige of the LACFL leadership and the willingness of local unions to follow its lead. But the limits of what the LACFL can do are defined by the structure of the union movement and its dependence on Democratic Party politics.

For most leftists this situation presents a difficult set of questions: How do we influence the transformation and restructuring of the union and labor movements without alienating the pragmatists? And how do we assert a political vision that is independent of the Democratic Party?

Some researchers on the topic of union transformation (e.g., Eisenscher 1999) have attempted to influence pragmatists by providing excellent organizational consulting that helps unionists to understand how the transformation to a more democratic, organizing-oriented union can help to create a more active union membership and make the union movement bigger. This method helps persuade unionists that they can serve their own interests of building the union movement by transforming. There are others who argue that until the union movement becomes antiimperialist, it will not be able effectively to fight for the long-term interests of the working class and thus the creation of independent community organizations is an important alternative to AFL–CIO unions. Still, some leftists believe that their role is to protect the positive actions of the pragmatists in the union movement, and they tend to discourage any significant criticisms or the development of outside organizations.

We believe that leftists have an important role to play in both the union movement and the broader labor movement. It is vital that leftists within the union and labor movements be able to assert a political perspective that is independent of the traditional American political parties. We also recognize that leftists have been historically weakened by traditional unionists and the hegemony of capitalist ideology. If the union and labor movements are to meet the challenge of neoliberal ideology, policies, and imperialism, these movements must consider whether they are adequately structured to meet the challenge. We think they are not. A key to this broad-based change will be the ability of the left and its allies to proliferate alternative visions of what the union and labor movements should look like. And while the main locus of change will be the local central labor councils, local unions, and their communities, a broad national discussion must also occur. Once agreed to, the implementation of such wide-scale transformation will require an unprecedented alliance between leftist and pragmatic unionists. But such an alliance is possible only if leftists can bring more to the table than their ideas. The leftists within the union and labor movement have to create space in existing structures where their ideas can take hold and influence outcomes. History has shown us that the ability to create movement within the union movement requires the power to move existing social systems. Simply stated, the left needs to have citizenship within the union movement, as well as in independent mass organizations within the labor movement. The left must create space in these movements in order to challenge the status quo and create a basis for forming the alliances that are necessary if the global challenge is going to be met.

Notes

1. For some of the difficulties, especially those facing the apparel industry, see Bonacich (2000).

2. We recognize that some authors on the left challenge the view that globalization has progressed that much (e.g., Moody 1997; Wood 1998). They claim that foreign direct investment (FDI) is relatively small in scope and limited mainly to other developed countries. However, limiting the discussion to direct investment misses the boat. The bulk of globalization is occurring through arm's length transactions: contracting and licensing. A good proportion of the billions of dollars' worth of products that flow into the United States each month is a product neither of FDI nor of independent exporters in other countries, but results from the activities of U.S. corporations in arranging production offshore.

3. We are not able to quantify the extent of interindustry movement among low-wage workers and base this statement on anecdotal evidence. We hope to be able to investigate the proposition more systematically at a later date.

4. California, in general, and Los Angeles, in particular, appear to be leading the nation in terms of the growth of the working poor. These are full-time workers who nevertheless make wages that are well below the poverty line. The living wage movement, which is gaining support around the nation, has sought to bring the families of the working poor up to the official poverty line—a sign of how low wages have sunk for this segment of the population (Los Angeles Alliance for a New Economy 2000).

5. Unfortunately, there is a long tradition of anticommunist activity by the AFL–CIO in its international work, especially in Latin America by the CIA-backed

American Institute for Free Labor Development (AIFLD) (Sims 1992). The New Voice leadership has made an impressive effort to alter this orientation, but damage was done that is hard to undo.

6. One exception has been the Unite for Dignity effort in South Florida. Here UNITE has been able to create organizing opportunities by taking a cross-sector and geographic approach to organizing mainly Haitian workers.

7. The Los Angeles Labor/Community Strategy Center and its Bus Riders Union (BRU) is an excellent example of how workers all across Los Angeles have been organized and mobilized around the community issue of mass public transportation, while at the same time antiracist and anti-imperialist politics have been integrated.

References

Bonacich, Edna. 2000. "Intense Challenges, Tentative Possibilities: Organizing Immigrant Garment Workers in Los Angeles." In ed., Milkman, pp. 130–149.

Bronfenbrenner, Kate, Sheldon Friedman, Richard W. Hurd, Rudolph A. Oswald, and Ronald L. Seeber, eds. 1998. *Organizing to Win: New Research on Union Strategies*. Ithaca: Cornell University Press.

Carre, Francois J., Virginia duRivage, and Chris Tilly. 1994. "Representing the Part-Time Contingent Workforce: Challenges for Unions and Public Policy." In Friedman et al., eds., pp. 314–323.

Eisenscher, Michael. 1999. "Labor: Turning the Corner Will Take More than Mobilization." In *The Transformation of U.S. Unions: Voices, Visions, and Strategies from the Grassroots*, ed. Ray M. Tillman and Michael S. Cummings, pp. 61–85. Boulder, CO: Lynne Rienner.

Fletcher, Bill, and Richard W. Hurd. 2000. "Is Organizing Enough? Race, Gender, and Union Culture." *New Labor Forum* (Spring/Summer): 59–69.

Friedman, Sheldon, Richard W. Hurd, Rudolph A. Oswald, and Ronald L. Seeber, eds. 1994. *Restoring the Promise of American Labor Law*. Ithaca: Cornell University Press.

Gapasin, Fernando. 2000. "The Los Angeles County Federation of Labor: A Model for Transformative or Traditional Unionism?" In *Central Labor Councils and the Revival of American Unions: Organizing for Justice in Our Communities*, ed. Immanuel Ness and Stuart Eimer. Armonk, NY: M.E. Sharpe.

Gapasin, Fernando E., and Howard Wial. 1998. "The Role of Central Labor Councils in Union Organizing in the 1990s." In Bronfenbrenner et al., eds., pp. 54–68.

Harvey, David. 1982. *The Limits to Capital*. London: Verso.

Larson, Simeon, and Bruce Nissen, eds. 1987. *Theories of the Labor Movement*. Detroit: Wayne State University Press.

Los Angeles Alliance for a New Economy. 2000. *The Other Los Angeles: The Working Poor in the City of the 21st Century*. Los Angeles: LAANE.

Mantsios, Gregory. 1998. "What Does Labor Stand For?" In Mantsios, ed., pp. 44–64.

———, ed. 1998. *A New Labor Movement for the New Century*. New York: Monthly Review Press.

Milkman, Ruth, ed. 2000. *Organizing Immigrants: The Challenge for Unions in Contemporary California*. Ithaca: Cornell University Press.

Moody, Kim. 1997. *Workers in a Lean World: Unions in the International Economy*. London: Verso.

Nissen, Bruce, ed. 1999. *Which Direction for Organized Labor: Essays on Organizing, Outreach, and Internal Transformations*. Detroit: Wayne State University Press.

Sims, Beth. 1992. *Workers of the World Undermined: American Labor's Role in U.S. Foreign Policy*. Boston: South End Press.

Wood, Ellen Meiksins. 1998. "Labor, Class, and State in Global Capitalism." In *Rising from the Ashes? Labor in the Age of "Global" Capitalism*, ed. Ellen Meiksins Wood, Peter Meiksins, and Michael Yates, pp. 3–16. New York: Monthly Review Press.

8

DOES NEOLIBERAL RESTRUCTURING PROMOTE SOCIAL MOVEMENT UNIONISM?

U.S. DEVELOPMENTS IN COMPARATIVE PERSPECTIVE

IAN ROBINSON

In the last decade, the concept of "social movement unionism" (SMU) has become popular among students of labor movements in countries such as South Africa, Brazil, South Korea, and the Philippines (Webster 1998; Scipes 1992, 1996; Seidman 1994; Adler 1996). More recently, analysts and activists have begun applying the concept to organized labor in the United States as a characterization of some unions within the larger movement (Dreiling and Robinson 1998; Johnston 2000), as an ideal toward which organized labor ought to be moving if it wishes to regain lost economic and political power (Goldfield 1987; Moody 1997), or both (Hurd and Turner 2000; Robinson 2000).

This chapter addresses a cluster of questions raised by these developments. What is SMU? Has there been a shift toward SMU in the United States in recent years? If so, has "neoliberal restructuring" (NLR) contributed to this shift?[1] If so, by what causal paths has it had this effect? If the U.S. labor movement is indeed moving toward SMU, how far is it likely to go in that direction? Can the experience of SMU in other countries help us to answer this last question? Conversely, can we generalize from the U.S. experience to the impact of NLR on the prospects for SMU in other countries?

The chapter is divided into four sections. The first offers a definition of SMU and identifies ten variables expected to affect strongly the likelihood that SMU will gain a dominant position in a national labor movement. The second section examines how NLR has affected most of these variables in the United States via three causal pathways. The third summarizes the evidence that the U.S. labor movement has moved toward SMU in recent years. The last section examines union political and economic opportunity structures—and labor movement political dynamics—in several other countries in which SMU is more fully developed in order to address our comparative questions.

SMU

What is SMU, and what conditions favor its development? Discussions of SMU generally focus on a set of characteristics that, taken together, distinguish it from other types of unionism. The ideal type of SMU sketched below would probably be endorsed by most of the analysts cited above, though it differs from the variant each analyst presents in various ways owing to the authors' focus on the particularities of SMU in the countries that they study.

A Definition

SMUs have a high degree of autonomy from the state, from political parties, and from employers. Membership in SMUs is largely voluntary, and such unions are very democratic in their internal political process. As a result, union leaders are highly accountable and responsive to the membership. This means that while union officers and activists have leading roles in shaping the culture of their unions, they do so in a close interaction with the membership. Leaders can lead, but they cannot dictate, oblivious to members' views on the issue at hand. Members, because they are not required to join the union to keep their jobs and because they believe that their leaders are accountable to them, typically have a strong sense of identification with, and ownership of, their union. This means that union leaders can usually rely on high levels of membership commitment to their union and the goals it pursues, provided there is continuity with the union goals and values that motivated members' decision to remain active in their union to that point. This high level of membership commitment gives such unions an unusually high capacity to mobilize their members.

SMU leaders and activists typically believe that their union—and the larger labor movement of which it is a part—has a social change mission, a *projet de société*, as the French put it. The changes sought are generally quite fundamental: the abolition of the colonial (or neocolonial or, more recently, neoliberal) subordination of the nation, the democratization of the political order, the abolition or radical transformation of the capitalist mode of production, the abolition of apartheid or other forms of oppression based on ethnoracial categories—all of these have been championed as core SMU goals in one country or another. In this sense, SMUs have a radical culture, one that is highly critical of very basic features of the existing social order.

SMUs typically claim to pursue these fundamental social change goals on behalf of very broad groups of people: all members of the subordinated nation (except collaborators in that subordination); all workers, regardless of race, ethnicity, religion, gender, or sexual orientation (and sometimes regardless of nation). Their radicalism may derive, in part, from their sense of how basic are the changes required to bring about a society in which these groups are not divided from, and pitted against, one another by those in power. Conversely, their inclusive sense of identity may derive in part from widespread popular support for the movement's social change goals. SMUs' unusually high inclusivity will be associated with intense efforts to organize very broadly. Where successful, these efforts result in high levels of union density and with it, the capacity to mobilize an exceptionally large percentage of the society.

An inclusive union collective identity, combined with commitment to a project of fundamental social change, implies particular kinds of strategies for building union power and harnessing it to advance movement goals. One source of this particularity is the constraint imposed by the fact that established economic and political elites—as defenders and beneficiaries of the existing social order—will usually have little genuine desire to cooperate with, or even tolerate the existence of, SMUs. As a result, SMUs search for allies among other social movements that share (some of) their social change goals. The breadth of the constituency that SMUs seek to represent and the hostility of governments and employers typically pull and push SMUs into community organizing as an important supplement to—or sometimes, early in the organizing process, a substitute for—workplace-based organizing.

Since SMUs cannot usually rely on supportive—or even neutral—states and employers but can count on high levels of membership commitment and strong community support, they typically rely heavily on large-scale mobilizations (e.g., mass strikes or mass civil disobedience) to advance their political agenda. They may be closely allied with a political party and support it between and during elections, but they seldom rely solely on electoral politics to advance their political agenda. Substantial energy is devoted to member and public education and "consciousness raising" with a view to building commitment to the movement's long-term goals. These efforts aim to change the popular culture within which economic and political elites must try to explain and legitimate their power and their policies. Success in this regard can yield important political gains even when the labor movement's political allies lose the election or, indeed, when there are no elections because the regime is authoritarian.

A key assumption that informs this account of SMUs is that union culture is one of two critical factors that shape the goals unions pursue and the strategies that they adopt in order to realize these goals. (The second factor is the environment in which unions operate, discussed below). Particularly important are the beliefs of union leaders (broadly defined to include activists at all levels) and members with respect to (a) for whom the union should speak and fight; (b) how the political economy works; (c) what the people that the union represents want and what is in their interests; (d) what conception of fairness and justice ought to govern the political economy; and based on all of these (e) what kinds of changes ought to be made to the existing social order.

Out of this complex of interrelated but distinct beliefs come the two key dimensions of union culture that lie at the heart of the analysis in this chapter: how critical the union is of status quo institutions (i.e., union moral economy), and how inclusive it is in terms of those whose interests and conceptions of justice it seeks to articulate and fight for (i.e., union collective identity).

This is perhaps the place to make clear that I assume that most (if not all) unions include members and leaders with a range of beliefs on these matters. Talk of "union culture," therefore, is really a shorthand way of speaking about the version of these beliefs that is dominant among the leadership of the union. This dominance may have been achieved by a democratic process, in which case the dominant culture will be closely aligned with the prevailing views among the majority of the union's members. In less democratic unions, it will reflect the views of whichever faction of union leadership was able to secure its control over positions of union power. In many cases, initial dominance will have been established by a process of political struggle, more or less open and fair. Once a particular position—or, more accurately, range of positions—is established as the dominant organizing assumptions under which decision-making will be made, open conflict may disappear. But differences of views are likely to continue and may resurface as conflict at moments when the dominant view is called into question by new developments in a union's environment.

Environmental Conditions Favoring SMU

The environment in which unions attempt to realize their goals is the second basic type of factor that favors (or disfavors) SMUs, relative to unions with very different leadership cultures, strategies, and action repertoires. Why are some environments more conducive to SMU than others? At root, the environment affects the dominant type of unionism in two distinct ways: first, by influencing the outcome of political struggles within unions that will directly determine the dominant union culture within particular unions, and, second, by differentially affecting the capacity of different types of unionism to advance their objectives by means of their characteristic strategies. I will first flesh out these causal pathways and then identify ten environmental variables that, by one or more of these paths, have a powerful impact on the variables that affect the prospects for a labor movement dominated by SMUs.

Paths from Environment to Dominant Union Type

Figure 8.1 shows that there are two distinct routes by which the economic and political environment can affect the dominant culture of a particular union. The first, indicated by the 1a beside the causal arrow, runs directly from environment to union culture. Variables of this sort that would favor SMU include economic outcomes, social structures, or political institutions that promote critical perceptions of the political economy while minimizing differences in worker collective identities that might be obstacles to an inclusive form of unionism. For example, if the real wages of unskilled workers (including union members) fall year after year, these workers are likely to become more critical of the system that generates these results, unless they can be persuaded that something else (e.g., a racial or ethnic scapegoat) is to blame.

Figure 8.1   **Paths from Environmental Conditions to Union Culture and Type**

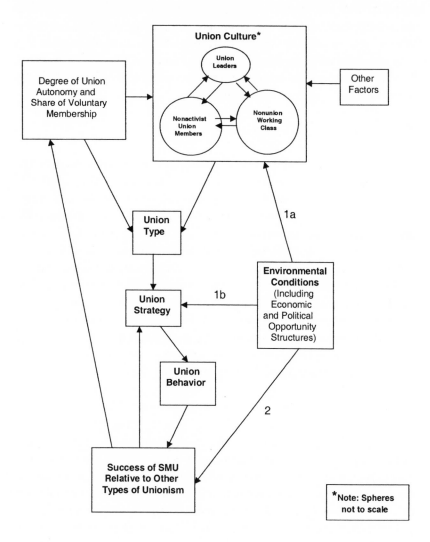

A less direct route to union culture, a side road of route 1a and designated 1b, runs from the environment to the declining effectiveness of traditional union strategies for realizing their goals and from there to innovations in union strategy that impact union culture over the longer run. This route involves changes in union behavior in response to shifts in the economic or political opportunity structure that unions face.[2] For example, changes in employer behavior may stimulate new organizing strategies that increase the diversity of union membership. A more inclusive union collective identity may, in turn, result as more women and people of color become union members and begin to fill union leadership positions.

The other basic pathway by which changes in the environment can affect the prevalence of SMU within a national labor movement, designated (2) in Figure 8.1, works through its effect on the viability of SMU in its competition with rival types of unionism. For example, if business unionism's characteristic strategies cannot secure the kinds of economic and political gains that workers have been encouraged to expect from such unions, space will be opened up within the labor movement for unions willing to adopt other strategies and corresponding discourses. In the United States, the greatest increase in the relative strength of industrial unions espousing a more inclusive and critical union culture occurred when the Great Depression rendered weak and ineffective the standard strategies and repertoires of the craft unions that championed an exclusive and uncritical "business unionism" culture.

Routes 1a and 1b are about how the environment affects the beliefs of union leaders, union members, and nonunion workers. By contrast, route 2 is about how the environment affects the kind of union that is most successful in organizing workers and realizing at least some of their economic and political objectives. The kind of unionism that "works best" in a particular political economy—given prevailing levels of state and employer repression, among other aspects of the economic and political opportunity structures—may not be the one whose culture most closely mirrors what most workers or even most union members would prefer. For example, it may be that most U.S. workers preferred something more critical and inclusive than the business unionism of the AFL's craft unions between 1885 and the 1930s. However, with employers and governments supporting the AFL in its struggles against more radical forms of "dual unionism" (e.g., the Knights of Labor, the IWW), AFL business unionism "worked best" in the sense that it alone survived on any scale prior to the 1930s (Voss 1993; Dubofsky 1969).

Ten Conditions Favoring SMU Dominance in Labor Movements

We can now restate the question posed at the outset of this section as follows: What environmental conditions are most conducive to SMU—and in particular to its characteristically inclusive collective identity and/or its relatively radical moral economy? We are interested in direct impacts (i.e., changes to people's beliefs) and indirect impacts (i.e., changes to union strategies) that are relevant to these dimensions of union culture. And we are interested in environmental conditions that enable more radical and inclusive unions to realize their objectives more effectively than rivals that are less inclusive and radical.

Direct Effects on Union Culture

Three environmental conditions will tend to produce highly *inclusive* union collective identities, other things being equal:

- Worker collective identities other than class (i.e., those based on language, religion, ethnicity, race, gender, etc.) are either of low political and social salience relative to class or, where their salience is high, they reinforce rather than crosscut class identity.
- State policies restrict or repress all autonomous unions and worker organizations equally, sending the message that all workers unwilling to comply with the state's denial of these rights are essentially the same, regardless of differences in skill, occupation, social status, etc.
- Economic changes adversely impact most or all wage workers (e.g., high levels of unemployment that drive down real wages even for those who remain employed, or economic restructuring that increases work intensity and reduces job security for workers in diverse strata and sectors).

The rationale for this list is that the three most powerful factors shaping collective identities in modern nation-states are (i) the constructions of identity promoted by powerful organizations (e.g., states, corporations, churches, social movements); (ii) state policies that group people in particular ways and treat them differently on that basis; and (iii) economic dynamics that result in growing differences in the lived experiences and life chances of people in different classes. The above conditions will minimize differences among workers that might make a highly inclusive definition of union collective identity more difficult to achieve.

Four conditions will strongly encourage the *radicalization* of union culture, other things being equal:

- Significant deterioration of most workers' standard of living over a prolonged period.
- An obvious connection between this deterioration and state policies, rather than factors that are seen to be beyond the control of the state—and by extension—union efforts to influence state policy (e.g., NAFTA was a very high-profile change in state economic policies).
- A state that excludes autonomous unions from political participation by repressing them (common in authoritarian regimes) or by regulating the competition for power so that organizations without extensive financial resources are marginalized (typical of low-quality democracies).
- An authoritarian state that responds to efforts by unions to make the regime more democratic with levels of repression that are high enough to alienate many but not intense enough to neutralize labor movement growth.

The rationale for the first two items on the list is that the legitimacy of the economic order, in the eyes of working people, depends heavily on whether it improves—or at least does not undermine—their standard of living. If the government is widely seen to be responsible for economic outcomes, its legitimacy will be more closely linked with economic performance than if economic problems seem to come from exogenous sources despite the best efforts of a competent government. Where both the economic order and the political regime are regarded as illegitimate, radicalism is broadened and probably also deepened. The third and fourth items reflect my assumption that the more the state excludes and/or represses workers, the less legitimate it will be with them and their organizations. The above conditions seem likely to delegitimate the political and/or the economic order among many workers, enabling unions that are highly critical of the existing order to organize broadly. They should also be able to secure high levels of commitment and mobilization from members animated by such an assessment of existing institutions.

Indirect Effects on Union Culture

What environmental conditions will have the greatest positive impact on the inclusiveness and/or radicalness of union cultures via their impact on union strategies? Conditions that encourage unions to put a larger share of their resources into organizing, particularly if that organizing is targeted on sectors and communities that have been underrepresented within organized labor, could result in a more inclusive union culture over the longer run. Conditions that cause a rapid loss of existing union membership and frustrate traditional organizing targets and methods are likely to be the most powerful spur to such a shift in the priority and focus of union organizing efforts.

As to radicalness, Marks (1989) has argued that conditions that frustrate union capacity to secure member economic objectives through collective bargaining tend to politicize unions. The politicization of the economy is itself a radicalizing step because it breaks with the illusion that market outcomes are either the product of "natural laws" or neutral institutions. State repression also forces strategic changes by unions that could have radicalizing effects. For example, in the 1980s, the black South African unions that made up COSATU developed a practice of rotating all leaders back to the shop floor. The policy was part of a strategy to increase the number of activists and shop stewards with leadership experience, to make it more difficult for the state to "decapitate" the union's most able leaders by putting a few top officers in jail. The initial motive was increased leadership "bench strength" to better cope with repression, but a side effect was to enhance the power of the shop stewards within these unions. While not always true, shop stewards are often more militant—and sometimes more radical as well—than top union leadership. Certainly this has been the case with the British shop steward movement (Coates and Topham 1988, 143–171). Doubtless, other connections could be made, but these will suffice for now.

Conditions that Give SMUs a Competitive Advantage

Under what conditions are SMUs most likely to prevail in competition with rival unions that are less inclusive and/or less radical? If the conditions considered under routes 1a and 1b, as indicated in Figure 8.1 are conducive, SMUs can count on high levels of allegiance and commitment from members. In that case, the question becomes whether SMUs are also able to secure the tolerance—if not support—of governments and employers. Usually such tolerance is secured only when labor movements have sufficient power to make the political risks associated with their repression too high. Under what conditions are SMUs able to gain sufficient power to raise the risks to such a level?

SMUs have the advantage of unparalleled mobilization capacity. Provided that they can harness it effectively to a sound strategy, this is the most important power resource that unions and labor movements (and other social movements) have. However, SMUs have at least two significant disadvantages. First, their greater inclusiveness renders them more vulnerable to divisions among their members that can weaken internal solidarity and make strategic coordination more difficult. The national (or sometimes subnational) political agenda can minimize or maximize these internal tensions. The optimal situation is one that minimizes such problems by focusing public attention on conflicts that unify rather than divide the membership.

Second and probably more important, the radical agenda of SMUs means that governments and employers often target them with higher levels of repression than rival union types. We have seen this dynamic recur in U.S. labor history, and the result was clear: SMUs were marginalized except during the great economic crisis of the 1930s. The lesson, it seems, is that even with superior mobilization capacity, SMUs will be crushed by the superior power resources of the state, employers, and more conservative unions—if they are willing and able to cooperate. Less inclusive and radical forms of unionism will thus come to dominate unless such a coordinated repressive response proves impossible.

What environmental conditions make such repression more difficult or costly? The optimal condition for the competitive success of SMUs is a situation in which state elites and/or employers are divided on whether to repress SMUs. This is most likely where the state elites are themselves deeply divided and where the balance of power among them is quite even. In such circumstances, the elite faction more open to alliance with organized labor may decide that the best way to win power is to strike a deal with the labor movement and use its mobilization capacity to tip the scales of national political power in its favor. Franklin Delano Roosevelt's second New Deal can be interpreted in this way, as can moments of "incorporation" in the history of other countries (Gourevitch 1986; Collier and Collier 1991). Public support for SMUs can also be important in restraining employers who might otherwise repress all unions or favor more conservative ones.

Of the twelve optimal conditions for SMU outlined above, two—the repression of autonomous unions and deteriorating economic conditions for most workers—were identified as important on two causal pathways. So we have ten different optimal conditions based on the above analysis. No doubt more could be listed, but I think these are the most important ones.

How NLR Affects Conditions Favoring SMU in the United States

How has the NLR of the last twenty years affected each of these ten variables in the U.S. case? Has it shifted their values closer to, or further from, those that are optimal for SMU? The left-hand column of Table 8.1 lists the ten variables discussed in the previous section: 1a–e are the five that affect union culture directly via path 1a in Figure 8.1; 1f–g are the two that affect union culture indirectly via path 1b; and 2a–c are the three that affect SMU competitiveness independent of union mobilization capacity via path 2.[3]

The table's center column summarizes the most important impacts that NLR has on each of the ten variables. The right-hand column of the table reflects my assessment of whether—and by how much—these changes move the variable in question closer to (or further from) the optimal value for SMU. Changes that are conducive to SMU are indicated by P (Positive impact) or PP (Very positive impact); changes that push in the opposite direction are indicated by N (Negative impact) or NN (Very negative impact); "0" designates little or no effect.

It would be tedious to run through the impacts reported in the middle column for all ten variables. However, three examples focusing on some of the less obvious variables may be helpful. As regards condition 1a, NLR has promoted increased labor migration from Central America to Mexico and the United States and from rural Mexico to urban and northern Mexico and the United States. In the past, great waves of immigration from diverse sources divided the U.S. working class in myriad ways, making the construction of highly inclusive forms of unionism more difficult, though certainly not impossible. However, a larger share of recent immigration stimulated by NLR comes from one linguistic group (Latinos) and reinforces an already substantial Latino population. The

Table 8.1

NLR Impact on Conditions Favoring SMU in the United States

Optimal conditions for SMU causal paths: 1a, 1b, and 2 variables under each path: a–g	NLR impact on conditions favoring SMU, Ceteris Paribus	Direction of NLR impact
1a. Collective identities crosscutting class among working people are weak.	Promotes more labor migration within United States and from Latin America, increasing Latino share of low-skilled workers.	P
1b. Substantial, sustained negative economic changes for most workers.	Exacerbates class inequalities of income and wealth and reduces living standards of most unskilled workers, especially men.	PP
1c. Moderate state repression of all types of autonomous unions.	Reduces union economic power and often worker rights and justifies reductions in legal or de facto worker rights.	P
1d. High level of state economic intervention.	Reduces visibility of state's economic role (except for high-profile trade pacts).	N
1e. Absence of democracy or low quality democracy.	Narrows scope and quality of democracy in several ways.	P
1f. Substantial decline in union membership and traditional organizing methods ineffective	Heavy loss of membership in manufacturing sector + increasing employer hostility to unions provoked by intensified international competition => dramatic decline in organizing victories and union density levels.	PP
1g. Substantial decline in union capacity to secure gains through collective bargaining.	Substantial decline in union collective bargaining power in most sectors, especially in trade-exposed manufacturing.	PP

(continued)

Table 8.1 *(continued)*

Optimal conditions for SMU causal Paths: 1a, 1b, and 2 variables under each path: a–g	NLR impact on conditions favoring SMU, Ceteris Paribus	Direction of NLR impact
2a. Political agenda minimizes intra–working-class cleavages.	Impact on political agenda limited, but effect is to raise profile of economic inequality and social justice issues.	P
2b. State and corporate elites cannot agree to repress SMUs.	Little if any impact on this condition.	0
2c. Economic and political power of traditionally dominant union type in sharp decline.	Highly detrimental to the traditional economic and political strategies of business unionism.	PP

Key: PP = Very Positive impact.
      P = Positive impact.
      0 = Little or no impact.
      N = Negative impact.
      NN = Very negative impact.

rapid growth of the Latino population makes it more difficult for unions to ignore or marginalize this group, and it makes immigration less problematic for inclusive unionism. Indeed, because of the cultural traditions and personal experiences that many Latino immigrants bring with them, the growth of this particular group may make a significant contribution to the development of more critical and inclusive unionism in the United States (see Milkman 2000; Grenier and Nissen 2000; and Johnston in this volume).[4] The impact of this trend is therefore expected to be positive, and the magnitude of the effect moderate.

On condition 1e, neoliberal policies narrow the *scope* of U.S. democracy by transferring policymaking power, *de facto* and *de jure*, from elected governments to unelected national (e.g., central banks) and supranational organizations (e.g., the IMF, WTO, and transnational corporations [TNCs]). Neoliberal policies also reduce the *quality* of democracy by exacerbating income and wealth inequalities, resulting in increased inequalities in political power (Robinson 1993a, 1995).[5] This effect is particularly powerful in the United States, where income and wealth inequality translate into larger inequalities in political power than in polities where private political advertising and campaign contributions are more restricted. By significantly reducing the scope and quality of U.S. democracy, neoliberal policies shift the environment in which unions operate *toward* the type of exclusionary polity in which SMUs tend to thrive, other things being equal. How far in this direction NLR shifts the U.S. polity is open to debate. I think the change will probably result in a moderate improvement in conditions for SMU.

Finally, consider condition 2c. NLR has reduced the economic bargaining power of all types of unions throughout the world by increasing international capital mobility and, often, unemployment.[6] Declining economic bargaining power is a blow to any union, but it is particularly costly for business unions because their culture encourages members to judge them mainly on their ability to deliver services and economic benefits. Moreover, because they typically have less mobilization capacity than the other three types of autonomous, voluntary unionism, business unions are liable to suffer greater losses in economic bargaining power given the same adverse change in the economic opportunity structure.[7]

We can see the difference by comparing data from the United States and Canada. Business unionism was the dominant tendency in the United States when the labor movement encountered NLR, while social unionism was (and remains) the dominant type in Canada (Robinson 1993b).

Table 8.2 summarizes data for the two countries on (1) union density,[8] (2) union member volunteerism levels,[9] (3) union societal mobilization capacity,[10] (4) the "relative involvement" of workers in strikes,[11] and (5) trends in the real compensation–productivity gap in the manufacturing sector.[12]

Row 3 of the table indicates that the Canadian labor movement had roughly three times the societal mobilization capacity of its U.S. counterpart in 1989 (i.e., after a decade of NLR). Row 4 shows us that as a share of the total workforce, eight times as many Canadians were involved in strikes as their U.S. counterparts in 1989. The higher level of mobilization in Canada was not enough to prevent the deterioration of the growth rate for real compensation relative to productivity growth in the 1980s and 1990s. However, the gap grew 85 percent faster in the United States than in Canada in the 1980s and 48 percent faster in the 1990s.

Canada–U.S. differences other than the dominant type of unionism (e.g., differences in economic policy or labor market regulations) might help to account for the differences in Table 8.2. Space does not permit a systematic accounting of such factors to assess the relative contribution of each. However, it is indisputable that NLR had a devastating impact on the economic bargaining power of the dominant form of unionism in the United States. As a result, NLR created space for the emergence of more inclusive and critical forms of unionism, particularly in the United States.

In sum, in the United States, NLR shifts the values of eight out of our ten variables toward the optimal conditions for SMU. For five of these variables, this positive impact has probably been substantial. I therefore conclude that NLR has altered environmental conditions in the United States in ways that favor a shift toward a more inclusive and critical form of unionism, *ceteris paribus*. Are there other factors that partially offset or completely overrode these tendencies? The best way of assessing this is to look at the actual behavior of U.S. unions. If they fail to move toward SMU as we would expect, then there must be other factors that are counteracting the effects of the conditions discussed here. If unions do move in the expected direction, then any countervailing effects must be relatively weak.

Evidence of a Shift toward SMU in the United States

If NLR has indeed helped to shift the culture of many U.S. unions toward SMU since 1979, we should be able to see evidence to this effect along one or more of the pathways that are supposed to connect NLR to

Table 8.2

Union Power Resources and Economic Power under NLR for Canada and the United States

Measures of union power resources and economic power (year of data)	Canada	United States
1. Union density (percent of workforce) (1999)	33.3	13.9
2. Member Volunteerism (percent of members) (1989)	26.5	18.6
3. Union societal mobilization capacity (percent of workforce) (1989)	9.1	3.0
4. Relative strike involvement (striking workers per 1,000 in workforce)		
1960–1969	23	17
1968–1973	45	24
1974–1979	59	15
1980–1988	33	4
5. Real compensation–labor productivity growth rate gap, manufacturing sector (mean annual percent change)		
1961–1971	–0.9	–1.0
1971–1981	0	–1.1
1981–1988	–1.3	–2.4
1991–1997	–2.1	–3.1

Sources: (1) Canada: Statistics Canada (1999); United States: Hirsch and Macpherson (1999); (2) World Values Survey Association (1994); calculated by author; (3) Calculated from data in (1) and (2); (4) Shalev (1992): 102–132; (5) Canada: 1961–1988: Courchene (1989): 11; business sector data, 1989–1998, Statistics Canada, *The Daily* (January 18, 2000) at http://www.statcan.ca/Daily/English/ 000118/ d000118c.htm; service and manufacturing sector data, 1991–1997, Statistics Canada, *The Daily* (July 21, 1998) at: http://www.statcan.ca/Daily/English/980721/ d980721. htm#ART2; United States: Manufacturing sector output per hour, annual change (Series ID : PRS30006091); business sector output per hour, annual change (Series ID : PRS84006091); manufacturing real hourly compensation (Series ID : PRS30006151); business sector real hourly compensation (Series ID PRS84006151)—all available from Department of Labor, Bureau of Labor Statistics, Selective Access Website: http://www.bls.gov/sahome.html.

such an effect. Changes traced along those pathways should be reflected in the beliefs and behavior of most U.S. unions and, through them, in the dominant coalition of affiliates that determines the culture and policies of the AFL–CIO.

Path 1a (NLR => Union Culture)

Path 1a runs from changes in the political and economic experiences of workers to changes in their sense of who shares their fate and/or in their perceptions regarding the justice of the existing order and the possibility of something better. Changes in worker—especially union member—

beliefs drive (or permit) parallel changes in union leadership culture, which then reciprocally influences members and workers insofar as the union has significant discursive capacity.[13]

Neoliberal policies were responsible for a substantial part—probably more than half—of the decline in the real wages of unskilled workers in the United States during the 1980s and most of the 1990s.[14] In an effort to maintain family incomes (among other things), more and more women have gone into the workforce over the last two decades. While a growing number of women are highly skilled, most still went into the poorest paying and most "contingent" private service sector jobs. There they worked beside the growing share of the workforce from the minority communities. The result was that NLR was associated with the growth of women and minority workers as a share of the total workforce.[15]

Most union membership growth in the neoliberal era took place in the service sector—particularly its public component—where women and people of color make up an unusually large share of employment. As a result, these groups also grew as a share of all union members in these years.[16] These union members are likely to favor more inclusive unions because they are members of groups that have long been excluded from, or marginalized within, unions. The growth of these groups within unions also implies that a growing share of union members are concerned about racial, ethnic, and gender forms of oppression as well as class oppression and are active in social movements that address these issues. Their subordinate position in these status hierarchies, as well as in segmented labor markets, makes them particularly likely to have a critical stance on the existing political economy. These workers should therefore support a more inclusive and critical union culture in the unions where they constitute a growing share of union membership.

Path 1b (NLR => Union Strategy => Union Culture)

Path 1b in Figure 8.1 runs from NLR-induced declines in the effectiveness of traditional union organizing and collective bargaining methods to strategic innovations with important (though often unforeseen) implications for union culture. The first widespread union response to NLR was an acceleration in the pace of union mergers.[17] The second strategic response—which some unions undertook in the 1980s but most did little about before the mid-1990s—was a substantial increase in the share of union funds allocated to organizing. Such increases were usually accompanied by increased experimentation with nontraditional approaches to union certification (e.g., finding ways to bring sufficient pressure on employers that they would consent to have certification determined on the basis of a card count rather than a National Labor Relations Board [NLRB] election and increased reliance on member volunteers in organizing campaigns) (Bronfenbrenner 1997).

The wave of union mergers in the neoliberal era meant that by the late 1990s, most large U.S. unions were no longer craft or industrial unions but "general" (or conglomerate) unions encompassing workers with varying skills in many different types of jobs and sectors. Craft and industrial unions relied on common workplace skills and/or common product markets to create a "community of interest" among their members, making solidaristic collective action easier.[18] In general unions, however, this particular source of common identity, interest, and solidarity does not exist across all members. As a result, general unions must either accept a lower level of mobilization capacity or develop alternative sources of worker collective identity and commitment. In an insightful paper on the Service Employees International Union (SEIU), Piore argues that

> despite its appearance as a conglomerate union, *par excellence*, it is actually an organic organization; its diverse membership and its staff have a single identity and share a sense of common purpose and mission. The source of that identity is not their industry or occupation, but it is a moral vision. That moral vision comes out of the fact that the union is really composed of low income workers . . . and the helping professions. The professionals have a commitment to the people they serve which goes beyond mere income or career, and the low income workers, actual and potential, are an important part of the group to whom that commitment extends. (Piore 1989, 29)

Such a culture does not naturally arise within general unions. The largest general union in the United States for many years was the Teamsters, and its dominant leadership culture was—and is—very different. The new collective identity that emerged in the SEIU in the 1980s was promoted by John Sweeney and the new staff that he hired at the international level after becoming international president. But leaders could not have developed the union's identity in this direction had not the membership been open to such a possibility by virtue of its work and other experiences. Most Teamster members are not found in the "helping professions," and this might make it more difficult for equally motivated leaders to promote a culture like that which Piore found in the SEIU.

Increasing the share of union resources devoted to organizing poses a much greater political challenge for business unions than mergers with smaller unions. Under traditional business unionism, most union dues went to pay staff to provide collective bargaining, grievance, and other "services" to members. On average, the largest U.S. unions get about 75 percent of their operating income from member dues (Masters 1998, 14–15). So if union expenditures on organizing are to be substantially increased, either member dues must be increased commensurately or members must be persuaded to continue paying dues at past levels while performing more "services" for themselves. It is likely to be difficult to persuade union members to do either if they have long been encouraged to think that top union officials and staff receive salaries far in excess of the members' because they have special skills that enable them to provide services that members could not supply for themselves.[19] While implicit, the idea that union spending and general operations ought to be shifted from a "servicing" to an "organizing" model is thus an assault on the self-understanding of business unions. Member resistance to efforts to move in this direction since 1995 makes it clear that officers and staffers are not the only source of resistance in unions to moving beyond business unionism (Hurd and Turner 2000; Lopez 2000).

If servicing is to be turned over to members, they must not only be trained in the skills required to perform these tasks, but they must also be motivated to substantially increase their volunteer contributions to their fellow members and their organization. Member volunteers must also be found in large numbers to assist in local organizing drives, for reasons made clear by Richard Bensinger, director of the Organizing Institute from its founding and of the AFL–CIO's Department of Organizing from 1995 until 1998:

> We will never have nearly enough professional organizers to organize the number of workers we need to [if union density is to be increased]. And if you look at history, that's not how the labor movement organized in the first place. We need more staff, and unions need to hire more organizers. But I think unless the fight is owned by the membership, and unless union leaders give ownership to the membership, it won't succeed.[20]

What is to motivate the much higher level of member volunteerism required? Bensinger links member volunteerism with "ownership," meaning increased membership control over union decision making. On this analysis, the challenge posed by a large-scale increase in union organizing investment goes beyond business unionism's self-understanding as a service-providing business to its internal power relations. Levels of member ownership and control are not the only factors affecting levels of membership commitment and volunteerism. Significant increases in member "ownership" have taken place in AFL–CIO affiliates where there were significant rank-and-file insurgencies—notably the United Mine Workers (Benson 1999), the Teamsters (La Botz 1999), and the SEIU (Johnston 1994). However, improvements in the quality of democracy have been quite limited in most U.S. unions over the last twenty years (Early 1999; Parker and Gruelle 1999; Benson 1999).[21] Yet union membership volunteerism levels increased substantially in the 1980s, as we saw in Table 8.2. This implies that members are motivated by something other than increased rank-and-file and/or local control, such as an increased sense that the union is fighting for things about which the volunteers care deeply.[22]

Successful organizing creates further challenges. Suddenly there are new voting members in the locals into which they are organized—or entirely new locals in some cases—and new leaders have been forged in the organizing process. If the organizers made heavy use of volunteer organizing committees in the workplace or member mass mobilizations or if they built support for the organizing drive within the community by stressing the union as a force for inclusion and social justice, then these new members will have expectations about how their union should be run that are very different from business union traditions. The case of SEIU Local 399 in Los Angeles is a good example. Its campaign succeeded in organizing 90 percent of the janitors working in the city's commercial jurisdiction by the early 1990s. In 1995, these new members became the political base for a dissident slate calling itself the Multiracial Alliance, which successfully challenged the established leadership of Local 399 (Williams 1999).[23] Such a dynamic is likely where new members are folded into existing locals with a different ethnic composition or a different culture from that of the new members brought in through organizing.

Path 2 (NLR => SMU Competitiveness)

This brings us to Path 2 in Figure 8.1: the impact of NLR on the competitiveness of SMUs vis-à-vis rival union types. While one business union—the United Food and Commercial Workers (UFCW)—was able to achieve membership growth rates similar to those of the SEIU through a combination of mergers and organizing in the 1980s, it was the exception that proved the rule. In the neoliberal era, the organizational bastions of business unionism suffered dramatic membership losses. In aggregate, U.S. union membership fell from 21 million in 1979 to 16.2 million (about 23 percent) in 1998. However, the growth of the public and private service sector unions masked much more severe losses by the unions in which business unionism had always been strongest—the building trades and the Teamsters.[24] Industrial unions whose dominant leadership culture had been conservative at birth (e.g., United Steel Workers [USW] and the International Union of Electrical Workers [IUE]) or had drifted toward a more conservative and exclusive vision in the 1980s (e.g., the United Auto Workers [UAW]) were even harder hit.[25]

These dramatic declines had two important effects. First, in the neoliberal era, for the first time, the membership of the public and private service sector unions combined exceeded that of the building trades and manufacturing sector unions that had dominated the AFL–CIO and the labor movement since the 1930s.[26] This mattered because several major service sector unions were gravitating toward more inclusive and critical positions. The SEIU under John Sweeney was the most important example, but this trend can also be observed in the Hotel Employees and Restaurant Employees (HERE) since John Wilhelm became international president in 1998. The largest public service sector union, the American Federation of State, County, and Municipal Employees (AFSCME), had been closely allied with and shaped by the civil rights movement since the 1960s and so had less far to move than the SEIU or HERE.

The second important effect was on the industrial unions, which became increasingly critical of the direction in which the national and international political economies were moving as economic restructuring cut deep into their manufacturing sector membership due to plant closings and downsizing. Some also became more inclusive as they sought to organize outside their traditional industrial jurisdictions to recoup their membership losses.

In short, the leaders of most service sector and industrial unions responded to the traumas of the neoliberal era by becoming more inclusive, more critical, or both. The leaders of most building trades unions did not change to nearly the same degree, but their influence within the labor movement and the AFL–CIO was greatly reduced by their membership losses in conjunction with the growth of the service sector unions.

Impact on AFL–CIO Strategy and Action

The dominant culture within the AFL–CIO reflects the beliefs of the leaders of the dominant coalition of its affiliates, albeit with some qualification (due to the desire to keep dissenters within the federation) and with a lag time (owing to the difficulty of displacing entrenched leaders at the federation level). How were the cultural changes in key affiliates and the shift in the balance of political power among different elements of the labor movement reflected in the behavior of the AFL–CIO? Between 1979 and 1994, there was little evidence of the cultural and strategic changes occurring in key affiliates at the federation level, where the president, Lane Kirkland—George Meany's right-hand man in the 1970s—led the old guard coalition that determined AFL–CIO strategy.

The old guard's strategy for recouping its economic and political power reflected business unionism's logic of collective action. Kirkland and his supporters did not believe that they could significantly increase union membership through organizing under the existing labor law because it was too easy for employers to frustrate union organizing efforts and employers were increasingly hostile to unions. Increasing union investment in organizing was therefore a waste of money in the absence of labor law reform. In any case, most union members (customers, from the business unionism standpoint) would be unlikely to increase their commitments (dues, volunteer time) to their unions in a period of declining union economic bargaining power and performance (diminished services). Favorable changes in labor laws were expected only if the Democrats regained control of the White House (while maintaining control of both houses of Congress) and a significant segment of the business community supported the reforms.

The old guard's political strategy flowed from these premises. To put Democrats back in the White House and secure Congress, union funding of the Democratic Party was dramatically increased in the 1980s.[27] To persuade business to support labor law reform, the federation argued that unions would become partners with employers in increasing the international competitiveness of their firms. Labor's contributions to this partnership were supposed to be greater flexibility in workplace organization and the promotion of productivity-enhancing employee "voice" (AFL–CIO 1985).[28]

The strategy seemed to have a chance of success when Bill Clinton was elected president in 1992. The Dunlop Commission was quickly constituted and mandated to explore the potential for a labor–business compromise on labor law reform. Both houses of Congress were, of course, still in Democratic hands. Two years later, however, the strategy lay in ruins. Unions had divided on the advisability of the kind of compromise that the Dunlop Commission was exploring,[29] and few employers seem interested (Dunlop Commission 1994).[30] Thus, the old guard's strategy for securing labor law reform came to naught, and on its own premises, U.S. unions were doomed to continued decline in the absence of such reform. Meanwhile, President Clinton put more effort into pushing NAFTA through Congress—over the strong opposition of organized labor—than into fighting for any policy backed by the labor movement. The coup de grâce was the loss of the Democratic majorities in the House and Senate in the November 1994 elections.

The bankruptcy of the old guard's survival strategy was the precipitating cause of the New Voice slate's challenge in the AFL–CIO executive board elections of October 1995 (Meyerson 1998). However, the success of this challenge reflected the longer-term impacts of NLR on many AFL–CIO affiliates over the previous fifteen years (Early 1999). The other critical factor was the government-mandated, first-ever postal ballot election that enabled a reformist slate led by Ron Carey to capture the international executive board of the Teamsters in 1991. In one fell swoop, the largest and most powerful union in the business unionist camp shifted into the New Voice camp, making the New Voice victory possible.[31]

How much more inclusive and critical have the policies of the AFL–CIO become since the triumph of the New Voice slate? Three good *indicators of increased inclusiveness* are (1) an expanded commitment of scarce union resources to helping unorganized workers by investing a larger share of the union budget in efforts to organize them and by fighting for public policies that will benefit those who are not members; (2) new policies signifying that women and minorities are welcome in unions and reducing barriers to their rise to top leadership positions; and (3) new policies that aim to change the rules of international competition in ways that will benefit workers in all countries, as opposed to those that aim to make U.S. workers more competitive relative to all other workers. The most important changes along these lines since 1995 have been the following:

- A substantial increase in AFL–CIO spending on organizing and institutional and strategic innovations (Union Cities, Union Summer, rethinking the role of central labor councils, etc.) aimed at encouraging affiliates to make similar commitments; promoting new organizing strategies; and disseminating organizing "best practices" widely and quickly (Cooper 1996; Early and Cohen 1997; Moberg 1997; Weinbaum, ed. 1999; Nissen and Rosen 1999; Rathke 1999).
- An immediate increase in representation of women and minorities on the AFL–CIO executive board.[32]
- An intense focus on the need for real increases in the minimum wage at all levels and legislative successes in realizing this goal (Greenhouse 1996b, 1997).
- An important shift in the AFL–CIO's long-standing position on illegal immigration, arguing for "blanket amnesty for illegal immigrants and an end to most sanctions against employers who hire them" (Greenhouse 2000).
- A post–Cold War "foreign policy" that rejects both protectionism and the neoliberal model of globalization in favor of an alternative approach to global economic regulation centered on increasing protections for core worker rights throughout the world; this goal to be pursued through a combination of building protections for such rights into trade agreements and efforts to promote cross-border solidarity among unions (AFL–CIO 2000a; Blackwell 1997, 1998; Shailor 1998; Cohen and Early 1999; Babson 2000; Frundt 2000).
- Increased outreach to students, university faculty, clergy, and social movement organizations with whom the AFL–CIO shares— and seeks to expand—common ground on its new domestic and international policy priorities (Greenhouse 1996a, 1996d, 1999b; Russo and Corbin 1999; Acuff 1999).

Union criticalness can pertain to the economic order, the political order, or both. On the economic side, deeper critiques focus on systemic features—capitalism per se or neoliberal forms of market economy— rather than more superficial features such as particular labor law provisions, corporate actors, or trade law provisions. A more critical stance will directly challenge corporate power, rather than accommodating to it by endorsing "producer alliances" in the name of superior U.S. competitiveness. It will also stress the common interests of working people over and above their particular employers and the sectors in which they work. On the political side, a more critical standpoint might go beyond particular candidate positions and party policies (e.g., campaign finance rules) to raise questions about how democratic the society as a whole is (e.g., lack of democracy in workplaces, narrowing scope of political democracy under neoliberal rules, and expanding Supreme Court and Federal Reserve powers). Another important question is how efforts to communicate such critiques and to build support for them are organized. Do these efforts focus primarily on electoral politics, with political parties and candidates as the principal vehicles for their articulation? Or are increased resources put into education and consciousness-raising by the unions and their social movement allies? The most important changes along these lines at the AFL–CIO since 1995 have been the following:

- Development of a discourse that targets TNCs as the principal architects of the neoliberal agenda instead of treating them as partners in a competition with corporations (and workers) from other countries (Blackwell 1997).
- Federation endorsement of and (for the first time in 1998) financial support for Jobs with Justice (JwJ), which pioneered the development of networks among union and community activists in most major U.S. cities to engage in solidaristic support work for other unions and to promote policies such as living wage campaigns that advance the interests of nonunion as well as union workers (Early and Cohen 1997; Mort, ed. 1998).
- Increased participation in efforts to develop international and cross-movement consensus on alternatives to the neoliberal model of globalization (e.g., the AFL–CIO now participates in efforts of the Hemispheric Social Alliance and challenges IMF and World Bank policies, as well as trade policies such as NAFTA and the World Trade Organization [WTO]) (AFL–CIO 1999, 2000b, 2000c).
- A shift in how union political money is spent: more is now devoted to member education about the issues and getting out the vote, rather than handed over to the Democratic Party (Greenhouse 1999a; Hurd and Turner 2000), and since the 2000 presidential election, the AFL–CIO has announced that it will be giving

much more money to Republican candidates who support at least some of labor's top legislative priorities than has been the case for many years (Wallison 2001).

These lists suggest that the AFL–CIO has become considerably more inclusive and somewhat more critical since the election of the New Voice slate in 1995. It is therefore accurate to say that the mainstream of the U.S. labor movement has moved *toward* SMU, even though it remains a long way from the full realization of this ideal type, and some unions have moved very little at all.

NLR and SMU in Other Countries

How far toward the ideal type of SMU is the dominant tendency within the U.S. labor movement likely to move over the next ten years? To get some purchase on this question, it is useful to consider developments in the labor movements of other countries that are further down the road to SMU. The Canadian case highlights some of the internal political difficulties associated with the shift toward SMU in the labor movement that, despite important differences, is most like that of the United States. Comparison with the paradigm cases of SMU highlights the fact that the United States is unlikely to move all the way to the kinds of conditions that are optimal for the dominance of SMU, particularly if current efforts to reverse the declining political power of the U.S. labor movement begin to bear more fruit.

Canada and the Internal Politics of Labor Movement Cultural Change

The Canadian labor movement emerged from World War II with a dominant culture that was highly inclusive and moderately critical of the decentralized Fordist mode of economic regulation that prevailed in Canada between 1945 and 1979 (Robinson 1993b). In the 1970s and 1980s, something like Scandinavian social democracy represented the dominant conception of a morally superior political economic order within the Anglo-Canadian wing of the movement (Smith 1990).[33] The actual Canadian political economy was seen as a long way from this ideal, but progress in this direction had been made in the 1960s and 1970s as the labor movement grew in strength, public ownership (particularly at the provincial level) increased, and the welfare and regulatory dimensions of the state expanded. The fact that the system was trending in a progressive direction, from organized labor's perspective, offered a kind of meta-legitimation that began to erode when these trends were reversed in the neoliberal era.

This began to change in the 1980s, however, as this progress was first halted and then rolled back at an accelerating pace. Table 8.3 indicates that the economic opportunity structure (EOS) facing Canadian unions deteriorated accordingly. So, too, did the economic power of Canadian unions in the neoliberal era.[34] In this context, union leaders' perceptions of the economy—and the direction in which it was moving—became increasingly critical in the 1980s (Kumar and Ryan 1988). They also became more critical of the political system that generated the policies that produced these economic results. At the same time, the movement became more inclusive as efforts to organize the unorganized intensified and attention to racial and gender issues within the movement increased.

As the mainstream of the movement became more critical and inclusive, it moved further toward the ideal type of SMU. Compared with the business unionism culture dominant in the U.S. labor movement, the Canadian labor mainstream was closer to SMU before the neoliberal era began.[35] By the 1990s, it also had even greater economic impetus to move in this direction than its U.S. counterpart (Table 8.3), and it had greater power resources with which to attempt to make the transition (Table 8.2).

We might therefore expect the Canadian shift toward SMU in the 1990s to be relatively rapid and unproblematic. But this has not been the case. Aggregate statistics notwithstanding, the shift toward SMU in Canada has occurred at different rates from different baselines in different unions. As a result, cultural differences and strategic disagreements among Canadian unions are probably greater today than they were in the Fordist era. This has resulted in intensified conflict among Canadian unions over two issues: basic political strategy and the principles that ought to regulate inter-union competition.

Inter-union competition has increased because Canadian unions' first response to the massive loss of traditional members due to NLR was to merge with other unions that shared a similar union culture. The result was that most of the largest unions in the country were transformed from industrial unions with fairly clear jurisdictional boundaries into general unions with members in a wide range of sectors and occupations.

Table 8.3

Elements of Union EOS, Canada and United States, 1969–1998

Elements	1969–1978		1979–1988		1989–1998	
	Canada	United States	Canada	United States	Canada	United States
1. Real interest rates (short term, mean annual percent)	–0.8	–0.3	4.9c	5.0	5.9e	1.2f
2. International capital mobility (private foreign investment: private domestic investment)	—	11	—	12	—	22
3. Exposure to international competition (manufacturing imports: domestic manufacturing)	.69	14	.72	.28	.90d	40f
4. Manufacturing employment > (mean annual percent change)	1.31a	0.5	0.95	–0.2	–0.16	–0.2
5. Economic growth rate (real GDP, mean annual percent change)	4.4	3.0	3.1	2.6	1.7	2.6
6. Employment growth rate (mean annual percent change)	2.7b	2.2	1.8	1.8	0.9e	1.4
7. Unemployment rates, official (mean annual percent)	6.5	5.9	9.3	7.3	9.7e	5.9
8. Public debt/GDP (percent) (1978)	35.5 (1988)	27.1 (1997)	70.2	33.2	1.01	47.0
9. Social security transfers/GDP (percent)	9.4	10.2	11.6c	11.0c	14.9e	12.2e
10. Changes to basic labor laws and/or enforcement	PP	NN	0	N	N	0

(continued)

Table 8.3 *(continued)*

Elements	1969–1978		1979–1988		1989–1998	
	Canada	United States	Canada	United States	Canada	United States
11. Changes in public opinion on (a) role of state,	O	N	N	N	N	O
and (b) union legitimacy	N	NN	O	P	P	P
12. Changes in employer (a) power resources,	P	NN	N	N	N	N
and (b) strategies	N	NN	NN	N	N	O

Sources: Row 1: OECD, Historical Statistics 1960–1981, and Historical Statistics, 1960–1995; Row 2: OECD, Historical Statistics 1960–1981, and Historical Statistics, 1960–1995; Row 2: Berman Press, Business Statistics of the United States, 1997; DOC, BEA, Survey of Current Business, May 1999, and StatCan, Canada = s International Investment Position, 1998; Row 3: Mean Annual Share of Imports, UN, Yearbook of International Trade Statistics, 1969–84 and UN, International Trade Statistics Yearbook, 1985–97; Rows 4 and 5: OECD, Historical Statistics, 1960–1994 and OECD, Main Economic Indicators, September 1998; Row 6: OECD, Economic Perspectives, 1995 and OECD, Main Economic Indicators, September 1998; Row 7: OECD, Statistics on the Active Population, 1974–1994 and OECD, Main Economic Indicators, September 1998; Row 8: Congressional Budget Office, http://www.cbo.gov/ showdoc.cfm?indix=1063&sequence=0&from=7, and StatCan CANSIM for consolidated (fed, provincial, and territorial) public debt, and OECD, National Accounts, 1969–1997 (1998) for GDP; Row 9: Social Security transfers, Congressional Budget Office, http://www.cbo.gov/ showdoc.cfm?index=1063&sequence=o&from=7; for GDP; DOC, BEA, http://www.bea.doc.gov/bea/dn/0898nip3/maintex.htm, and OECD, Historical Statistics, 1960–1981 (1983) and Historical Statistics, 1960–1995 (1997). Rows 10–12: author estimates.

Key: PP = Major positive change
P = Minor positive change
0 = No change
N = Minor negative change
NN = Major negative change.

a 1971–1978.
b 1970–1978.
c 1980–1989.
d 1989–1993.
e 1989–1995.
f 1989–1996.

Thanks to Cedric DeLeon for compiling the data in this table.

The fact that these new general unions espoused increasingly distinctive visions of unionism made them more like rival labor federations than they had ever been before. This greatly increased the potential for—and the reality of—competition among unions.

The most intense conflicts occurred when workers disaffected with one union went to another and asked to join it. In the late 1980s, eastern fisheries workers originally affiliated with the UFCW asked to join the then new Canadian Auto Workers (CAW), precipitating a very bitter clash that resulted in new CLC rules relating to "raiding" and new processes for dealing with such cases in the future. Then in 2000, eight Ontario SEIU locals made the same kind of request of the CAW, by this time the largest private sector union in the country as a result of aggressive organizing and mergers with a number of smaller unions (e.g., the United Electrical Workers) from the left of the Canadian labor movement spectrum. The SIEU charged that the CAW had violated the CLC's new rules regarding how to proceed in the matter, and the CLC agreed. After refusing to give the SEIU "its" members back, the CAW was expelled from the CLC in the spring of 2000 (Oziewicz 2000), though one year later a deal had been worked out that permitted its readmission (CAW 2001; SEIU 2001).

The CAW has also led the push to put more resources into an extraparliamentary political strategy, which, while not abandoning labor's traditional alliance with the New Democratic Party (NDP), supplements it with sustained efforts to forge alliances with other progressive social movements. The CAW, together with the Canadian Union of Public Employees (CUPE), Canada's largest union, has also advocated the escalating use of mass civil disobedience tactics—notably, the Days of Action in Ontario—both as a method of educating and increasing the commitments of members and as a way of challenging the power of neoliberal governments where the NDP no longer seems capable of mounting an effective parliamentary opposition (Gindin 1997; Benzie 2001).

Support for social movement coalition building, in particular, has precipitated conflicts with other unions, whose leaders have also traditionally been strong supporters of the NDP and the traditional strategy building political power primarily through an alliance with a political party. Thus there have been running skirmishes on a wide range of issues between the CAW and CUPE, as champions of the need for change, and a group of unions sometimes called the "Pink Paper" group. Led by the USW and the UFCW, this group has argued that extraparliamentary strategies of social movement alliance tend to rob the NDP of badly needed resources at the very moment when it most needs them to rebuild its flagging political power. This conflict came to a head in the immediate aftermath of the 1993 federal election, when the NDP lost most of its seats in parliament. The deep split among its major affiliates has forced the CLC to take an in-between position on the issue, with the result that there is no overall labor movement position on the matter at this time.

In short, both internal political dynamics and the impacts of changes in union economic opportunity structures brought about by NLR vary greatly from one union to another. As a consequence, unions have not all responded to the challenges and opportunities of NLR by moving in the same direction at the same pace. Most building trades unions, as in the United States, have clung tightly to their traditional business unionism culture. Some unions that had strong business and social union elements in deep tension with one another—notably the UFCW in Canada, owing to the U.S.-driven merger of two unions with very different cultures—moved firmly into the social unionism camp in the 1990s. Some, such as the USW, moved toward SMU as regards their inclusiveness and critical stance on the neoliberal economy but held firmly to their traditional social democratic political strategy. Others began to advocate a new combination of electoral and extraparliamentary strategies.

The result has been intensified conflict and fragmentation, which have weakened the Canadian labor movement's capacity for inter-union coordination and solidarity. The imperative of keeping as many unions as possible on speaking terms within the same federation slows the pace of the shift toward SMU at the CLC level. This dynamic of fragmented and uneven change in union culture and strategy is unlikely to change in the foreseeable future. It seems likely that we will see the same kinds of dynamics in the United States as its labor movement moves toward SMU from its more distant business unionism baseline. The recent announcement that the UBC would leave the AFL–CIO should probably be interpreted in this light (see endnote 35).

Three SMU-Dominated Labor Movements

In addition to the internal political difficulties of maintaining some semblance of labor movement solidarity while moving toward SMU, there are also external structural constraints on how far movement in this direction is likely to go. In its paradigmatic form, SMU is a rare and paradoxical phenomenon. It is rare even where the dominant union culture is favorable (i.e., highly critical and inclusive) because it can reach its strongest form only where most of the ten optimal conditions discussed above and summarized in Table 8.4 are found. It is paradoxical because to the degree that SMUs are successful in realizing their political and economic reform goals, they usually become less critical of the new political economic order that they have helped to build. Put another way, as their social change projects advance, SMUs usually shift toward the kind of social unionism that one finds in the social democratic countries of Western Europe (i.e., still highly inclusive but now much more integrated into the existing political economy, and so much less critical of it).

Table 8.4 compares the optimality of the ten variables most important to the prevalence of SMU in the paradigm cases of Brazil, South Korea, and South Africa with the United States and Canada for the 1970s and 1990s. The conditions in the 1970s contributed greatly to the emergence of SMU as the dominant form within the labor movements of Brazil, South Korea, and South Africa in the 1980s. In the 1970s, the average number of optimal conditions met in these countries ranged from 8.0 in Brazil and South Korea to 7.0 in South Africa. By the 1990s, SMUs dominated the labor movements of each country. A good deal of the credit for the democratization of each of these countries must go to these labor movements (Adler and Webster 1995). But democratization eliminates optimal condition 1e and, less obviously, tends to undermine condition 1c.

What independent effect did NLR have on these countries? As already indicated, the natural tendency of these labor movements, given their political successes in the 1980s (or, in South Korea's case, 1990s) would have been to become less critical, shifting them toward the kind of social unionism found in Canada and social democratic Europe. However, NLR significantly increased the "exclusion" of unions in the economic sphere, despite their recent gains in political power. High levels of labor movement political power mitigated the negative economic impacts that NLR would otherwise have had on the standards of living of most workers and the economic and political power of their unions, but its impact on these things was still negative. The result is indicated by a small or large positive impact for conditions 1b, 1g, and 2c in these

Table 8.4

Change in Ten Conditions Favoring SMU

Country	Direct impacts on union culture via beliefs					Indirect impacts via strategies		Impacts on SMU competitiveness with other types			Total plus factors[a]
	1a	1b	1c	1d	1e	1f	1g	2a	2b	2c	
Brazil, 1970s		1.0	1.0	1.0	1.0		1.0	1.0	1.0	1.0	8.0
Brazil, 1990s		1.0		0.5			0.5	?	1.0	0.5	3.5
South Korea, 1970s	1.0		1.0	1.0	1.0	1.0	1.0	1.0		1.0	8.0
South Korea, 1990s	1.0	1.0		0.5			0.5	?		1.0	4.0
South Africa, 1970s	0.5	0.5	1.0	1.0	1.0		1.0	0.5	1.0	0.5	7.0
South Africa, 1990s	0.5	0.5		0.5			0.5	0.5	1.0	0.5	4.0
United States, 1970s		0.5				1.0	1.0		1.0	1.0	4.5
United States, 1990s		0.5		1.0		1.0	1.0	0.5	1.0	1.0	6.0
Canada, 1970s				1.0		0.5			1.0		1.5
Canada, 1990s		0.5		0.5		0.5	0.50	0.5	1.0	0.5	4.0

Optimal Conditions:

1a Collective identities crosscutting class among working people are weak.
1b Substantial, sustained negative economic changes for most workers.
1c Moderate state repression of all types of autonomous unions.
1d Negative changes (1b) clearly linked to well-known state economic policies.
1e Absence of democracy or low-quality democracy.
1f Substantial decline in union membership and traditional organizing methods ineffective.
1g Substantial decline in union capacity to secure gains through collective bargaining.
2a Political agenda minimizes intra–working-class cleavages.
2b State and economic elites divided, but important component opposes repression of SMUs.
2c Economic and political power of dominant union type is declining significantly.

Values:

1.0 = Strongly positive, that is, the optimal condition in question is close to fully satisfied.
0.5 = Weakly positive, that is, the optimal condition is not fully satisfied, but some positive influence.

[a]This system of accounting is obviously very crude since it admits of only three possible values while the reality would have a continuous range, but it has utility as a first approximation.

countries. Thus NLR contributed to maintaining a degree of criticalness in the dominant union culture that might not otherwise have existed.

NLR, as mitigated by relatively pro-union states, was less harmful to the economic and political power of the dominant type of unionism in the 1990s than was the repression of authoritarian states in the 1970s. So conditions 1g and 2c are less favorable to SMUs than they were in the 1970s, even though they remain mildly favorable in the 1990s. I expect the same pattern to hold for worker living standards, as indicated by the value of condition 1b in the 1990s relative to the 1970s. However, this needs to be confirmed or rejected based on a careful examination of the data on worker living standards—something I have not yet undertaken. Whatever the findings of such research, at least two additional conditions became less optimal for SMU in the 1990s. All together, then, the average number of variables on which conditions for SMU were close to optimal was halved in these three countries between the 1970s and the 1990s, despite—not because of—NLR.

The SMU culture of the three paradigm cases was forged in a period when conditions were extremely favorable to this kind of unionism. Even after two decades of NLR, conditions in Canada and the United States remain much less favorable than they were in these three countries in the 1970s, when SMU was forged there. NLR alone will not be enough to push the conditions in Canada and the United States to such a high level of optimality. For example, while it does erode the scope and quality of democracy, NLR is unlikely to result in authoritarianism of the sort that prevailed in all of the paradigm countries in the 1970s. Thus it seems unlikely that SMU will ever become as strong in the United States or Canada as it did at its high point in the paradigm countries, and if it does, it will not be due to NLR.

Conclusions

NLR has changed the conditions in which U.S. unions operate in ways that have promoted a shift away from the long dominant business unionism toward SMU. NLR is not the only factor responsible for this shift; the changing demographics of the workforce are also very important, and these are only partly determined by NLR. Nor do structural changes dictate any particular response from unions. The business union culture remains strong within some unions and may continue to do so whether or not it "works" as measured by union membership growth or power.

For some leaders, any other orientation is unacceptable, even if the failure to change seems likely to doom the organization to decline or even obliteration.

For this reason, the shift toward SMU, in the United States as in Canada, is likely to be both less universal and less rapid than many who favor SMU would hope. These changes may also be associated with new kinds of conflict among U.S. unions that may be as intense as any we have witnessed in a long time. The process of change will not be politically simple or easy for the U.S. labor movement. Still, NLR has given unionists powerful reasons to be more critical of the political economic order; it has accelerated structural changes that create major incentives for unions to move toward a more inclusive collective identity, and it has undermined the effectiveness of the strategies employed by the business unionists, who are most strongly opposed to a shift toward SMU in this country. It therefore seems likely that the overall trend toward SMU will continue. While no guarantee, such a shift is probably the best chance that the U.S. labor movement has for increasing its political and economic power under NLR.

How much farther will the U.S. labor movement move in this direction? It is not possible to say at this point. However, one important indicator of progress in this direction will be the spread of the policies currently advocated by the AFL–CIO to more of its affiliates. Another will be the degree to which U.S. union leaders are willing and able to increase the quality of democracy and member participation within their organizations. Union democracy is no panacea and is problematic in cases where years of business unionism have led members to assess the quality of union leaders and strategies based on its norms. Still, a high level of internal democracy is essential to SMU, for the reasons we have explored. Developments along these lines can therefore be seen as litmus tests for the progress of U.S. unions toward SMU.

Notes

The theoretical framework and empirical argument outlined here are elaborated in a forthcoming study of the labor movements of the three NAFTA countries under neoliberal restructuring. My coresearchers and coauthors in this endeavor are Graciela Bensusán (FLACSO and Universidad Autónoma Metropolitana-Xochimilco in Mexico City), Maria Lorena Cook (School of Industrial and Labor Relations, Cornell University), Gregor Murray (Département des Relations Industrielles, Université de Laval), and Bodil Damgaard (formerly at FLACSO and now at the Danish National Institute of Social Research); all had a hand in the development of our theoretical framework. Thanks also to Julia Adams, Glenn Adler, Steve Babson, Michael Dreiling, Muge Gocek, Howard Kimeldorf, Gabe Lenz, Steve Lopez, Bruce Nissen, Jeff Paige, Kim Scipes, George Steinmetz, and Mayer Zald for their comments on earlier versions of this chapter.

1. "Neoliberal" economic policies flow from the following more or less explicitly articulated premises: (a) a competitive market form of economic regulation is generally the best means of increasing allocative efficiency; (b) increased allocative efficiency is the best way to promote aggregate economic growth; and (c) maximizing economic growth (as opposed to, say, meeting the basic needs of all or minimizing poverty or reducing economic inequality) ought to be the principal goal of economic policy. These claims derive most of their intellectual support from the dominant—if not quite hegemonic—neoclassical strand of academic economics. "Neoliberal restructuring" refers to changes in economic institutions, rules, and dynamics that can be directly traced to neoliberal economic policies.

2. I use "political opportunity structure" (POS) in the objective sense, as defined in social movement analyses such as McAdam (1982) and Kriesi et al. (1997). Economic opportunity structure (EOS) is a parallel concept developed by Robinson and his coauthors in their comparative analysis of North American labor movements (see acknowledgments above). As POS is a set of structural factors that affect unions' capacity to change state policy, EOS is a set of structural factors that affect unions' capacity to transform their power resources into collective bargaining power with employers.

3. Conditions that were important in particular cases but less general in application are not included in the table. For example, a number of authors have pointed to the rapid growth of an urban, semiskilled industrial proletariat, in a manufacturing sector protected from international competition as part of the state's import substitution industrialization strategy, as a key factor in the emergence and subsequent dominance of SMU in South Africa and Brazil (Adler 1996; Seidman 1994). While undoubtedly important in these cases and some others (e.g., South Korea), the rapid growth of this type of worker does not seem to have been an important part of the rise of SMU in Spain or Nicaragua in the 1970s or in Poland in the 1980s. Nor, Scipes (1996) argues, is SMU in the Philippines more deeply rooted in protected industries than in the agricultural sector and the newer factories in the export processing zones that began to expand rapidly in the Marcos era.

4. See also the essays by La Luz and Finn and Adams in Mantsios, ed. (1998).

5. The criterion of democratic quality employed in making this judgment is taken from Dahl (1989), who argues that in the ideal democracy, the concerns of all citizens should have equal weight in the decision-making process. The further we move away from this ideal, the lower the quality of democracy.

6. On the impact of increased international capital mobility on union economic bargaining power in the United States, see Bronfenbrenner (1997). For a more general argument that applies to unions in the global North and South alike, see Rodrik (1997).

7. Business unions have lower levels of societal mobilization capacity than SMUs for two reasons: first, owing to their exclusivity, they typically organize a smaller percentage of the workforce (i.e., low union density); second, business unions cannot call on the same level of commitment from their members because it is easier

to mobilize people to fight perceived injustices than to defend the status quo that they may broadly endorse. This is a general problem of "consensus" movement organizations, including business unions (Schwartz and Paul 1992).

8. Union density is measured differently in different countries. But the core concept is union membership as a share of the total workforce that might plausibly belong to unions (i.e., excluding managers, business owners, and family farmers).

9. Member volunteerism levels—the share of the union's members who volunteer time to union activities—are used here as an indicator of the percentage of members who have a significant commitment to their unions. On union member commitment and the factors that motivate it, see C. Kelly and J. Kelly (1994); J. Kelly and Heery, eds. (1994); Kuruvilla et al. (1993); Kuruvilla and Sverke (1993); Sverke (1995); Sverke and Sjoberg (1994).

10. The labor movement's societal mobilization capacity is the share of the society's labor force that are committed supporters of the unions to which they belong. This is estimated as the product of union density and membership volunteerism levels for 1989.

11. Shalev (1992) argues that "relative involvement" (i.e., the number of workers involved in stoppages per thousand employees in the workforce) is the best single measure of strike levels for comparative purposes. In the years 1960–1969, relative involvement in Canada and the United States was quite similar (twenty-three and seventeen workers per thousand respectively). But the gap widened dramatically thereafter: forty-five versus twenty-four in 1968–1973, fifty-nine versus fifteen in 1974–1979, and thirty-three versus four in 1980–1989.

12. The size of the gap in the growth rate of real worker compensation (wages plus benefits) relative to labor productivity is a good indicator of union bargaining power with employers. If the gap is zero, compensation rises at the same rate as productivity and profits, so that both parties improve their situation without any redistribution in the shares going to capital (profits) and labor (compensation). We focus on the manufacturing sector because it has the highest productivity growth, the strongest unions, and the highest wages for unskilled workers. It is also the sector most affected by the intensified international competition and capital mobility that results from neoliberal trade policies.

13. Union discursive capacity has two components: first, the union's capacity to frame its understanding of events and its objectives in ways that its intended audience finds plausible and compelling, and, second, the union's capacity to reach its intended audience, either by using the mass media effectively or through its own communications networks.

14. After falling in real terms since the early 1970s, the wages of unskilled workers in the United States finally began to pick up in 1997, as unemployment levels fell below 5 percent (Passell 1998). There is heated debate over the precise contribution of trade liberalization to these wage trends (Bound and Johnson 1995; Kapstein 1996; Lawrence 1998; Leamer 1995; Wood 1994). However, all of the participants in these debates concede that trade liberalization accounts for a substantial share of the increase in income inequality and poverty. A figure of 25–30 percent has become popular among economists who promote neoliberal trade agreements and who might therefore be expected to wish to minimize its negative impacts on wages. If we assume, as they do not, that declining manufacturing sector union density and increased substitution of capital for unskilled labor are also related to trade liberal-

ization and increased international capital mobility, the figure would rise a good deal more. If we then added the effects of another neoliberal policy—very high real interest rates designed to discipline organized labor by keeping unemployment relatively high—the figure would surely climb to well over half by most calculations.

15. At the outset of the neoliberal era, women made up about 41.6 percent of the U.S. workforce, but by 1997 they made up more than 49 percent. In 1997, blacks and Hispanics accounted for 9.6 and 8.5 percent of the workforce respectively. White males accounted for 44.2 percent of the workforce in 1997 (Hirsch and Macpherson 1998). A Bureau of Labor Statistics study estimates that by 2005, 87.5 percent of new entrants into the workforce will be either minorities or women (Kim 1993).

16. In 1978, about 28 percent of union members were women; by 1997, 39.4 percent were. In 1997, blacks and Hispanics accounted for 14.9 and 8.7 percent of union members respectively. White males accounted for 50.7 percent of union members in 1997 (Hirsch and Macpherson 1998).

17. The most common kind of merger was what Chaison (1996, 25) calls "absorptions," in which a large union merges with a much smaller union. There were twenty-one absorptions (2.3 per year) between 1970 and 1979 and fifty-two (3.7 per year) between 1980 and 1994.

18. The degree to which a common skill or working in a common industry generates a sense of common identity and interest among union members can easily be exaggerated. Still, the number of sources of difference among members in a general union will normally be even larger than those in industrial or craft unions. So I would grant Piore's (1989) premise that the challenge of building common identity is greatest in general unions, though I would not place too much weight on the difference.

19. It can, however, be done. Within a couple of years of becoming international president of the SEIU in 1980, John Sweeney expanded its staff from 20 to 200. To fund this expansion, Sweeney persuaded members to double the SEIU's per capita dues, traditionally the lowest in the AFL–CIO, from $4 to $8 per month (Piore 1989, 26).

20. The quote is from Bacon (1997), cited in Eisenscher (1999).

21. One reason for the slow pace is that in unions with a long tradition of business unionism, many members have been socialized into accepting the defining assumptions about what unions should do and how they should do these things. In such cases, increasing local membership control before changing this culture would likely frustrate leadership efforts to shift resources from servicing to organizing. Jimmy Hoffa, Jr.'s victory in the recent Teamsters elections should underscore this point. Many Teamsters evidently think that a union's strength depends as much (or more) on a "strong" leader as it does on democratic reforms (Greenhouse 1996c, 1998). How do the cultures of very large organizations like U.S. unions get changed? Leadership is essential, though it will be much more effective if, as was the case in the Teamsters, it is responding to pressures from a strong rank-and-file movement for democratic reform. The Teamsters Union was characterized by this ideal reform situation from 1991 to 1998, yet seven years of sustained effort by dedicated reformers were not enough to turn a majority of Teamster members—or even a majority of the minority who were sufficiently engaged in union politics to cast ballots—into active supporters of the reformers' ideals of good unionism and good leadership. On the other hand, to win, Hoffa was forced to adopt many planks of the reformers' agenda (e.g., cutting multiple salaries), so the efforts of the reformers

did have an important impact on what members are understood by all leaders to demand.

22. Analyses of the sources of variation in levels of union member participation indicate that members are motivated to participate for a variety of reasons. Among the most important reasons are a belief that the movement's goals are morally and politically important and a belief that the movement's strategies for realizing those goals have a reasonable prospect of success (Klandermans 1986, 1988). Data from the World Values Surveys indicate that the share of U.S. union members who were currently volunteering time without pay to their union increased from 6.8 percent in 1981 to 18.6 percent in 1990—a 173.5 percent increase.

23. The initial response of the SEIU's international executive board was to place Local 399 under trusteeship. It is hard to imagine that this would not have a serious dampening effect on the energies and commitments built during the organizing process. If so, such a reaction undermines the momentum of the organizing victory that precipitated the political crisis of Local 399.

24. Between 1978 and 1997, the International Brotherhood of Electrical Workers (IBEW) lost 20 percent of its members, the operating engineers' union (IUOE) and the plumbers' union both lost about one-third of their members, the laborers' union (LIUNA) lost 46 percent, and the United Brotherhood of Carpenters (UBC), 56 percent of their members. Between 1975 and 1987, when the old guard was still in charge of the Teamsters, it lost one-third of its members.

25. Between 1978 and 1997, the membership of the UAW fell by 49 percent, that of the IUE by 50 percent, and that of the USW by 60 percent.

26. In 1978, of the twenty largest unions in the United States, eighteen were affiliated with the AFL–CIO, accounting for 67 percent of its members. At that point, the ten manufacturing and building trades unions accounted for 61 percent of the members—and the votes—of the eighteen affiliates. By 1997, with the Teamsters reaffiliated to the AFL–CIO, nineteen of the twenty largest unions were affiliated with the AFL–CIO. (The exception was the National Education Association [NEA]). Within this group, the manufacturing and building trades unions combined accounted for only 38 percent of the members and votes. (Data for 1978 from Troy, 3–16; data for 1997 from AFL–CIO, unpublished data. Data for NEA for 1988 and 1997 from the membership records department of the NEA national office in Washington, D.C.). In all cases, these data are for dues-paying members.

27. Between 1979–1980 and 1991–1992, union contributions to labor PACs registered with the Federal Elections Commission doubled in real terms.

28. The "down with adversarialism, up with voice" strategy was first articulated in the report of the AFL–CIO's Committee on the Evolution of Work (AFL–CIO 1985). Harvard labor economist Richard Freeman, who served on the committee, developed the idea of unions as worker voice at about this time (Freeman and Medoff, eds. 1984).

29. The Teamsters' general counsel, Judith Smith, Communications Workers of America (CWA) organizing director Larry Cohen, and Oil, Chemical, and Atomic Workers Union (OCAW) president Bob Wages all criticized such a trade-off in their testimony to the Dunlop Commission (Boal 1994).

30. The report noted that the commission heard from "many business representatives who believe that the current law is working well, at least for the vast bulk of employers and workers, and does not need any major revision." These businesses, the report went on, condemned the illegal actions of (a growing number of) employ-

ers but saw the remedy as improved enforcement rather than more basic innovations (Dunlop Commission 1994, 76).

31. SIEU president John Sweeney, who led the New Voice slate, won 7.3 million votes (56 percent) to Tom Donohue's 5.7 million. The difference—about 1.6 million votes—was equivalent to the Teamsters' block vote (1.3 million) plus that of one medium-sized union (300,000 members) such as the Union of Needletrades, Industrial, and Textile Employees (UNITE). Sweeney's core supporters were his own union, four major industrial unions (the UAW, USW, International Association of Machinists [IAM], and United Mine Workers [UMW]), and two other major service sector unions (AFSCME and the Teamsters). Tom Donohue, the old guard's presidential candidate, had the support of most building trades unions—the UFCW, CWA, HERE, and American Federation of Teachers (AFT) (Sweeney and Kusnet 1996).

32. The AFL–CIO secured the convention's support for the creation of a third full-time executive position—executive vice president—to be filled by Linda Chavez-Thompson, formerly a vice president in AFSCME. It also expanded the federation's executive council from thirty-five to fifty-four members. This expanded the representation of women and minorities on this key body from 17 percent of the total under the old system to 27 percent.

33. The Quebec labor movement is different in many ways from the Anglo-Canadian movement outside that province and is probably best understood as a separate national labor movement. Its overarching social project by the early 1970s was the formation of a Quebec nation-state run along socialist lines. The Quebec movement from the 1960s forward was closer in a number of ways to the SMU ideal type than its Anglo counterpart. The discussion here focuses on the Anglo movement.

34. Table 8.3 indicates that in the last decade before neoliberal restructuring, the EOS facing Canadian unions was more favorable than that facing U.S. unions in seven of the eleven categories for which data are available. In the first neoliberal decade (1979–1988), this fell to six of eleven categories, and in the second neoliberal decade (1989–1998) the EOS facing U.S. unions was better in nine of eleven categories. Other things being equal, a deterioration of union EOS implies a loss of union power vis-à-vis employers. This, in turn, is a stimulus to the search for strategic innovations aimed at increasing union power resources and the effectiveness with which they are deployed.

35. Thus the building trades unions quit the Canadian Labour Congress (CLC) to form a rival federation in 1979 because of the CLC's growing support for the social democratic New Democratic Party (NDP) and its insistence that the Canadian leadership of international unions be elected by Canadian members rather than appointed (Ryan 1986). The recent exodus of the UBC from the AFL–CIO may signify the growth of parallel tensions between the New Voice AFL–CIO and the building trades unions, in which business unionism remains dominant. At the time that the UBC withdrew from the federation, UBC secretary-treasurer Andris Silins said that "The AFL–CIO has strayed to social and environmental issues that have nothing to do with getting better wages and working conditions for working people" (cited in Nichols 2001).

References

Acuff, Stewart. 1999. "Expanded Roles for the Central Labor Council: The View from Atlanta." In Nissen, ed., pp. 133–142.

Adler, Glenn. 1996. "Global Restructuring and Labor: The Case of the South African Trade Union Movement. In *Globalization: Critical Reflections*, ed. James Mittelman, pp. 117–143. Boulder, CO: Lynne Rienner.

Adler, Glenn, and Eddie Webster. 1995. "Challenging Transition Theory: The Labor Movement, Radical Reform, and Transition to Democracy in South Africa." *Politics and Society* 23, 1 (March): 75–106.

AFL–CIO. 1985. *The Changing Situation of Workers and Their Unions*. Washington, DC: AFL–CIO.

———. 1999. "Resolution 6. New Rules for the Global Economy." AFL–CIO website: http://www.aflcio.org/convention99/res1_6.htm.

———. 2000a. "Campaign for Global Fairness." AFL–CIO website: http://www.aflcio.org/publ/estatements/feb2000/globaires.htm.

———. 2000b. "Make the Global Economy Work for Working Families Petition on WTO." AFL–CIO website: http://www.aflcio.org/globaleconomy/petition.htm.

———. 2000c. "Union Members Join Thousands to Protest Anti-Worker World Bank, IMF Policies." AFL–CIO website: http://www.aflcio.org/globaleconomy/global_imf_rally.htm.

Babson, Steve. 2000. "Cross-Border Trade with Mexico and the Prospect for Worker Solidarity: The Case of Mexico." *Critical Sociology* 26, 1: 13–35.

Bacon, David. 1997. "The Promise of a Raise Is Not Enough." *Dollars and Sense*, September–October.

Benson, Herman. 1999. "The Rising Tide of Union Democracy." In Tillman and Cummings, eds., pp. 27–47.

Benzie, Robert. 2001. "Labour Declares War on Harris: 'It's Time for Increased Militancy on Our Picket Lines,' CUPE Head Tells Delegates." *National Post*, June 2.

Blackwell, Ron. 1997. "Globalization and the American Labor Movement." In *Audacious Democracy: Labor, Intellectuals, and the Social Reconstruction of America*, ed. Steven Fraser and Joshua B. Freeman, pp. 94–105. New York: Houghton Mifflin.

———. 1998. "Building a Member-Based International Program." In Mantsios, ed., pp. 320–328.

Boal, Ellis. 1994. "The Dunlop Commission Fact Finding Report, May 1994: Analysis and Comment." Labor notes (unpublished paper).

Bound, John, and George Johnson. 1995. "What Are the Causes of Rising Wage Inequality in the United States?" *Federal Reserve Bank of New York: Economic Policy Review* 1, 1: 9–17.

Bronfenbrenner, Kate. 1997. "We'll Close! Plant Closings, Plant-Closing Threats, Union Organizing and NAFTA." *Multinational Monitor* (March): 8–13.

———, et al., eds. 1998. *Organizing to Win: New Research on Union Strategies*. Ithaca, NY: Cornell University Press.

CAW (Canadian Auto Workers). 2001. "CAW–CLC–SEIU Agreement." *Contact*, June 10.

Chaison, Gary N. 1996. *Union Mergers in Hard Times: The View from Five Countries*. Ithaca, NY: ILR Press.

Coates, Mary Lou, and Tony Topham. 1988. *Trade Unions in Britain*, 3d ed. London: Fontana Press.

Cohen, Larry, and Steve Early. 1999. "Defending Workers' Rights in the Global Economy: The CWA Experience." In Nissen, ed., pp. 143–166.

Collier, Ruth Berins, and David Collier. 1991. *Shaping the Political Arena: Critical Junctures, the Labor Movement, and Regime Dynamics in Latin America.* Princeton, NJ: Princeton University Press.

Cooper, Marc. 1996. "The Boys and Girls of (Union) Summer." *The Nation*, August 12–19.

Cowichène, Melanie. 1988. "Wages, Productivity and Labour Costs, Reference Tables." In *The Current Industrial Relations Scene in Canada*, ed. Pradeep Kumar and Ken Coates. Kingston, Ontario: Centre for Industrial Relations, Queen's University.

Dahl, Robert. 1989. *Democracy and Its Critics.* New Haven, CT: Yale University Press.

Dreiling, Michael, and Ian Robinson. 1998. "Union Responses to NAFTA in the USA and Canada: Explaining Intra- and International Variations." *Mobilization* 3 (October): 163–184.

Dubofsky, Melvyn. 1969. *We Shall Be All: A History of the Industrial Workers of the World.* Chicago: University of Illinois Press.

Dunlop Commission (Commission on the Future of Worker–Management Relations). 1994. "Fact Finding Report." Washington, DC: U.S. Department of Labor and U.S. Department of Commerce.

Early, Steve. 1999. "Checking the Union Labels." *The Nation*, February 8.

Early, Steve, and Larry Cohen. 1997. "Jobs with Justice: Mobilizing Labor–Community Coalitions." *Working USA* (November–December): 49–57.

Eisenscher, Michael. 1999. "Labor: Turning the Corner Will Take More than Mobilization." In Tillman and Cummings, eds., pp. 61–85.

Freeman, Richard, and James Medoff, eds. 1984. *What Do Unions Do?* New York: Basic Books.

Frundt, Henry. 2000. "Models of Cross-Border Organizing in Maquila Industries." *Critical Sociology* 26, 1: 36–58.

Gindin, Sam. 1997. "Notes on Labor at the End of the Century: Starting Over?" *Monthly Review* 49, 3 (July–August): 140–157.

Goldfield, Michael. 1987. *The Decline of Organized Labor in the United States.* Chicago: University of Chicago Press.

Gourevitch, Peter. 1986. *Politics in Hard Times: Comparative Responses to International Economic Crises.* Ithaca, NY: Cornell University Press.

Greenhouse, Steven. 1996a. "Labor and Clergy Are Reuniting to Help the Underdogs of Society." *New York Times*, August 18.

———. 1996b. "Unions Putting Ambitious Aims on Agenda for the New Congress." *New York Times*, December 17.

———. 1996c. "Teamster Counter-Revolution: Why It Nearly Won the Election." *New York Times*, December 23.

———. 1996d. "With Summer Program, Unions Try to Recruit Students." *New York Times*, August 11.

———. 1997. "Analysis: Unions Shift Focus to Low-Wage Workers." *New York Times*, August 10.

———. 1998. "For Hoffa, the Challenge Is Getting Beyond the Name." *New York Times*, December 7.

————. 1999a. "AFL–CIO. Approves $40 Million Political Action Plan." *New York Times*, February 18.

————. 1999b. "The Labor Movement's Eager Risk-Taker Hits Another Jackpot." *New York Times*, February 27.

————. 2000. "Labor Urges Amnesty for Illegal Immigrants." *New York Times*, February 17.

Grenier, Guillermo, and Bruce Nissen. 2000. "Comparative Union Responses to Mass Immigration: Evidence from a Union City." *Critical Sociology* 26, 1: 82–108.

Hirsch, Barry T., and David A. Macpherson. 1998, 1999. *Union Membership and Earnings Data Book: Compilations from the Current Population Survey*, 1998 ed. Washington, DC: Bureau of National Affairs.

Hurd, Richard, and Lowell Turner. 2000. "Revitalizing the American Labor Movement: Progress, Shortcomings, Comparisons." Paper presented to the annual meeting of the Industrial Relations Research Association.

Johnston, Paul. 1994. *Success Where Others Fail: Social Movement Unionism and the Public Workplace*. Ithaca, NY: ILR Press.

————. 2000. "The Resurgence of Labor as Citizenship Movement in the New Labor Relations Environment." *Critical Sociology* 26, 1: 139–160.

Kapstein, Ethan B. 1996. "Workers and the World Economy." *Foreign Affairs,* (May/June): 16–37.

Kelly, C., and J. Kelly. 1994. "Who Gets Involved in Collective Action? Social Psychological Determinants of Individual Participation in Trade Unions." *Human Relations* 47: 63–88.

Kelly, John, and Edmund Heery, eds. 1994. *Working for the Union*. Cambridge: Cambridge University Press.

Kim, Marlene. 1993. "Overview: Losing Ground, Increasing Hate—Workers and Minorities Today." *Labor Research Review* 12, 1 (Spring/Summer): vii–ix.

Klandermans, Bert. 1986. "Psychology and Trade Union Participation: Joining, Acting, Quitting," *Journal of Occupational Psychology* 59: 189–204.

————. 1988. "Union Action and the Free-Rider Dilemma." In *Research in Social Movements, Conflicts, and Change*, ed. Louis Kriesberg et al., pp. 77–92. Greenwich, CT: JAI Press.

Kriesi, Hanspeter, Ruud Koopmans, Jan Willem Duyvendak, and Marco Giugni. 1997. "New Social Movements and Political Opportunities in Western Europe." In *Social Movements: Readings on Their Emergence, Mobilization, and Dynamics*, ed. Doug McAdam and David A. Snow, pp. 52–65. Los Angeles: Roxbury Publishing.

Kumar, Pradeep, and Dennis Ryan. 1988. *Canadian Union Movement in the 1980s: Perspectives from Union Leaders*. Kingston, Ontario: Centre for Industrial Relations, Queen's University.

————. 1988. *Canadian Unions' Response to the Challenge of the 1980s: Perspectives of the Leaders*. Kingston, Ontario: Industrial Relations Centre, Queens University. Working paper 1999–86.

Kuruvilla, Sarosh, and Magnus Sverke. 1993. "Two Dimensions of Union Commitment Based on the Theory of Reasoned Action: Cross-Cultural Comparisons." *Research and Practice in Human Resource Management* 1, 1: 1–16.

Kuruvilla, Sarosh, D.G. Gallagher, and K. Wetzel. 1993. "The Development of Members' Attitudes Towards Their Unions: Sweden and Canada." *Industrial and Labor Relations Review* 46: 499–515.

La Botz, Dan. 1990. *Rank-and-File Rebellion: Teamsters for a Democratic Union.* New York: Verso.

Lawrence, Robert Z. 1998. "Does a Kick in the Pants Get You Going or Does It Just Hurt? The Impact of International Competition on Technological Change in U.S. Manufacturing." In *North American Seminar on Incomes and Productivity,* ed. Secretariat for the Commission on Labor Cooperation, Dallas, TX.

Leamer, Edward. 1995. "A Trial Economist's View of U.S. Wages and Globalization." in *Imports, Exports, and the American Worker,* ed. Susan Collins. Washington, DC: Brookings Institution.

Lopez, Steven. 2000. "Contesting the Global City: Pittsburgh's Public Service Unions Confront the Neoliberal Agenda." In *Global Ethnography,* ed. Michael Burowoy et al., pp. 268–298. Berkeley: University of California Press.

Mantsios, Gregory, ed. 1998. *A New Labor Movement for the New Century.* New York: Monthly Review Press.

Marks, Gary. 1989. *Unions in Politics: Britain, Germany, and the United States in the Nineteenth and Early Twentieth Centuries.* Princeton, NJ: Princeton University Press.

Masters, Marick F. 1998. "Unions at the Crossroads." *Working USA* (January–February): 10–23.

McAdam, Doug. 1982. *Political Process and the Development of Black Insurgency, 1930–1970.* Chicago: University of Chicago Press.

Meyerson, Harold. 1998. "A Second Chance: The New AFL–CIO and the Prospective Revival of American Labor." In Mort, ed., pp. 1–26.

Milkman, Ruth. 2000. "Immigrant Organizing and the New Labor Movement in Los Angeles." *Critical Sociology* 26, 1: 59–81.

Moberg, David. 1997. "The Resurgence of American Unions: Small Steps, Long Journey." *Working USA* (May–June): 20–31.

Moody, Kim. 1997. *Workers in a Lean World: Unions in the International Economy.* New York: Verso.

Mort, Jo-Ann, ed. 1998. *Not Your Father's Union Movement: Inside the AFL–CIO.* New York: Verso.

Nichols, John. 2001. "Teamsters Not Turtles: Bush's Strategy to Divide the Democrats." *In These Times,* June 25.

Nissen, Bruce, and Seth Rosen. 1999. "Community-Based Organizing: Transforming Union Organizing Programs from the Bottom Up." In Nissen, ed., pp. 59–74.

Nissen, Bruce, ed. 1999. *Which Direction for Organized Labor?* Detroit, MI: Wayne State University Press.

Oziewicz, Estanislao. 2000. "CAW Refuses to Yield to CLC Tactics: Won't Halt Bid to Sign up Members of Rival Union; Hargrove Contemplates National Alternative." *Globe and Mail,* June 28.

Parker, Mike, and Martha Gruelle. 1999. "Democracy Is Power: Rebuilding Unions from the Bottom Up." Detroit: Labor Notes.

Passell, Peter. 1998. "Benefits Dwindle for the Unskilled Along with Wages." *New York Times,* June 14.

Piore, Michael. 1989. "Administrative Failure: An Hypothesis about the Decline of the U.S. Union Movement in the 1980s." Working paper, Department of Economics, MIT.

Rathke, Wade. 1999. "Letting More Flowers Bloom under the Setting Sun." In Nissen, ed., pp. 75–94.

Robinson, Ian. 1993a. *North American Trade As If Democracy Mattered: What's Wrong with NAFTA and What Are the Alternatives?* Ottawa, Canada: Canadian Centre for Policy Alternatives and International Labor Rights Education and Research Fund, Washington, DC.

———. 1993b. "Economistic Unionism in Crisis: The Origins, Consequences, and Prospects of Divergence in Labour-Movement Characteristics." In *The Challenge of Restructuring: North American Labor Movements Respond*, ed. Jane Jenson and Rianne Mahon, pp. 19–47. Philadelphia, PA: Temple University Press.

———. 1995. "Globalization and Democracy." *Dissent* (Summer): 373–380.

———. 2000. "Union Strategic Responses to Neoliberal Restructuring, Canada and United States, 1979–2000." Paper presented to the Panel on Labor Movement Strategic Responses to Neoliberal Restructuring, Twenty-Second International Congress of the Latin American Studies Association.

Rodrik, Dani. 1997. *Has Globalization Gone Too Far?* Washington, DC: Institute for International Economics.

Russo, John, and Brian R. Corbin. 1999. "Work, Organized Labor, and the Catholic Church: Boundaries and Opportunities for Community/Labor Coalitions." In Nissen, ed., pp. 95–112.

Ryan, Dennis. 1986. *Division in the 'House of Labour': An Analysis of the CLC–Building-Trades Dispute*. Kingston, Ontario: Industrial Relations Centre, Queen's University.

Schwartz, Michael, and Shuva Paul. 1992. "Resource Mobilization versus the Mobilization of People: Why Consensus Movements Cannot Be Instruments of Social Change." In *Frontiers in Social Movement Theory*, ed. Aldon D. Morris and Carol McClurg Mueller, pp. 205–247. New Haven, CT: Yale University Press.

Scipes, Kim. 1992. "Social Movement Unionism and the Kilusang Mayo Uno." *Kasarinlan* 7, 2–3: 121–162.

———. 1996. *KMU: Building Genuine Trade Unionism in the Philippines, 1980–1994*. Quezon City, Philippines: New Day Publishers.

Seidman, Gay W. 1994. *Manufacturing Militance: Workers' Movements in Brazil and South Africa*. Berkeley: University of California Press.

SEIU (Service Employees International Union). 2001. "Georgetti Announces Resolution of SEIU–CAW Dispute." http://www.seiu.ca/news_frames523.html, May 23.

Shailor, Barbara. 1998. "A New Internationalism: Advancing Workers' Rights in the Global Economy." In Mort, ed., pp. 145–155.

Shalev, Michael. 1992. "The Resurgence of Labour Quiescence." In *The Future of Labour Unions*, ed. Marino Regini, pp. 102–132. New York: Sage.

Smith, Miriam. 1990. "Labour Without Allies: The Canadian Labour Congress in Politics, 1956–1988." Ph.D. dissertation, Department of Political Science, Yale University.

Statistics Canada. 1999. *Union Statistics, First Half of 1999*. Ottawa: Statistics Canada. August 24.

Sverke, Magnus. 1995. *Rational Union Commitment: The Psychological Dimension in Membership Participation.* Department of Psychology, Stockholm University.

Sverke, Magnus, and Anders Sjoberg. 1994. "Dual Commitment to Company and Union in Sweden: An Examination of Predictors and Taxonomic Split Methods." *Economic and Industrial Democracy* 15: 531–564.

Sweeney, John, and David Kusnet. 1996. *America Needs a Raise.* New York: Houghton Mifflin.

Tillman, Ray M., and Michael S. Cummings, eds. 1999. *The Transformation of U.S. Unions: Voices, Visions, and Strategies from the Grassroots.* Boulder, CO: Lynne Rienner.

Troy, Leo, and Neil Sheflin. 1988. *U.S. Union Sourcebook: Membership, Finances, Structure, Directory.* West Orange, NJ: Industrial Relations Data and Information Services.

Voss, Kim. 1993. *The Making of American Exceptionalism.* Ithaca, NY: Cornell University Press.

Wallison, Ethan. 2001. "Unions Retool Grassroots Plan." *Roll Call,* May 10.

Webster, Eddie. 1988. "The Rise of Social Movement Unionism: The Two Faces of the Black Trade Union Movement in South Africa." In *State, Resistance, and Change in South Africa,* ed. Philip Frankel, Noam Pines, and Mark Swilling. London: Croom, Helm.

Weinbaum, Eve S. 1999. "Organizing Labor in the Era of Contingent Work and Globalization." In Nissen, ed., pp. 37–58.

Williams, Jane. 1999. "Restructuring Labor's Identity: The Justice for Janitors Campaign in Washington, D.C." In Tillman and Cummings, eds., pp. 203–217.

Wood, Adrian. 1994. *North–South Trade, Employment and Inequality: Changing Fortunes in a Skill-Driven World.* Oxford: Oxford University Press.

World Values Survey Association. 1994. *The World Values Surveys, 1981–1984 and 1990–1993.* Ann Arbor: ICPSR 6160.

9

CITIZENSHIP MOVEMENT UNIONISM

FOR THE DEFENSE OF LOCAL
COMMUNITIES IN THE GLOBAL AGE

PAUL JOHNSTON

The arrangements that govern labor and employment relations are part of an ensemble of public institutions that together define the terms and conditions of citizenship in a society. For fortunate groups in favorable times, such arrangements are likely to be taken for granted and thus be invisible. But even for these groups, this seemingly immutable public order becomes problematic in times of economic upheaval, and so the conditions of economic citizenship themselves become contested. So it is that the era of globalization, industrial restructuring, and political retrenchment launched in the 1970s has produced a resurgence of what is here labeled citizenship movement unionism.

Every historical era is a crucible of change for the labor movement and its unions. In the United States, the past two decades of union failure and insecurity in the private sector and success and security in the public sector were no exception. In the private sector of the 1980s and 1990s, as in the public sector of the 1960s and 1970s, painful confrontations with the failures of what had become taken-for-granted union agendas forced unionists to question operating assumptions taken for granted in union practice and enshrined in labor law. Helped by the passage of an aging generation of labor leaders, this process has produced a new cohort of activist leaders, themselves often the products of social movements of recent decades. Consequently there are today more activists dedicated to the revival of labor as a social movement in the rank and file and staff and other leadership positions than in any period since at least the 1930s.

By no means at this writing has labor yet erupted once again as a history-shaping social movement in the United States. During the past two decades of crisis in the private sector labor movement unions in fact virtually abandoned their main form of collective action, the economic strike. Increasingly, however, unions are broadcasting agendas for social change. Most recently, after a hiatus of nearly twenty years, the strike has returned with a vengeance. Suddenly, union after union is finding itself transformed: from a small circle of staff and activists "servicing" a large body of passive members into a large body of mobilized members caught up in the disruptive, transformative effervescence of strike action. Conditions appear to be ripe for the reemergence of labor as a social movement.

But social movements require more than organizational resources and more than collective action. They depend as well on the presence of what sociologists call, after Erving Goffman (1974), a social movement frame: a shared interpretation of our goals and methods and role in history.

So what is unionism when it is a social movement? This is more than a theoretical question. No social movement can thrive and develop without a shared understanding of what is at stake and what it stands for. And despite encouraging signs of revival, the U.S. labor movement is profoundly disoriented because in the aftermath of business unionism, we lack a shared sense of who we are and where we are going. Yes, we know, we must organize or die. But organize for what?

Both in theory and in practice, moreover, making sense of the labor movement as a social movement is particularly difficult because of the great diversity of conditions faced by workers and their unions. The goals, resources, shared identities, forms of organization and collective action, patterns of change over time, and ultimately the historical possibilities of labor movements all depend on the kind of employment relations and the historical circumstances within and against which they surface. This too is a practical as well as a theoretical problem because solidarity itself depends in part on shared vocabulary and a common project.

I argue here, however, that all the strands of today's embryonic labor movement revival can be grasped as citizenship movements. The language and theory of citizenship, I claim, offer both powerful conceptual tools for scholars and compelling self-understandings for participants.

Despite their diversity, labor movements all appeal to, rely upon, and seek in some sense to achieve the promise of citizenship.

This chapter offers a new interpretation of social movement unionism as a movement for expanded and deepened democracy or, in the language used here, as a citizenship movement. I rely on a conceptual framework developed in research in immigrant and transnational workers' movements in California and on the U.S.-Mexican border (Johnston 2001). This framework—labor as citizenship movement—speaks equally to struggles around and across the boundaries of citizenship and struggles over the terms and conditions of "actually existing citizenship" within the U.S. polity.

"Social movement unionism" evokes both labor's renewed mobilization in challenge to the status quo and its growing tendency to align itself and even merge with other social movements for gender and racial justice, environmental protection, immigrant rights, and urban social change. Here I focus on the first meaning of this term. By defining our labor movement as a citizenship movement, however, I suggest that we see ourselves as part of a larger family of democratizing social movements.

I begin by briefly reviewing the recent resurgence of social movement unionism in the United States; I then introduce the idea that "citizenship" can serve as a powerful framework for research and practice in this field. I relate this notion to the great body of citizenship theory, suggesting avenues for research and practice opened up by this new view. The following section focuses on diverse strands of social movement unionism, finding in each patterns of collective interest, action, and identity associated with the promise of citizenship. A final section focuses on the convergence of these diverse "citizen worker" movements in the defense of local communities and considers the practical implications for labor councils and urban public life.

The Resurgence of Social Movement Unionism

The new AFL–CIO has escaped from the clutch of Cold War politics, overcome its conservative cultural politics, and abandoned its adversarial relationship to other social movements. Today many unions, some labor councils, and a lively crop of new community-based labor organizations are exploring the possibilities opened up by this shift: innovating, testing new strategies, building new coalitions, and rethinking their agendas. If the basic orientation of a labor federation makes a difference in a country's historical development, then the consequences are likely to be profound.[1]

Significantly, this resurgent unionism is finally opening the doors of labor to first-generation immigrant workers, and it also taps into the energies of civil rights and other social justice movements. Also evident is a new commitment to organizing, including ambitious industrywide organizing drives and some still more ambitious regional campaigns. Other evidence includes a revitalized labor movement in agriculture and the hotel and restaurant industries and surges of organizing among Latino immigrants in other low-wage industries; growing militancy and increasingly political unionism among nurses and other health care workers; on the strike front, a trend away from the debacles of the post-Professional Air Traffic Controllers Organization (PATCO) era, which appears to have sparked renewed worker confidence and led to a greater volume of strike activity; in local government across the country, a wave of "living wage" initiatives and home health care campaigns, both targeting contracted-out public workers; on the college campuses, a steady pattern of militancy among graduate student employees; among other temporary employees and occupational groups, a variety of new worker associations often not affiliated with the AFL–CIO; at all levels of electoral action, sharply intensified grass-roots mobilization; on the international front, a break with the past half-century of collaboration with reactionary and repressive forces against democratic unionism and the beginnings of cross-border organizing and global solidarity; quietly and behind the scenes, a new degree of nonsectarian cooperation among the networks of long-time left-wing activists now well entrenched in unions formerly hostile to their involvement; and now in community after community across the United States, the emergence of a great variety of creative new labor/community organizing projects and coalitions addressing social and economic justice issues.[2] Along with the living wage campaigns, these last initiatives are bringing into focus an important feature of the new labor movement: it mobilizes and represents working people beyond the boundaries of the bargaining unit, in dealings not limited to employers and on issues not limited to the scope of recognition.

The importance of this process might best be illustrated by imagining the state of the unions in the United States today were it not for social movements among just two groups of workers. Before the emergence of their labor movements, both public workers and low-wage immigrant workers had long been scorned by the labor establishment. Now (despite real vitality in a variety of other sectors) it is probably fair to say that labor clings to life mainly thanks to the phenomenal force of public worker movements from the 1960s to the 1980s and to the growth of industrial militancy among immigrant workers in a variety of industries, from agriculture to the service sector, in more recent years.

These energies have surfaced in many international unions, but they intersect in the Service Employees International Union (SEIU), with its strong public sector and private building maintenance divisions. Were it not for these episodes of social movement unionism, the successful challenge to Lane Kirkland and his anointed successor for leadership in the AFL–CIO in 1995 would have been unlikely to occur, and SEIU's John Sweeney might well be the failed leader of a second-rate international union.

The Challenge of Diversity

Work and labor relations today are characterized by extraordinary diversity, and both scholars and practitioners can be faulted for drawing conclusions about all labor relations from one piece of the workforce. Too often, for example, scholars have focused either on the higher-waged corporate workforce (e.g., Kochan et al. 1986) or on contingent employment in the new informational workforce (e.g., Hecksher 1988) and have tended to generalize from that part to the whole of the workforce and its labor movements.[3] Meanwhile, "in the real world," unionists relying on repertoires similarly transplanted from one sector to another have frequently paid a more painful price.

The public and the private sector, for example, have displayed contrary patterns of change for decades, with crisis coming in the former and relative stability in the latter during the expansive 1960s and 1970s, followed by crisis in the private sector and unprecedented stability and union security in the public during the 1980s.[4] Despite this, most industrial relations scholars (and organizational researchers more generally) neglect the public–private sectoral difference. And within the public and private sectors, trends in employment and labor relations have also displayed wide and sometimes contrary patterns of variation: intense and bitter conflict alongside consolidated labor–management partnerships, the growth of "union-free environments" alongside fully reorganized industries; unprecedented union security and job security alongside massive subcontracting of professional work for still higher wages and low-wage work for still lower wages, the wholesale expulsion of many workers from the organization into contingent status, and the simultaneous expansion of both high-wage/high-skill and low-wage manual and service work. Also, labor movement activity in the United States has lately concentrated in the service sectors, and conventional wisdom remains convinced that the time of industrial unionism among semiskilled blue collar workers—with its historic contribution to democratic development—is long dead.[5] But clearly, oppressive industrial employment continues and is continuously renewed in the United States, especially in workforces formed by in-migration to work in agriculture, food processing, light manufacturing, and garment work, as well as hotel and restaurant, building maintenance, and health services.

Virtually all these patterns of diversity, moreover, coincide with and are reinforced by basic fault lines of racial and ethnic difference. Among the various segments of the U.S. workforce, labor movements typically surface within groups bounded by language, culture, residential, and other circumstances associated with race and ethnicity. As a result, within a given urban region, participants in different labor movements typically inhabit different social universes. How then, in the face of all this diversity, is it *conceivable* that we might both analyze and orient our practice with a single theory of the labor movement?

Labor as a Citizenship Movement

Despite this diversity, *the various labor movements emerging in each of these circumstances all seek to defend, exercise, and extend the boundaries of citizenship.* All these labor movements converge, moreover, with other citizenship movements that seek to develop public institutions that defend and rebuild local communities, in an increasingly globalized economic and public order.

Practically speaking, this implies a new way of framing our claims and orienting our strategies: no longer is the fate of a particular bargaining unit at stake, but the status and future of a community.[6] No longer does our power depend mainly on market position or on homogenous coalitions with similar workers in the same labor market, but rather also on heterogeneous coalitions assembled around a vision of the future— implicitly, at least, a potential governing agenda.

To forestall misunderstanding: "citizenship" refers not only to formal political participation, but also to a variety of relationships to a variety of public institutions. "Citizenship rights" refer not only to legally recognized rights, but also to rights that may be denied but are nonetheless claimed by participants and so may orient and motivate social movements. Citizenship refers, moreover, not only to the status of U.S. citizens, but also to that of citizens of all countries. Although mainly associated with the nation-state today, citizenship also surfaces within other political organizations, from the labor union and local government to the transnational and global levels. Citizenship is here defined in this expansive and developing sense as our relationship to public institutions.

Historically, to be sure, citizenship has always meant exclusion as well as inclusion. Citizenship is always the imposition of an extreme power upon a population: the power to define and implement "the public interest." Citizenship legitimizes a power that typically, behind the veil of that public interest, always favors one private interest over another. But on the one hand, the question is not whether or not we like citizenship, but whether or not it is a social force moving in our world and informing our labor movements. And on the other hand, the promise of citizenship may still be valid if we can discern a developmental logic within which the hidden tyrannies, biases, hypocrisies, and other boundaries of citizenship are challenged by social movements that themselves arise from, appeal to, and seek to strengthen the institutional structure of citizenship. In theory and in practice many of citizenship's critics, it seems, are themselves oriented by the promise of citizenship.

The notion of labor as citizenship movement has rich implications, ranging from the methods and practice of individual organizers in particular workplaces to the strategic agendas of local unions and labor councils to our grasp of the role of the labor movement in history. Unlike Marxism, however, it does not privilege the labor movement above all other forces for social change. It suggests, in fact, that the labor movement achieves its full potential only when it aligns itself and even merges with other democratic social movements, or when it enables its participants to express themselves and act not only as workers, but also as members of a community with multiple interests and identities.

This perspective does propose to anchor the labor movement in the broader and still far from finished movement for expanded democracy. Citizenship theory offers a unifying social movement frame, an essential explanatory tool, and a practical and strategic orientation for scholars and other participants. Successful labor movement initiatives draw upon the resources, resonate with the themes, and defend or extend the boundaries of citizenship.

Moving as it does around and against rather than through the exercise of market power, this "citizenship movement frame" certainly does not fit the familiar inherited routines, organization, and self-concept of business unionism in the postwar United States. It points in fact to connections with historical processes beyond the conventional boundaries of the labor movement and the realm of industrial relations. But it also resonates with other approaches that similarly link labor movement revival to broader agendas (Brecher and Costello 1990; Banks 1991–1992; Waterman 1993; Sweeney 1996; Eisenscher 1999; Fine 1998; Scipes 1992). Most though not all of these views also anchor resurgent unionism in the defense of local communities, a theme to which we turn below. It resonates as well with the social movement unionisms of countries like Brazil, South Africa, South Korea, and the Philippines, where the most dynamic and powerful labor movements in the world today take on issues of democracy, human rights, and social justice not only in the context of labor relations, but also in the larger society (Foweraker and Landman 1997; Scipes 1992). It reclaims our roots in the citizenship movements of the nineteenth century, as revealed by social historians tracing the relationship between class conflict and the emergence and development of citizenship (Marshall 1950; Hobsbawm 1968; Thompson 1974; Barbelet 1988; Rueschemeyer et al. 1992; Montgomery 1993; Steinberg 1995). It observes, however, that the West European and U.S. path through industrialization to expanded citizenship is neither unique nor the final expression of this force for global democratic development. And it lends support to the already rather evident notion that this larger democratic revolution is an unfinished business and we are participants in it.

Labor Relations and the Civic Regime

For reasons rooted in half a century of social and intellectual history, research on contemporary labor relations, social movements and other political processes, citizenship, public organization, and the state more generally is not well integrated. I am convinced that citizenship theory can produce historic breakthroughs in both social theory, which has for centuries wrestled unsatisfactorily with the problem of the state, and social practice, long haunted as well by the problem of power in political organizations ranging from the labor union to the political party to, most tragically, the socialist state.

But even a survey of the field of citizenship theory—much less the integration of these related literatures, and much, *much* less the exploration of the terrain revealed by their integration—is beyond our scope here. Nor does space permit an examination of the role of citizenship status or public institutions in the various forms of labor process. All of this work, moreover, is likely to meet with varying degrees of disagreement. A better way to introduce this paradigm is to review a set of widely shared understandings about the institutions of citizenship, pointing to fairly obvious connections between them and the challenges faced by the labor movement.

Participants in today's dialogue and struggle over citizenship are generally familiar with several basic dimensions of citizenship, each associated with a particular set of institutions. Though interpretations vary, most would agree that these include the triad of basic (1) *civil rights*, (2) *political rights*, and (3) *social welfare rights,* which were the focus of T.H. Marshall's (1950) classic theory of citizenship. Each is associated not only with a particular set of rights, but also with a particular set of complex public institutions (this suggests, incidentally, a clear avenue for integration of citizenship theory and research on public institutions), and each can be easily associated with a particular variety of "pro-citizenship" social movement. The first are associated with individual rights and the civil and criminal legal system; the second, with electoral processes and other forms of participation in the political system; the third, with "family needs" for social insurance and the social welfare programs that comprise much of local and state government.

Most follow Marshall by including educational resources in the last category on the grounds that, like minimal subsistence, education is a necessary condition of political participation. I will not address the merits of this approach but simply suggest that there may be good reason to follow Talcott Parsons (1966) in understanding educational institutions as part of a distinct field of (4) *cultural citizenship*, or stratified participation in and exclusion from the accumulated cultural resources of a society.[7]

More recently, anthropologists and others have advanced another concept of cultural citizenship, through which groups occupy or claim public space for the expression of their identities and recognition of their own membership in public life (e.g., Flores and Benmayor 1997). Historically, democracy has always emerged in institutions that seek to impose a homogenous cultural identity on their citizenry. The incompatibility of homogenous cultural identities with core principles of citizenship is evident, however, in today's multicultural and increasingly transnational society. So this concept of cultural citizenship is a useful way to grasp the struggle by excluded groups and their allies for public institutions that embrace heterogeneity, toward a more fully developed citizenship. This is a recurrent struggle in a country like the United States, continuously transformed due to war, conquest, slavery, and immigration. It may be possible to synthesize these views of cultural citizenship, though that too is beyond our scope here.

Finally, many scholars have recognized labor market institutions, workers' rights, and labor–management relations as a distinct and particularly problematic domain of citizenship under the label of (5) *economic or industrial citizenship*. Economic citizenship refers to the complex of *public* law, policy, regulation, places, "opinion," interests, identities, activities, and resources that surround, pervade, shape, and orient our economic lives. Like other forms of citizenship, economic citizenship is both an empirically observable status and a normative ideal. It is our answer to the question: if we want to take our conditions of employment out of competition, where do we want to take them? Or, responding to the direction coming from the new leadership of the AFL–CIO, "Organize for what?" Our answers range from an enforceable employment contract to a living wage to worker control of the labor process to full-fledged "economic democracy" or workers' self-government.[8]

However we define it, however, economic citizenship is inevitably problematic because citizenship claims conflict fundamentally with the workings of the labor market and the institutions of private ownership. This fault line of conflict between capitalism and democracy is built into the system, so to speak, and so produces tensions and other effects in the social structure and at deeper levels of personal experience.[9] It results in struggles that may drive changes not only along the boundaries of industrial citizenship, but also in other citizenship domains, and so has been associated with citizenship development from its earliest known emergence in ancient Greece to the modern world. Most obviously, for example, such conflict may lead to changes in the social wage. Expanded or contracted "social welfare" may in turn change the economic balance of power by changing workers' vulnerability to unemployment.

Connections are evident between the status and rights of workers and their unions, or economic citizenship more generally, and each of the other citizenship domains. Thus, for example, whether workers enjoy basic civil rights such as freedom of association and travel or freedom to enter into and leave employment will have a decisive effect on their conditions of employment (as is evident in recent patterns of change in the status of unauthorized immigrant labor in the United States and elsewhere). Whether and how political processes produce public policies that regulate labor unions, capital mobility, employment practices, labor–management relations, the social wage, apprenticeship and training programs, or the direction of economic development itself obviously has profound effect on the status of workers and the interests of their unions. Whether workers have access to what kind of educational resources in today's increasingly flexible and skill-centered labor markets and who controls these resources and the learning that occurs within them, and whether and how these educational resources mediate between the needs of workers—especially educationally disadvantaged workers—and those of employers are of tremendous interest to workers and workers-to-be and of increasing interest to labor unions and other worker organizations as well. The struggle to open labor unions to a multicultural, often racialized membership has been visible for decades, as have efforts to open them up to women's participation and leadership. Once again, recent gains on these fronts are mainly the product of social movements among public workers and among immigrants.

Thus we have five distinct concepts of citizenship: four—civil, social, political, and cultural—indirectly important, particularly in circumstances where crisis drives workers and their unions to grope for ways to outflank employer power, and one in particular—economic citizenship—in perpetual tension with capitalism and clearly central to labor's agenda, whatever it might be.[10] Variation in citizenship status includes, then, not only differences in whether a constituency has a political voice in a community, but also differences in protection from abuses of authority and power, differences in access to social services and health care, differences in educational opportunities, differences in coverage by labor relations or related laws, etc.

I do not suggest that this descriptive list is a theory of citizenship; for that, we would need to treat public institutions as a whole. But we can observe that every set of public institutions is characterized by a particular set of such arrangements, which together might be termed "the civic regime." For our purposes, it should be clear that certain social movements emerge and develop within and against the terrain, so to speak, of the civic regime; that it is also a product of such movements, at least in part. It should be clear that this territory is sufficiently broad and its geography sufficiently varied and complex that it might give rise to a variety of different struggles over the terms and conditions of citizenship—not only a variety of labor movements, but also other social movements expressing the interests and identities of other groups within the framework of public life.

This suggests the notion of a family of social movements, shaped (at least in part) by the civic regime or the citizenship status of their participants and distinguished by their appeal to the promise of democracy. According to a compelling current of social movement scholarship, these democratizing social movements are evoked and oriented and sustained in a particular kind of conversation, which occurs within and is evoked around them. In these public conversations, people address one another in a manner that assumes a fundamental equality and openness to dialogue over questions of common concern. Issues are decided, in this kind of encounter, on the basis of argument rather than authority or tradition. These conversations may help to constitute people as citizens of a shared public and equip democratic social movements with exceptional learning and adaptive abilities.[11]

Other such citizenship movements would include movements for democratic revolution or reform; consumer rights; welfare rights; corporate accountability; international human rights; student movements; movements for racial justice; some urban social movements; and some currents of feminist, gay, lesbian, and environmentalist movements. By no means homogenous or oriented toward a single vision, all these democratic social movements are informed by a culture of critical discourse (Gouldner 1976). All share a commitment to communicative competence (Habermas 1979), which drives a collective learning process (Elder 1993). All are best evoked or organized by methods that rely on such discourse to challenge conventional codes in ways that constitute and reconstitute public spaces (Melucci 1996). Because of the instability of any definition of "the public" or its "interest," all share a tentative, decentered attitude that leaves them always incomplete, nicely postmodern.

A Unifying Agenda for a Diverse Movement

The U.S. workforce appears to face at least four radically dissimilar types of labor relations environment: *public employment, corporate employment* in large organizations, *low-wage work in a wide variety of industries* with high concentrations of African American and immigrant labor, and *temporary employment*, slicing across all three of the above sectors.

These four categories are neither exhaustive nor exclusive, but they allow us to capture the main patterns of recent labor movement activity in the United States. To what extent, then, do variations within and among the labor movements that surface in these settings reflect changes and differences in the civic regimes that constitute them, and to what extent can all be grasped as citizenship movements that converge with other democratic social movements on the defense of local communities? A very brief overview of developments in each of these arenas will at least suggest an answer.

Public Service Unionism

The only truly significant U.S. union growth of the past half century came, of course, in the public workplace, mainly in schools and other local government institutions, formerly despised and excluded in the house of labor. Recent progress in health care and educational organizing continues this trend.

Virtually invisible to date in political theory, public workers play a unique part in public life. They produce it. They are employed, that is, in the production of politically defined "public needs" and so have a unique relationship to the local communities through the local agencies where they are concentrated. Accordingly, their labor movements follow a distinct logic of labor–management relations, defined first of all by their emergence within and against political bureaucracy. Their movements surface and their strategic coalitions are located in the complex political universe that surrounds each single agency rather than in homogenous labor markets that slice across organizations. They are empowered mainly by their status in political coalitions and by their capacity to articulate their particular claims as legitimate public interests. Public employee strikes are more likely to succeed, for example, when they combine economic with noneconomic demands, frame economic demands as legitimate claims or principles of good government, and ally different kinds of workers in collective action (Johnston 1994).

The sectoral difference has had decisive consequences for patterns of change over time in public versus private sector labor relations. Thus while the private sector labor movement drifted into steady decline in the 1960s and 1970s, those parts of the public workforce empowered by growth in the social welfare state and the racialized, gendered urban upheavals of that era produced new labor laws, explosive union growth, and a new species of adversarial employee associations. These organizations grew not so much through conventional organizing strategies, but through the transformation of long existing (and essentially similar) employee associations and unions into social movement organizations.

Public worker movements thus achieved the first major beachheads of clerical and professional unionism, established new work environments of freer speech and less arbitrary and abusive supervision, and proved themselves powerful new constituencies for expanded (and occasionally improved) public services.[12] They produced new African American and female union leadership, and in the comparable worth movement, a wave of feminist unionism. Despite the often bureaucratic character of the organizations they left in their wake, these social movements rearranged the political and organizational landscape not only of unionism, but also of urban life, creating the possibility—still unrealized—of progressive new urban coalitions between labor and neighborhood movements, with far-reaching implications. And they disclosed a dimension of public life still unrecognized in political theory—the status, organization, activity, and historical role of the working people who produce what is politically defined as "the public interest."

By the time of the PATCO strike, however, most public employee unions had already experienced their own PATCO-like traumas at the local level, typically brought on by their own mechanical application of radically inappropriate bargaining agendas and strike strategies borrowed from the private sector.[13] By and large they failed to fully grasp the power of labor–community coalitions in campaigns for good government. By and large they were relieved to join in new labor–management coalitions against the Republican assault of the Reagan era, alongside their erstwhile adversaries in local government.

But though most public worker movements have subsided to a simmer, the unions they left in their wake represent a distinct kind of unionism, uniquely related to local communities, that continues to play a powerful role in the defense of local government, universities, and other education, health care, and social services (Piven and Cloward 1988). As we will see below, moreover, the more recent emergence of new urban leadership out of the private sector labor movement may provide yet another opportunity to assemble these new resources into progressive new urban coalitions.

Community-Based Corporate Unionism

Out of the private sector came the great resistance movements sparked by the failure of the industrial relations model of bargaining unionism by the early 1980s: resistance to concession bargaining, two-tier wage systems, plant closures, and subcontracting. Early on, these mainly took the form of movements within unions to vote down concessionary agreements and to unseat those who negotiated them; more often than not failing, but still beginning to transform unions into arenas for participation. Increasingly, though, local unions began to take a stand against concessions and plant closures. In case after case, beleaguered workers and their unions discovered new resources as they reached out for support to other community members in their churches, schools, and neighborhood organizations and across the country and the world in "corporate campaigns" patterned on the United Farm Workers' (UFW) early efforts.

These were (and are) often poignantly painful battles mobilizing whole communities against the seemingly inexorable logic of capitalist development, and more often than not they failed (and they fail). Catastrophic defeats like the mid-1980s strike by Local P- 9 of the United Food and Commercial Workers' union at the Austin, Minnesota, Hormel plant and the six-year-long Caterpillar strike by the United Auto Workers' Local 751 in Decatur, Illinois, displayed both the challenges facing this segment of the workforce and the response by labor organizations shaped in previous decades of collective bargaining. Both local unions resisted the tide of concessionary bargaining, both inspired broad support among grass-roots labor activists across the United States, and both were ultimately abandoned by their respective international unions.

On the other hand, the 1988–1990 Pittston coal miners' strike showed that other directions are possible. In that successful struggle, whole communities mobilized in defense of their right to health care, deploying tactics and discourse consciously adopted from the civil rights movement and the UFW. Importantly, in contrast to the P-9 and Caterpillar debacles, they were solidly backed by an international union with its leadership already renewed through internal rebellion. More recently, the massive Teamsters' strike at United Parcel Service in 1997 also ended in success. Again, not coincidentally, the strikers framed their claims as a public issue—opposing the expansion of part-time work—and again they enjoyed the solid support of an international leadership renewed through internal upheaval.[14] That strike emboldened other workers and their unions, like the United Auto Workers in Flint, Michigan; their eight-week 1998 strike snowballed into a massive shutdown of GM production and secured similar support through its public challenge to downsizing and contracting out. It ended, to be sure, in a standoff rather than a union victory. But this was still a far cry from the wrenching Caterpillar debacle.

Then a hiatus ensued. The volume of traditional economic strikes declined still further, and many wondered whether the strike was perhaps dead after all. Even as the economic strike continues to fade away, however, the political strike increasingly takes its place. The April 2000 Los Angeles-area strike victory of the Justice for Janitors (JfJ) campaign, to be discussed below, was a dramatic demonstration of the power of the political strike.[15] At this writing, while recourse to the economic strike continues to fade, pioneering local unions are once again enrolled in "the school of the strike." There, they are relearning old lessons about strike organization and strategy while exploring new possibilities for the political strike in the informational age.

In every case, moreover, in the process of articulating their appeals, these unionists found their particular concerns translated into the general interests of their community. To be sure, even as they began to take up the tools of grass-roots political action to moderate the impact of plant closures and even began to envision new institutions that would allow local communities to control capital investment, participants did not always rely on the language of citizenship. And, to be sure, most of these campaigns did little more than slow the erosion of labor's industrial base.

Among unionists, however, these experiences produced a radically new grasp of the relationship between corporate decision making and community interests and new language linking their claims to those interests. New levers of power began to become visible, and this stimulated a great deal of innovation as organizers groped for new strategies to outflank the overwhelming bargaining position of corporate employers.

These include growing recognition of the potential power of labor–community coalitions, the importance of economic development planning, the value of research (not only for strategic planning, but also to identify avenues for political action to influence employer decisions), and the imperative of transnational solidarity in the face of global competition.

Low-Wage and Immigrant Workers' Movements

Most if not all of the innovations employed in today's labor movement were developed decades ago by the UFW, which maneuvered as we maneuver today to outflank the superior market position and political power of employers.[16] Agriculture differs from other low-wage sectors in the terms of both labor law and the citizenship status of workers and more generally in terms of the civic regime. Despite this, common patterns of labor movement activity in agriculture, building maintenance, and the hotel and restaurant industries suggest that we revise the common view of the UFW as a unique case and see it rather as a pioneer.

Some of the earliest and least noted movements for union democracy and against concessions occurred, for example, among Latino and African American custodians in the SEIU's frequently corrupt building maintenance unions, which in many cities had been forced to adopt two-tier wage agreements by the mid- to late-1970s. Stimulated by racial succession in the workforce, those developments sparked democratic reform movements and other upheavals, to which the international union responded (as was its practice) with trusteeships and mergers.

By the mid-1980s, however, organizers influenced by the UFW and by organizing experience in comparable conditions in the garment industry assumed responsibility for SEIU's organizing department, and they in turn launched the JfJ campaign.[17] By the early 1990s, JfJ had demonstrated in city after city the power of direct and disruptive collective action, oriented by careful strategic planning, armed with corporate campaign tactics, allied with community coalitions, and framed as campaigns for economic and social justice, to tap the social movement potential of this workforce and the larger community in locally based industrywide organizing campaigns. The campaigns would generate economic and political power and use it to secure contracts with building maintenance firms through tactics targeting the major companies behind the building maintenance contractors and public agencies that contracted for their services.

Significantly, these campaigns reorganized the building maintenance industry during a period when a labor surplus in this low-wage labor market made it a poor target by conventional standards of union strategic planning. And more than any other factor, the JfJ campaign legitimized SEIU's John Sweeney in his 1995 bid for leadership in the AFL–CIO.

The JfJ campaign was only the most visible of a series of immigrant workers' movements that effectively rebuilt declining unions in this period. These included hotel and restaurant employees in San Francisco, Los Angeles, Boston, and elsewhere; drywall workers in southern California's construction industry; democratic upheavals in the Teamsters' food industry unions; and following Cesar Chavez's death, the resurgence of a somewhat more strategic and less sectarian UFW.

The 1990s were also a period of dramatic change in the formal citizenship status of immigrant workers, especially for Mexican immigrants concentrated in California. If, as we have argued, the labor movement is both strongly shaped by the civic regime and in turn a force for the expanded development of citizenship, then those changes should be closely related to variations in labor movement activity among these immigrant workers. The social history of the period reveals this to be the case.

Specifically, we find that patterns of industrial militancy across different industries and over time are directly related to the citizenship regime in effect in those industries and at those times (including both citizenship status and the intensity of enforcement). Evidence includes data on union membership trends in the 1980s, when relatively lax Immigration and Naturalization Service (INS) enforcement practices were accompanied by a 16 percent increase in Latino union membership while union membership rates collapsed in the rest of the private sector workforce (Freitas 1993). The Mexican and Central American workers' movement surged still further in the early 1990s among workers benefiting from the amnesty provisions of the 1986 Immigration Reform and Control Act and the continued lax enforcement regime of the period.

A sharp decline in the propensity to organize starting in 1995 reflected the passage of Proposition 187 (which denied public social services, health care, and education to undocumented workers) and subsequent exclusionary legislation and intensified enforcement of border policy and employer sanctions. While that legislation and enforcement failed to slow the flow of undocumented labor, it dramatically increased the likelihood and consequences of deportation, loss of access to health care, isolation, and general vulnerability of undocumented immigrants. The result was in effect a new apartheid, affecting workers in major portions of the low-wage labor market and their families.[18]

Importantly, however, legal permanent residents (and their unions) were deeply involved in mobilizations in the late 1980s in response to the amnesty process and then since 1995–1997 in a huge surge of demand for naturalization, expanded voter registration, language and social welfare rights, and political participation. The linkage between the labor movement and the broader citizenship movement among Mexican immigrants was strongest in those unions where immigrant leadership was itself the product of democratic upheaval. Unions characterized by more paternalistic and authoritarian rule, on the other had, failed to tap into the power of the citizenship movement and continued to be dogged by their own internal democratic distemper.

Throughout the entire labor movement, moreover, unionists began to grasp the importance of organizing among immigrant workers and began to share first-hand experience of the challenges of citizenship status among organizing workers. This learning experience led to the adoption of a new more inclusive stance toward immigrants by the executive council of the AFL–CIO in 2000. By then, proposals by major agricultural employers and their Republican allies in Washington, D.C. for a limited amnesty for agricultural workers had already generated intense interest among undocumented workers. The AFL–CIO's February 2000 call for "a general amnesty" both reinforced that interest and contributed a significant new change to the policymaking equation in Washington, D.C. As the AFL–CIO's previous exclusionary stance had been an essential ingredient in current federal immigration policy, this new stance is likely to trigger change in federal policies and practices affecting immigrants, or what Soysal (1994) terms the "incorporation regime."

Elsewhere, I examine the emergence of transnational citizenship in the most significant bloc of immigrant labor, Mexican immigrants in California (Johnston 2001). In realms that range from labor to education and local government, I find recent years have witnessed the greatest expansion in the circle of citizenship, or participation in public life, since the similar African American citizenship movement of the civil rights era.

If economists and historians like Piore (1979) and Mink (1986) are correct, moreover, this shift may have still more profound consequences for U.S. political, social, and economic development. As they argue, the segregation of recently arrived immigrants from rural areas into low-wage, less politically regulated labor markets and (in many cities) politically marginalized urban settlements has been an essential ingredient in an entire century of development characterized by deep inequalities or "dualism" in the U.S. economy, polity, and urban life. This suggests, then, that new horizons may now be opening toward a period of possibility for a more inclusive and egalitarian civic regime in the United States.

Temp Unionism

Still on the margins but increasingly the focus of innovation in organizing is the growing "permanently temporary" workforce of peripheralized employees. Temporary employment and contracted-out production is nothing new in agriculture, of course, where a resurgence of contracting has sharply reduced wages and benefits over the recent decade. But now major slices of the temp workforce can also be found in diverse occupational groups and subsectors, from the construction trades (the one great success story for temp unionism) to white collar and technical service work to colleges and universities.

Over the past decade, a wide array of new temporary workers' organizing projects has surfaced across the United States. Like the UFW in agriculture, many consciously or unconsciously imitate the craft union model of organizing their labor market through a hiring hall. These include a variety of local advocacy groups and worker-owned temp agencies, home health aide organizing campaigns, unions of cab drivers, freelance writers, and high-tech contract employees. The New York–based Working Today is a rapidly growing online network of independent workers and their associations that to date operates mainly as a consumer group of temporary workers and their associations.

Though this workforce slices across all sectors, the centrality of its information-age segment is underlined by the fact that by the 1980s, the new academic underclass of temporary faculty matched or surpassed the building trades in its rate of union membership.

Though an intense focus of innovation and organizing today, it certainly remains to be seen whether temp unionism will thrive. If the rise of a network society means that peripheral, boundary-spanning positions will acquire a new centrality, then these marginal efforts to organize this marginalized workforce may yet move to the center of the labor movement. If that is the case, then a particular vanguard role may fall to the part-time instructors—overwhelmingly public employees and typically leaders in their own trade or profession—who provide most postsecondary education and training to working adults in the United States.

Like many, and often most of the students whom they teach, these adult vocational and community college instructors are themselves typically temporary employees. Through the combination of their own work experience and their educational work, they are often at the center of informal and shifting local occupational networks. Their leadership role is anchored in circumstances where employment opportunities and economic security increasingly depend on continuous learning.

An organizing agenda responsive to this new terrain might focus, then, not on a particular employer but on such occupational networks in local labor markets. It might begin, moreover, with resources for temps who work in postsecondary education. There, its strength would depend partly on its ability to articulate and respond to the peculiar injuries of the new academic underclass. It might grow, however, through the occupational networks led by these worker/teachers, into the larger workforce.

Regardless, for our purposes here it is useful to note that all these efforts seek to replace the lost infrastructure of the membership in the organization with a local structure of information, training, and job opportunities—all new avenues for new ways of organizing—not unlike the locally rooted building trades unions. Formally or informally organized, such infrastructures of support and organizing among temp workers are likely to serve as vehicles for citizenship movements.

Historically, for example, the craft unions that represent the contingent workers of the building trades have been deeply engaged in public life through their stakes in the jobs associated with local development and redevelopment and in state and federal construction projects. If labor movements based in the new temp workforce thrive, they are likely to do so in alignment with educational interests, through demands for access to health care and other social insurance, and in other efforts to reregulate their employment relations. Owing to their public sector status, contingent academic workers also are likely to contribute leadership to movements in defense of public education and for educational equity and opportunity.

Convergence in Community Unionism

From the local to the global level, the phenomenon of citizenship is becoming increasingly complex, overlapping, and differentiated. At the same time that globalization drives the development of increasingly transnational citizenries, however, *local public spaces* remain at the center of much citizenship movement activity.

This pattern holds with most varieties of social movement unionism. The beginnings of resurgence in the U.S. labor movement are associated, accordingly, with a new emphasis on local organizing and local political action based in neighborhoods as well as workplaces. They challenge the insulation of unionism from community life that runs so deep in the twin histories of our labor movement and our urban politics: between labor relations, left to bargaining unions, and local politics, left to ethnic and racial urban political machines. They aim to overcome what Ira Katznelson (1982) calls the historical split between the politics of production and the politics of place—key, he persuasively argues, to the formation of our apolitical unions and our classless politics. In all strands of the new labor movement these two themes—citizenship and local communities—converge because, in a variety of different ways, each addresses what is in effect the same quintessentially political question: "What kind of community do we want to live in?"

Moreover, this shared urban space is the basic site and this common urban future is the actual stake in today's organizing drives. From this point of view, today's organizing campaigns are themselves urban agendas. They respond to the rise of low-wage and increasingly part-time and temporary work with a fight for an urban future that will permit families to support themselves. And through today's local living wage campaigns, public and private sector organizing agendas finally begin to converge. To the extent that they move beyond the contracted-out public workforce, tie organizing to living wage initiatives, and, perhaps, health care responsibility campaigns targeting employers who do not provide health care coverage, they may even evolve into labor's rejoinder to welfare reform.

Importantly, all the disparate movements sketched above move the center of decision making and responsibility for leadership down from the international unions and into the local unions and at that level channel our efforts beyond relatively homogenous workforces and across diverse local communities. As a result, all converge at the *local labor council.*

As a result, labor councils are themselves in renewal today. After decades when international unions (each narrowly focused on its own interests in its own industrial jurisdiction) served as the central institution in the house of labor, the local labor council is increasingly re-emerging as a center of labor movement activity (on this topic see Gapasin and Wial 1998; Kriesky, ed. 1998).

Thus it falls to labor councils to broker and hold together common or complementary organizing campaigns that mobilize the same allies, publicize the same themes to organize workforces residing in the same neighborhoods, and align these forces with the complementary resources of the public workers and others whose efforts similarly focus on the fate of local places. In this increasingly central local forum, the question noted above—"What kind of community do we want to live in?"—must be answered in a manner that speaks to *all* of these labor movements and its allies.

The local significance of these trends may best be seen when they are considered in the context of urban social change over recent decades. Almost universally, the regimes governing and reshaping urban life in the United States over the past half century have been centered on property or commercial development (Molotch and Logan 1987; Stone 1989). These regimes have been recurrently challenged both by justice-oriented movements based in African American and other dispossessed communities, and other neighborhood movements based among new middle class constituencies concerned about their quality of life. Both are typically infused, we should note, with a grass-roots feminist assertion of deeply gendered claims (Johnston 1994, 17–18, 100–104).

To date, these challenges have either failed, been coopted, or achieved power only to find themselves paralyzed due to the absence of their own viable governing agenda (DeLeon 1992). In the postwar period these contests occurred in circumstances where public and private sector unions were alienated from one another, private sector unions were politically dormant and largely contained by collective bargaining, and public employee unionism was dominated by police and construction trades groups allied with the probusiness status quo (Mollenkopf 1983). However, since the 1970s the addition of progressive (and, again, deeply gendered) public service unionism to the urban mix has produced the potential to tilt the balance of power toward the challenging groups through labor–community coalitions (Johnston 1994). Now, the new political energies and local focus of a resurgent private sector labor movement have further swung the potential balance of power toward the challengers. The emergent political voice of immigrants, documented and undocumented and increasingly organized, many now achieving U.S. citizenship, registering, and voting in unprecedented numbers, further strengthens the hand of neighborhood groups and both public and private sector unions. As a result, people who participate in various forms of community-based unionism and especially in local labor councils are beginning to grapple with the challenge of coalition building around a new vision of the city.

Notes

1. An example is the current shift in the AFL–CIO's stance toward immigrant workers' rights, which has further destabilized an already crisis-ridden immigration policy domain and is likely to lead to significant policy change at the federal level.

2. Jennifer Gordon (1999) provides a partial list that includes the Workplace Project in Long Island, the Latino Workers Center, Chinese Staff and Workers Association, and Workers Awaaz in New York City; the Tenants and Workers Support Committee in Alexandria, Virginia; the Korean Immigrant Workers Association in Los Angeles and the Asian Immigrant Women's Advocates in Oakland, California; the Workers Organizing Committee in Portland, Oregon; La Mujer Obrera in El Paso, Texas; the Immigrant Workers' Resource Center in Boston, Massachusetts; the Mississippi Workers Rights Project in Oxford, Mississippi; and the Coalition of Immokalee Workers in Immokalee, Florida. The author's own work is based at the Citizenship Project: a Mexican immigrant labor/community-based organization dedicated to expanded citizenship, broadly defined.

3. Their selective focus on less vulnerable slices of the workforce also helps these authors to compose new variations on an old theme: the nonadversarial, demobilized unionism that oriented and regulated the U.S. labor movement during its recent decades of decline.

4. Elsewhere, I analyze these contrary patterns of change in public and private sectors in considerable detail (Johnston 1994).

5. Mainstream scholars have (since Kerr et al. 1960) concluded that the traumas of early industrialism have long been left behind in "advanced" countries like the United States. In a parallel vein, the younger generation of new social movement scholars and post-Marxist radical intellectuals similarly pronounces the labor movement *passé*.

6. "Community," to be sure, is no less problematic than "citizenship." Here, however, the term refers to an aspiration or ideal. As it appears in the language of today's labor movements, the term is highly politicized. Its appearance is a crucial step toward the identification of labor's interest with "the general interest."

7. Liberals emphasize civil rights; republicans, political rights; social democrats and some feminists, social welfare rights; each is a vital interest for the labor movement. Pluralist political science, "public choice" political economy, orthodox Marxism, and some feminisms, on the other hand, are all profoundly cynical about the promise of citizenship. For our purposes here, it is necessary for them

only to acknowledge that though promises may be illusory, movements that appeal to them may not.

8. Typically, notions of economic citizenship emphasize what might be called "producer's democracy," neglecting the citizenship claims of consumers.

9. Marshall concludes his famous discussion of citizenship with a discussion of this tension as reflecting a "basic conflict between social rights and market value . . . not an invention of muddled brains [but] . . . inherent in our social system" (1950, 68–74). Bendix (1964), Giddens (1982), Bowles and Gintis (1986), Turner (1986), Barbalet (1988), Held (1989), and Janoski (1998) all wrestle with this issue.

10. We neglect here the important and contested arena of environmental rights and ecological identity (Van Steenbergen 1994). In my view, "social citizenship" refers not to the minimum prerequisites for the exercise of other forms of citizenship, but rather to politically defined social needs. This is an expansive concept, as much a product as a precondition of the exercise of other forms of citizenship. Increasingly in this view, clean air and water and shared access to a politically protected "nature" are just such social needs. While this does not capture the "deeper" ecological sense of connection to and responsibility for nature, it does describe the fusion of that movement with the citizenship movement.

11. These practices suggest discursive modes of citizenship organizing and participatory social research that may help to constitute and reconstitute public life and which are corrosive, potentially subversive, to more hierarchical groups.

12. Today's correctional officers' unions have similarly benefited from and increasingly organized the "law and order" coalition of recent decades, which of course provides the effective political demand for expansion of the prison–industrial complex.

13. Traumas promoted by a main current in the industrial relations research of that era, dedicated to the development and diffusion of strategies to contain those troublesome public worker movements (e.g., Wellington and Winter 1971; Kochan 1974; Sumners 1976; Katz 1974).

14. It was a mistake to assume that recent changes in the leadership of the Teamsters' union will reverse these trends. The Hoffa administration faces election and must cover its left flank. The apparently enduring achievement of what is in effect a loose two-party system in the Teamsters falsifies long-standing claims by venerable sociologists regarding the death of union democracy (Lipset et al. 1956).

15. In Los Angeles in 2000, SEIU campaigners finally demonstrated that it was possible to win the second stage in the Justice for Janitors campaign. *Stage one*: win recognition. *Stage two*: achieve significant improvements in wages and working conditions in the heavily competitive building maintenance industry. *Stage three*: start dealing with the "social wage" or conditions of urban life faced by low-wage and immigrant workers (e.g., housing costs), develop a political agenda, and seek to become part of a new urban governing coalition.

16. The UFW Organizing Committee (UFWOC, predecessor to the UFW union) was conducting fully developed corporate campaigns by 1970.

17. Johnston (1994) examines the character and course of public worker movements, the history behind the emergence of JfJ in California's major building maintenance union, and also the surge of feminist unionism associated with the pay equity movement in both sectors, in a set of comparative studies centered on strikes.

18. This view appears to depart from Hector Delgado's (1993) argument in his

widely regarded study of a successful organizing drive among mostly undocumented workers in the mid-1980s, which questions the significance of citizenship status (p. 11). Delgado's finding, however, is that "immigration status will have an adverse effect on the organizability of undocumented workers under certain, but not all conditions" (p. 141). The thrust of my argument in this respect, moreover, is not that workers with limited citizenship rights are "unorganizable," but rather that unions cannot expect to succeed in organizing this workforce without responding to those circumstances. Accordingly, unions should embrace immigrant workers' aspirations for expanded citizenship and associate their organizing efforts with challenges to the apartheid of citizenship status. Delgado agrees (personal communication).

References

Banks, Andy. 1991–1992. "The Power and the Promise of Community Unionism." *Labor Research Review* 10, 2: 17–32.

Barbelet, J.M. 1988. *Citizenship: Rights, Struggle, and Class Inequality.* Minneapolis: University of Minnesota Press.

Bendix, Reinhard. 1964. *Nation-Building and Citizenship.* New York: John Wiley and Sons.

Bowles, Samuel, and Herbert Gintis. 1986. *Democracy and Capitalism.* New York: Basic Books.

Brecher, Jeremy, and Tim Costello 1990. *Building Bridges: The Emerging Grassroots Coalition of Labor and Community.* New York: Monthly Review Press.

DeLeon, Richard Edward. 1992. *Left-Coast City: Progressive Politics in San Francisco, 1975–1991.* Lawrence: University of Kansas Press.

Delgado, Hector. 1993. *New Immigrants, Old Unions: Organizing Undocumented Workers in Los Angeles.* Philadelphia: Temple University Press.

Eisenscher, Michael. 1999. "Critical Juncture: Unionists at the Crossroads." In *Which Direction for Organized Labor? Essays on Organizing, Outreach, and Internal Transformations,* ed., Bruce Nissen. Detroit: Wayne State University Press.

Elder, Klaus. 1993. *The New Politics of Class: Social Movements and Cultural Dynamics in Advanced Societies.* Newbury Park, CA: Sage Publications.

Fine, Janice. 1998. "Moving Innovation from the Margins to the Center for a New American Labor Movement." In *A New Labor Movement for the New Century,* ed. Gregory Mantsios, pp. 119–145. New York: Monthly Review Press.

Flores, William V., and Rina Benmayor. 1997. *Latino Cultural Citizenship: Claiming Identity, Space and Rights.* Boston: Beacon Press.

Foweraker, Joe, and Todd Landman. 1997. *Citizenship Rights and Social Movements: A Comparative and Statistical Analysis.* Oxford: Oxford University Press.

Freitas, Gregory. 1993. "Unionization among Racial and Ethnic Minorities." *Industrial and Labor Relations Review* 46, 2 (January): 284–306.

Gapasin, Fernando, and Howard Wial. 1998. "The Role of Central Labor Councils in Union Organizing in the 1990's." In *Organizing to Win: New Research on Union Strategies,* ed. Kate Bronfenbrenner and Richard W. Hurd. Ithaca, NY: Cornell University Press

Giddens, Anthony. 1982. "Class Division, Class Conflict, and Citizenship Rights." In *Profiles and Critiques in Social Theory,* ed. Anthony Giddens, pp 164–180. Berkeley: University of California Press.

Goffman, Erving. 1974. *Frame Analysis: An Essay on the Organization of Experience*. Cambridge, MA: Harvard University Press.

Gordon, Jennifer. 1999. "The Campaign for the Unpaid Wages Prohibition Act: Latino Immigrants Change New York Wage Law: The Impact of Non-Voters on Politics and the Impact of Political Participation on Non-Voters." Carnegie Endowment Comparative Citizenship Program. Unpublished paper.

Gouldner, Alvin. 1976. *The Dialectic of Ideology and Technology: The Origins, Grammar, and Future of Ideology*. New York: Oxford University Press.

Habermas, Jurgen. 1979. *Communication and the Evolution of Society*. London: Heinemann.

Heckscher, Charles C. 1988. *The New Unionism: Employee Involvement in the Changing Corporation*. New York: Basic Books.

Held, David. 1989. *Political Theory and the Modern State*, pp. 189–213. Stanford, CA: Stanford University Press.

Hobsbawm, E.J. 1968. *Labouring Men: Studies in the History of Labour*. London: Wiedenfeld and Nicolson.

Janoski, Thomas. 1998. *Citizenship and Civil Society*. New York: Cambridge University Press.

Johnston, Paul. 1994. *Success While Others Fail: Social Movement Unionism and the Public Workplace*. Ithaca, NY: Cornell University, Industrial and Labor Relations Press.

———. 2001. "Citizens of the Future: The Emergence of Transnational Citizenship Among Mexican Immigrants in California." In *Citizenship Today: Global Perspectives and Practices*, ed. T. Alexander Aleinikoff and Douglas Klusmeyer. Washington, DC: Carnegie Endowment for World Peace.

Katz, Harry C. 1984. *The Impact of Public Employee Unionism on City Budgeting and Employee Remuneration: A Case Study of San Francisco*. New York: Garland Publishing.

Katznelson, Ira. 1982. *City Trenches*. Chicago: University of Chicago Press.

Kerr, Clark, Frederick Harbison, John Dunlop, and Charles Myers. 1960. *Industrialism and Industrial Man*. Cambridge, MA: Harvard University Press.

Kochan, Thomas A. 1974. "A Theory of Multilateral Collective Bargaining in City Governments." *Industrial Relations Review* 27, 4: 525–542.

Kochan, Thomas, Harry C. Katz, and Robert B. McKersie. 1986. *The Transformation of American Industrial Relations*. Ithaca, NY: ILR Press.

Kriesky, Jill, ed. 1998. *Working Together to Revitalize Labor in Our Communities: Case Studies of Labor Education–Central Labor Body Collaboration*. Orono, Maine: University and College Labor Education Association.

Lipset, Seymour Martin, Martin A. Trow, and James S. Coleman. 1956. *Union Democracy: The Internal Politics of the International Typographical Union*. Glencoe, IL: Free Press.

Marshall, T.H. 1950. *Citizenship and Social Class and Other Essays*. Cambridge: Cambridge University Press.

Melucci, Alberto. 1996. *Challenging Codes: Collective Action in the Information Age*. Cambridge: Cambridge University Press.

Milkman, Ruth, and Kent Wong, eds. 2000. *Organizing Immigrants: Unions and Foreign-Born Workers in Contemporary California*. Ithaca, NY: Cornell University Press.

Mink, Gwendolyn. 1986. *Old Labor and New Immigrants in American Political Development: Union, Party, and State, 1875–1920.* Ithaca, NY: Cornell University Press.

Mollenkopf, John. 1983. *The Contested City.* Princeton, NJ: Princeton University Press.

Molotch, Harvey, and John Logan. 1987. *Urban Fortunes: The Political Economy of Place.* Berkeley: University of California Press.

Montgomery, David. 1993. *Citizen Worker: The Experience of Workers in the United States with Democracy and the Free Market during the Nineteenth Century.* New York: Cambridge University Press.

Parsons, Talcott. 1966. *Societies, Evolutionary and Comparative Perspectives.* Englewood Cliffs, NJ: Prentice-Hall.

Piore, Michael J. 1979. *Birds of Passage: Migrant Labor and Industrial Societies.* Cambridge: Cambridge University Press.

Piven, Frances Fox, and Richard Cloward. 1988. "Popular Power and the Welfare State." In *Remaking the Welfare State: Retrenchment and Social Policy in America and Europe*, ed. Michael K. Brown. Philadelphia: Temple University Press.

Rueschemeyer, D., E.H. Stephens, and J. Stephens. 1992. *Capitalist Development and Democracy.* Cambridge: Polity Press.

Scipes, Kim. 1992. "Understanding the New Labor Movements in the 'Third World': The Emergence of Social Movement Unionism." *Critical Sociology* 19, 2: 81–101.

Soysal, Yasemin N. 1994. *Limits of Citizenship: Migrants and Postnational Membership in Europe.* Chicago and London: University of Chicago Press.

Steinberg, Marc W. 1995. "The Great End of All Government: Working People's Construction of Citizenship in Early Nineteenth-Century England and the Matter of Class." In *Citizenship, Identity, and Social History*, ed. Charles Tilly. *International Review of Social History* 40, Supplement 3.

Stone, Clarence. 1989. *Regime Politics.* Lawrence: University of Kansas.

———. 1993. "Urban Regimes and the Capacity to Govern: A Political Economy Approach." *Journal of Urban Affairs* 15, 1: 1–28.

Sumners, Robert S. 1976. *Collective Bargaining and Benefit Conferral: A Jurisprudential Critique.* Ithaca, NY: Cornell University, New York School of Industrial and Labor Relations, Institute of Public Employment.

Sweeney, John. 1996. "Labor's Role in a Meaningful Society." *Tikkun* 11, 4 (July–August): 37–39.

Thompson, E.P. 1974. *The Making of the English Working Class.* Hammondsworth: Penguin Books.

Turner, Bryan. 1986. *Citizenship and Capitalism: The Debate over Reformism.* London: Allen and Unwin.

Van Steenbergen, Bart. 1994. "Towards a Global Ecological Citizen." In *The Condition of Citizenship*, ed. Bart Van Steenbergen, pp. 141–52. London: Sage Publications.

Waterman, Peter. 1993. "Social Movement Unionism: A New Union Model for a New World Order?" *Review* (Fernando Braudel Center) 16: 245–278.

Wellington, Harry H., and Ralph K. Winter, Jr. 1971. *The Unions and the Cities.* Washington, DC: Brookings Institution.

10

CONCLUDING THOUGHTS

INTERNAL TRANSFORMATION?

BRUCE NISSEN

The chapters in this book point to a number of ways in which the changed environment facing the U.S. labor movement requires it to change its ways of operating if it is to be adequate to the tasks at hand. For example, continuing the relative isolation from, and absence of solidarity with, unions and workers abroad can lead only to continuing loss of power and relevance as the U.S. economy continues to integrate into the world economy. Likewise, an inability to organize immigrant workers or to establish a strongly positive relationship with immigrant communities can only harm organized labor in a country where immigrants—primarily from Asia and Latin America—will be an ever-increasing proportion of the U.S. labor force.

These chapters also provide many suggestions for specific measures that unions could undertake to be more effective. But virtually every suggestion carries with it the question of whether unions in the United States have the capacity and will to undertake the change in direction. As many of the authors state or hint, unions will need to "transform" or "reinvent" themselves to accomplish many of the tasks they are being asked to do.

In fact, more and more of the scholarship on unions in the United States concerns the need for transformation of unions as organizations. Sometimes metaphors are used to explain the change that is needed. Thus one article compares the AFL–CIO to a giant snapping turtle in its shell: either the shell must be broken or become more flexible, or the rigid shell may kill the attempt to grow a new more dynamic organism (Brecher and Costello 1998). Pocock (n.d.) concludes that in many settings unions need to "shed their institutional skin" if they are to renew themselves.

Between 1998 and 2001 there have been at least 10–20 academic articles or book chapters written on the transformation process needed to revitalize the U.S. labor movement. Very few of them are based on detailed empirical research; most are the result of observation coupled with viewpoints derived from long experience either in or examining organized labor in this country. Valuable though these contributions are, it must be admitted that scholarship on this topic is at a rather primitive level.

This chapter shares the limitations of previous recent efforts to address this subject. It is not based on rigorous research into attempted self-transformation by unions. Rather, it attempts to build on the insights provided by the previous chapters in this book to conceptualize clearly some of the dimensions involved and to offer a very preliminary assessment of the prospects for change.

All three chapters in the first section of this book make it clear that a key stumbling block to attaining stronger ties of solidarity with unions and workers abroad is the organizational dynamics inherited from the past, which make genuine cross-border organizing and solidarity decidedly out of the ordinary. For example, Rechenbach and Cohen note the tendency to make internationalism nothing more than a few meetings of top union functionaries. And Babson notes that "internal politics" or insistence on "proper channels" can derail cross-border auto solidarity. From these chapters it is clear that cross-border solidarity requires unions to act much less bureaucratically than they have in the past.

What would this entail? For one thing, unions would need to follow the latest business management trend to "push operational decisions and implementation down to the lower levels of the organization." This means that international solidarity is not carried out primarily by top union leadership and union functionaries hired at the national level, but at local and intermediate levels of the union. But almost any national union leader knows that the current internal state of most unions means that union locals and regional/district bodies would do virtually nothing in the area of international work if simply left to themselves. Therefore, as Rechenbach and Cohen note, extensive education about the importance of international solidarity must be carried out to induce genuine, unforced involvement from the local level. Beyond education, a union's national level leadership and staff need to provide structured, convenient ways for local and intermediate bodies to participate in an ongoing way. The Ameritech Alliance at least partially shows how this might be accomplished, as does the UE–FAT alliance referred to in Babson's chapter.

But needed changes go beyond that. If officers and/or staff at some level of a union see little need for international work and therefore attempt to block or ignore work of this nature, what is the solution? Centralizing power at the national level and attempting to run roughshod over intermediate or lower levels would ultimately be self-defeating; among other things, it would nullify the very decentralization of decisions and operations mentioned in the last paragraph, not to mention its impact on internal democracy. Rather, the opposite of such a bureaucratic solution is called for: union activists or leaders at lower levels of the union hierarchy need to be allowed and encouraged to participate in international solidarity efforts of many kinds, even if their regional or other local leadership levels are indifferent or opposed.

Such openness will be extremely hard to attain in most U.S. unions, for it requires some breaking of the "chain of command" and the rather rigid hierarchical organizational structures that most union leaders believe necessary in an effective organization. It would end reprisals against union activists for "unauthorized" contact with unionists abroad. It would encourage experimentation with many types of transnational solidarity, even those not currently prioritized by the union's leadership. It would require that the internal practice of many unions be more democratic, at least in the sense of allowing free rein to activists within the ranks.

Organizationally, changes of this nature could be characterized as *increased organizational flexibility* accomplished by less reliance on "protocol," "proper channels," or control from above of cross-border activities. From the point of view of the typical union leader, these changes are likely to appear to be *increased risk taking and experimentation* regarding organizational control over the activities undertaken by a union's various levels of personnel and membership. These changes will be very hard to accomplish with leaders who have felt themselves well served by relatively rigid and hierarchical structures prevalent during the heyday of business unionism in the post–World War II decades.

The chapters on union relationships with immigrant workers also demonstrate the need for more organizational flexibility. Unions unwilling or unable to incorporate "nontraditional" workers such as immigrants will become increasingly dysfunctional in a workforce that has ever-growing percentages of those born in another country. But beyond the organizational flexibility issue, they also highlight changes needed in attitudes. Anti-immigrant attitudes are not overwhelming, but they are present in virtually every sector of the U.S. working class. Union leaders and members are not exempt from such attitudes simply by virtue of their organizational membership.

The most immediate desirable attitudinal change raised by the immigration issue is *greater inclusiveness*. More inclusive unions would not only welcome immigrants more fully, but they would also welcome and champion the rights and interests of African Americans, women, and gays and lesbians. Attitudinal changes are among the most difficult any organization could attempt to undertake. Educational programs are one obvious part of the answer, as the AFL–CIO recommends in a recent publication on immigrants:

> The union movement should develop a broad internal education program that reaches all levels—elected leaders, staff, and members. A wide range of topics should be included, from providing basic information about immigration and immigrant rights to more detailed discussions about the political economy of globalization, immigration policy and union legal responsibilities in representations issues. A variety of education materials should be made available in multiple languages to all unionists. Ultimately, this educational work should be part of the union movement's efforts to advance a broad social and economic justice agenda that seeks to end discrimination against women and all minorities. (AFL–CIO 2000)

But of course education will have a relatively limited impact unless it is integrated with ongoing programs that bring immigrants and minorities in a practical way into the ongoing functions of the union, as Unite for Dignity does in South Florida.

Attitudes toward specific groups of workers (immigrants, African Americans, women, gays and lesbians, etc.) are also likely to be at least loosely linked with larger visions of an ideological nature. If the ideological complexion of U.S. unions moves them in the direction of *ever-expanding conceptions of solidarity*, they will very likely improve considerably their practice toward (and standing with) immigrant and minority groups. But ideological outlook is something that unions are even less likely to consciously and speedily change than attitudes about narrower issues. If the ideological orientation of unions is to move toward broader conceptions of solidarity, such change would require an outside "push" as well as an inside effort.

Gapasin and Bonacich argue strongly that the ideological orientation of the U.S. labor movement will have to move toward the left if it is to make progress. Traditionally the left has promoted broad conceptions of working-class solidarity. Every single advance made by the U.S. labor movement toward broader classwide solidarity or solidarity with oppressed peoples and nations abroad owes a great deal to the influence of the left. Likewise, the political left has historically been a force for greater inclusiveness and a more daring path for organized labor. Furthermore, as Gapasin and Bonacich note, the left is usually involved in the myriad "other" forms the labor movement might take beyond simply conventional unions. That is, the left tends to be involved in the "movement" aspect of the labor movement.

A further contention of the scholarship in this book is that U.S. unions need to move toward social movement unionism. Ian Robinson's argument that the neoliberal agenda is driving the U.S. labor movement in precisely this direction breaks new ground. Even if the measures he employs in his argument turn out to be somewhat rough approximations of the phenomena being measured, the overall argument is highly original and persuasive. The U.S. labor movement has at least partially begun to move out of its long-standing business unionism, even if to date the move seems to be only a partial transition into social unionism and not full-fledged social movement unionism.

Both the partial nature of the change and the reality of genuine change are apparent to anyone paying close attention to the recent trajectory of the U.S. labor movement. As for the limitations, consider the following: despite the post-1995 AFL–CIO's decision that organizing the unorganized should be the number one priority of the labor movement, according to ex-federation organizing director Richard Bensinger, only a "half dozen unions" (out of over sixty in the AFL–CIO) have begun to "reinvent themselves to focus on organizing" ("Tough Love for Labor," 118). Bensinger states,

> [Organizing] would require massive cultural change by unions. But only a handful of unions have even started down this road. . . .We still spend 90% of our resources servicing union contracts. . . . Most union still think of themselves as a special interest group whose sole job is to represent

their members. We need to get back to our original mission of bringing economic justice to millions of non-members. ("Tough Love for Labor," 118, 120)

Only a small minority of unions is seriously tackling the internal changes needed to carry out the very top goal set down by the nation's peak labor body. Clearly, only very small steps have been taken to transform unions enough internally to seriously undertake this top priority.

On the other hand, the focus and rhetoric of the U.S. labor movement are much changed from what they were less than ten years ago. At the time this was written (October 2000) the most recent issue of the AFL–CIO publication *America @ Work* contains a major centerfold article entitled "Member-to-Member Mobilization." The article stresses internal organizing and mobilizing, primarily in the political arena. Another article features the "New Alliance" program, an attempt to reinvigorate state federations and local central labor bodies through activist measures. Another article, "Where Is the Justice?," casts the right of U.S. workers to choose a union as an international human rights issue. Yet another article, "Growing Latino Workforce Needs a Voice at Work," highlights abuses of the country's growing Hispanic workforce and calls for major changes in the nation's immigration policy. Another article highlights the international campaign against the Nike shoe company and touts living wage activists and organizations. Not all articles have such an activist tinge, and many of the politically oriented ones aim to direct union members' votes toward a presidential candidate largely owned by business interests. But there is nevertheless an unmistakable change from the type of article one was likely to see in the old *AFL–CIO News* in the 1980s or early 1990s.

A cynic may read this as an indication that the rhetoric has changed more fully than the practice or the reality. While this may be true, rhetoric is not irrelevant; it is indicative of the image projected and the self-understanding of at least some of those now playing leading roles in the U.S. labor movement.

Rhetoric is also closely allied to the theoretical understanding held by labor leaders of the overall purpose and function of a labor movement. Here Paul Johnston's argument that the many strands of labor movement coalesce into a movement for citizenship rights is compelling. Such a self-understanding is probably prevalent among those working in nonconventional formations such as immigrant workers' centers, worker civil rights organizations such as Black Workers for Justice, and others linking labor and community issues. But it is highly unlikely that many leaders of established conventional unions conceptualize their organizations or their goals as oriented toward citizenship rights.

But such a reorientation may be taking place anyway. In the labor movement, practice often precedes conceptual self-understanding. The U.S. labor movement has not traditionally been strong on theorizing its activity. Instead, practical innovations are first attempted, and whatever appears to be working in the direction of building power is then ossified into "standard practice" and theoretical justification. Thus the labor movement may in fact be coalescing around a common goal and theme of citizenship rights without fully realizing it. Theorizing interventions such as Johnston's chapter could play a very useful role in clarifying the trajectory taken and in guiding future practice.

The citizenship theme highlights a number of needed changes that are partially taking place. One of them is the need for *more varied organizational forms*. Both the chapter by Gapasin and Bonacich and the chapter by Johnston note the growth in recent years of "unofficial" labor movements for workers' rights, including transnational anti-sweatshop movements, civil rights worker-based organizations, workers' centers, community-based organizing of workers, etc. This, combined with "official" union attempts at creating "members-only" or "minority" unions, points to some of the new directions that could potentially vary the organizational flexibility and variety of labor organizations or movements.

A second feature nicely captured by the citizenship frame of reference is the need for the labor movement to be *more rooted in communities*. Here again, at least small steps have been taken by both the official labor movement and fledgling workers' rights movements outside the confines of labor officialdom. The AFL–CIO's attempt to rebuild state and local central bodies is the most highly visible effort in this direction. An extremely hard task in a frequently fragmented and suburbanized living environment, rootedness is nevertheless a laudable and potentially viable goal.

The citizenship frame also draws attention to another change that the authors in this book find desirable: *less strict market orientation and more of a social orientation*. While the labor movement strives to improve the market position of workers, a social movement orientation also propels it to fight for numerous rights to be free from the market.

Rights are not something that can be sold, and they do not depend on one's market power. Ian Robinson's chapter points out that business unionism in the recent U.S. past has been a colossal failure, largely because of its reliance on a strictly market orientation in an era of neoliberal ascendancy. And both the Gapasin/Bonacich and Johnston chapters illustrate the greater promise and/or results of social movements far removed from a simple quest for more economic market clout.

Overall, the authors in this volume believe that a movement toward social movement unionism and an ideology well to the left of center is both desirable and, to a very limited degree, occurring. To accomplish such a movement, both organizational and conceptual internal transformations are necessary. Four organizational changes are highlighted:

1. Increased organizational flexibility in existing mainstream unions, including a more open and democratic internal practice;
2. More varied organizational forms, supplementing standardized collective bargaining unions with other formations;
3. More rootedness in communities, including communities of disadvantaged or oppressed peoples or communities not based on geography;
4. Greater inclusiveness, especially opening ranks to those workers considered "other," "foreign," or nontraditional to the traditional labor movement.

Three changes in outlook and attitude are seen as necessary to effective social movement unionism:

1. Greater willingness to take risks and to experiment with unconventional methods and organizational forms;
2. Broader conceptions of solidarity with different types of workers here and abroad (relationships with the "other"); and
3. Less strict orientation toward simply the market and more orientation toward social issues and rights.

Can the U.S. labor movement transform itself and change in the seven ways enumerated above? More empirical investigation, both through case study and broader methodologies, would aid us greatly in answering this question. It may well be that there are hidden contradictory aspects to the above list or that implementation of the suggested changes will have unintended consequences not perceived by those putting them forward. Or perhaps they are impractical or utopian given certain features of the environment or of labor organizations not factored in to the analyses leading to suggestions for their implementation. But lacking such detailed investigations, they give the appearance of being plausible, internally coherent suggestions for change. And if they are possible and realistic, they would likely lead to more powerful union organizations.

The prescription of social movement unionism is far removed from the recommendations of most mainstream industrial relations scholars in the United States. These scholars have also criticized the traditional "job control" model of unionism prevalent in the United States during the post–World War II years. But their prescriptions for new forms of worker representation depart widely from a social movement orientation. Rather, employee representation should take the form of nonadversarial organizations that participate with (and become part of) management of enterprises in an effort to resolve mutual problems. (For an example, see Kochan and Osterman 1994). A power base for workers and worker organization independent of whatever influence may be had through internal company or enterprise participative structures is either downplayed or ignored as unnecessary. Some are even attempting to revive company unions as legitimate forms of worker voice (Kaufman 1997; 1999). Clearly, social movement unionism is far removed from such a perspective.

Just as the official U.S. labor movement is experimenting with social movement approaches, it is also testing the participative approaches urged upon it by the mainstream scholars, albeit usually without an equal naiveté over the need for an independent power base or for weapons of coercion. The results have been quite mixed, giving both critics and supporters of the new participative, nonadversarial unionism (what Robinson calls the "up with voice, down with adversarialism" approach) grounds for arguing their case.

The fact that the AFL–CIO is simultaneously experimenting with social movement approaches and nonadversarial, business-friendly participative approaches underscores the essentially *pragmatic* nature of its current leadership. Ideological consistency is sacrificed for eclectic experimentation, and the mainstream unions will adopt on a wide scale only approaches that prove themselves with practical results over a relatively short time span. The essential pragmatism of current AFL–CIO president John Sweeney and some other top labor leaders is a welcome advance over the hardened Cold War business union perspective of his predecessor Lane Kirkland, but it should not be misread as a firm commitment to left-wing ideology or practice.

Which of the two (or perhaps more) directions the U.S. labor movement is likely to pursue more fully in the coming years therefore likely depends heavily on what "works" best in the short run. Of course the very meaning of the phrase "working well" is part of what is up for grabs. Nonideological pragmatism may be the central tendency, but ideology cannot be avoided entirely. To the extent that the ideology of union leaders has changed in the recent past, the movement has mostly been to the left, away from an ossified Cold War business unionism that was little concerned with the fate of workers throughout the world or those left out of the domestic union organizational boundaries. And so the conception of what it means to "work well" has evolved to a broader and somewhat more class-conscious view of self-interest.

The future trajectory of the U.S. labor movement will continue to depend heavily on changes in the broader environment, as well as the efforts of internal actors attempting to influence policies and initiatives. The evolution of U.S. capitalism and the broader U.S. society could push our pragmatic labor movement into either of the two fundamental directions mentioned in this chapter. The future is not preordained; multiple possibilities present themselves. If the authors in this volume are correct, the preferable path under contemporary circumstances is the path of social movement unionism.

References

AFL–CIO. 2000. *Building Understanding, Creating Change: A Report on the AFL–CIO Forums on Immigrant Workers' Rights*. Washington, DC: AFL–CIO. August.

America @ Work. 2000. Vol. 5, 10 (October). Washington, DC: AFL–CIO.

Brecher, Jeremy, and Tim Costello. 1998. "A 'New Labor Movement' in the Shell of the Old?" In *A New Labor Movement for the New Century*, ed. Gregory Mantsios, pp. 29–50. New York: Garland Publishing.

Kaufman, Bruce. 1997. "Company Unions: Sham Organizations or Victims of the New Deal?" In *Proceedings of the Forty-Ninth Annual Meeting of the IRRA*, p. 166–180. Madison, WI: Industrial Relations Research Association.

———. 1999. "Nonunion Employee Representation in the Pre-Wagner Act Years: A Reassessment." *Journal of Labor Research* 20 (Winter): 9–30.

Kochan, Thomas, and Paul Osterman. 1994. *The Mutual Gains Enterprise*. Boston: Harvard Business School Press.

Pocock, Barbara. N.d. "Union Renewal: A Theoretical and Empirical Analysis of Union Power." Unpublished manuscript.

"Tough Love for Labor: A Union Crusader Is Not Afraid to Criticize Unions and Managers." *Business Week*, October 16, 2000, pp. 118, 120.

ABOUT THE EDITOR
AND CONTRIBUTORS

Steve Babson is a Labor Program Specialist at the Labor Studies Center of Wayne State University. His current research and teaching focus on union strategies for workplace mobilization and cross-border solidarity, with a particular emphasis on the auto industry. He is the author of *The Unfinished Struggle: Turning Points in American Labor, 1877–Present* and *Working Detroit: The Making of a Union Town* and is co-coordinator of the International Research Network on Autowork in the Americas (IRNAA).

Edna Bonacich is Professor of Sociology and Ethnic Studies at the University of California at Riverside, where she has taught since 1970. Her major research interest has been the study of class and race, with special emphasis on racial divisions in the working class. Since 1989 she has been studying the garment industry, in both Los Angeles and the Pacific Rim region, coediting a book called *Global Production: The Apparel Industry in the Pacific Rim.* She has recently completed a coauthored volume entitled *Behind the Label: Inequality in the Los Angeles Apparel Industry*, published by the University of California Press. She has worked as a volunteer with the garment workers' union, UNITE, and has been active in the anti-sweatshop movement.

Larry Cohen is a member of the executive board of the 700,000-member Communications Workers of America, representing technical, customer service, and content workers, as well as electronics, production, and public service workers in many states. He is also Executive Vice President of the Communications Workers of America, with responsibility nationally for organizing and international work, as well as education, mobilization, civil rights, and health and safety. He is also a founder of Jobs with Justice, a national coalition for economic justice.

Henry J. Frundt convenes the Sociology program at Ramapo College, where he has been teaching for nearly thirty years. His previous works include *Refreshing Pauses: Coca-Cola and Human Rights in Guatemala* and *Trade Conditions and Labor Rights*. Currently an AFT state council delegate, he is also secretary of the Labor Studies section of the Latin American Studies Association and a board member of the U.S. Labor Education in the Americas Project.

Fernando Gapasin for over thirty-five years has been a union activist and elected leader in several national unions and is presently the president of AFSCME Local 1108. He is on the faculty at the UCLA Cesar E. Chavez Center and a member of the Center for Labor Research and Education. He comes to UCLA via the Pennsylvania State University, where he was a faculty member in the Department of Industrial Relations. His work focuses on strategic planning, leadership, and racial and gender diversity in the workplace. His publications are in organizational research and the dynamics of race and gender in the workplace. While at Penn State he was commissioned to do a national study of central labor councils for the AFL–CIO. His research on central labor councils was the basis for the AFL–CIO's "Union City" initiative.

Guillermo Grenier is the Director of the Center for Labor Research and Studies at Florida International University. He is the author of *Inhuman Relations: Quality Circles and Anti-Unionism in American Industry* (1988) and coauthor of *Employee Participation and Labor Law in the American Workforce* (1992). He has also written numerous scholarly articles and coedited several books, primarily on immigrant workers in the United States. Recent research interests include immigrant workers and unions, as well as labor in Eastern Europe during the recent transition to capitalism.

Paul Johnston is a research sociologist who studies public life as a participant. He is Executive Director of the Salinas-based Citizenship

Project and an Associate Researcher at the Department of Latin American and Latino Studies at the University of California at Santa Cruz. He served as an organizer for the UFW and the SEIU, received his Ph.D. in Sociology from the University of California at Berkeley, and was Professor of Sociology at Yale University for eight years. He left Yale in 1995 to develop the Citizenship Project in California. He is author of *Success While Others Fail: Social Movement Unionism and the Public Workplace* (Cornell ILR Press, 1994) and numerous other publications.

Ruth Milkman is Professor of Sociology at UCLA and Director of the new UC Institute for Labor and Employment. Her research and writing have ranged over a variety of issues surrounding work and labor organization in capitalist societies. She has written many articles and three books: *Gender at Work: The Dynamics of Job Segregation During World War II*, which won the 1987 Joan Kelly Prize from the American Historical Association; *Japan's California Factories: Labor Relations and Economic Globalization* (1991); and *Farewell to the Factory: Auto Workers in the Late 20th Century* (1997). She also has published two edited volumes: *Women, Work and Protest: A Century of Women's Labor History* (1985) and *Organizing Immigrants: The Challenge for Unions in Contemporary California* (2000). Her current research focuses on immigrant workers and their relationship to labor unionism in contemporary southern California.

Bruce Nissen is Program Director at the Center for Labor Research and Studies at Florida International University in Miami. He has published numerous scholarly articles and six books, including *Theories of the Labor Movement* (coeditor, 1987); *Grand Designs: The Impact of Corporate Strategies on Workers, Unions and Communities* (coeditor and contributor, 1993); *Fighting for Jobs: Case Studies of Labor–Community Coalitions Confronting Plant Closings* (1995); *Unions and Workplace Reorganization* (editor and contributor, 1998), and *Which Direction for Organized Labor?—Essays on Organizing, Outreach, and Internal Transformations* (editor and contributor, 1999). He is coeditor of *Labor Studies Journal* and an executive board member of the United Association for Labor Education (UALE). Recent research interests include living wage movements and immigrant experiences with organized labor.

Jeff Rechenbach is a member of the executive board of the 700,000-member Communications Workers of America, representing technical, customer service, and content workers, as well as electronics, production, and public service workers in many states. He has been Vice President of the Communications Workers of America, District 4, since October 1994. His responsibilities include coordination of all bargaining activities within the five states of District 4–Ohio, Michigan, Indiana, Illinois, and Wisconsin, consisting of 105,000 members. In addition, he is involved in a number of community and civic activities and serves as a board member of the Ohio AFL–CIO.

Ian Robinson teaches in the Department of Sociology and the Residential College at the University of Michigan–Ann Arbor. He is also Associate Director of the Institute of Labor and Industrial Relations' new Labor and Globalization Project. In recent years, his research has focused on how neoliberal economic restructuring has affected the objectives, strategies, power resources, and economic and political power of unions in the three countries of North America. He is also working on a book that compares systematically the determinants of labor movement character in Canada and the United States from the late nineteenth century to the present, a comparison that yields new insights relevant to the recently renewed debate on the origins of American exceptionalism. He has also contributed to the debates concerning how trade and capital liberalization agreements such as NAFTA affect the scope and quality of worker rights and democracy and the character of federal political systems.

INDEX